GRISWOLD
MUFFIN PANS

Jon B. Haussler

4880 Lower Valley Road, Atglen, PA 19310 USA

Acknowledgements

I would like to express my sincere thanks and appreciation for the encouragement and input I received for this effort. Over 50 collectors provided input and advice to this effort for which I am extremely grateful. It has been a real joy discussing "iron" with these fine people. I would like to specially thank my major consultants, Alan Stone, Joseph Noto, Richard Miller, and Joel Schiff for their patience, knowledge, advice, and willingness to share information from their collections.

Book Designed by Laurie A. Smucker

Printed in the United States of America
ISBN: 0-7643-0239-6

Published by Schiffer Publishing, Ltd.
4880 Lower Valley Road
Atglen, PA 19310
Phone: (610) 593-1777
Fax: (610) 593-2002
E-mail:Schifferbk@aol.com
Please write for a free catalog.
This book may be purchased from the publisher.
Please include $2.95 for shipping.
Try your bookstore first.

We are interested in hearing from authors
with book ideas on related subjects.

Table of Contents

Introduction

Muffin pans have been a significant product line of the Griswold Manufacturing Company throughout its long history. In fact, muffin pans were a significant product line of the predecessor company, Seldon and Griswold Manufacturing Company. Muffin pans were made in many different sizes and shapes, with a wide variety of markings. These wide ranging variations were produced to accommodate the many needs of the home baker.

Collecting Griswold muffin pans is enjoyable, affordable, challenging, somewhat mysterious, and addictive. They can be found in many different places, including yard sales, flea markets, auctions, and antique malls. They may also be acquired from other collectors and from dealers.

There are many very valuable Griswold muffin pans to be found. There are some pans and variations that have yet to be found by the collecting community. The lucky collectors or enthusiasts that find these will gain tremendous satisfaction and/or considerable financial reward.

This book is intended to serve both the novice and the very advanced collector by providing the information known on Griswold cast iron muffin pans and their variations clearly and concisely. The text, photographs, and line drawings provide all of the information necessary to identify Griswold muffin pans. Estimates of the rarity and retail value of Griswold muffin pans are also included.

Chapter 1.
History of
Griswold Muffin
Pans

Early Muffin Pans

The predecessor company of the Griswold Manufacturing Company, Seldon and Griswold Manufacturing Company, was started as a family enterprise in 1865. In 1884 the Griswolds bought the Seldons' portion of the business and changed the name to the Griswold Manufacturing Company. The business remained in operation as the Griswold Manufacturing Company until it was sold to Wagner in 1957.

There is almost a total absence of definitive literature available on Griswold muffin pans. The information that collectors would like to know, such as the shape of pans, markings, dates of manufacture, number made, etc., are totally non-existent. Newspaper advertisements and some sales catalogs and supplements are the only surviving information from this early era.

One of the first known ads is from the February 6, 1882 issue of the Erie Morning Dispatch and shows that muffin pans (gem, Vienna bread, French roll, biscuit, and muffin pans) were among the products of the Seldon and Griswold Manufacturing Company. The significance of this ad is that it gives factual evidence that muffin pans were made for many years prior to the 1890 catalog. In fact, because of the rather extensive list in the 1882 ad, one could reasonably infer that the Seldon and Griswold Manufacturing Company made some muffin pans in the 1870s and that muffin pans were a significant segment of their product line.

Pattern Numbers

During the 1880s and 1890s, as the Griswold product line expanded, it became necessary to develop a method to keep up with the various patterns. Griswold started using pattern numbers (P/N). These were assigned somewhat arbitrarily and were used strictly for internal control (within the factory). The placement of a pattern number on an individual product began in the 1880s; by the early 1900s virtually every item made by Griswold had a pattern number on it. The Griswold catalogs that are presently available were originally published for sales purposes only. They did not contain pattern numbers, further evidence that pattern numbers were for internal use. When an item was dropped from production, its pattern number was avail-

GENERAL FOUNDRY

Selden & Griswold Man'f'g Co.,
ERIE, PA
MANUFACTURERS OF

Copying presses,	Lid-Lifters,
Ink Stands,	Coal Shovels,
Umbrella Stands,	Coal Tongs,
Fire Pokers,	Parlor Fire Sets,

THE AMERICAN STOVE PIPE DAMPER,
STOVE PIPE SAFETY HEAD,

Gem Vienna Bread, French Roll, Biscuit and Muffin Pans,
THE NOVELTY CAKE MOLD.

FINE LIGHT CASTINGS A SPECIALTY.

Seldon & Griswold Manufacturing Company advertisement from the February 6, 1882 Erie Morning Dispatch.

able to be assigned to a new item. There are many examples of pattern numbers being reused. Pattern numbers used by Griswold are a significant identifying feature used by collectors. The pattern numbers for the Griswold cast iron muffin pans are listed in numerical order in the Appendix in the back of this book.

Evolutionary Changes

The Griswold Manufacturing Company produced a quality product line and was responsive to customer demands. This is evident by the evolutionary changes they incorporated in their line of muffin pans. They did many things to increase their sales and develop the leadership position that they attained in an industry that was extremely competitive.

Gate marks are the result of the casting process where the molten metal was poured into the mold. Early on this was done through the bottom of the pans. After about 1890 Griswold's process was to pour the molten metal into the mold through the top outside edge. The resulting excess metal was then ground off to create a smooth area. This was specifically stated in the 1890 catalog, "the process by which these pans are made not only avoids rough bottoms, caused by gate marks running across the pan, but also leaves the casting inside very smooth...".

Various Griswold sales catalogs gave different names to the same pan. The catalogs identified pans as whatever the users wanted them to be in order to maximize salability. An example of this is the No 32 pan which was referred to as an egg poacher, a Danish cake pan, and an apple cake pan at various times. There are many other examples of this. It is suggested that the terminology used in this book be considered as the standard among collectors when they refer to the various Griswold muffin pans. This would minimize misunderstandings and provide a clear consistent language to describe Griswold muffin pans since there presently is no standard.

Some very early pans were totally unmarked and some were marked only with the trade number and/or the pattern number. Trade numbers were assigned by Griswold and used to identify the products in Griswold's sales literature and to their customers. The pattern numbers were used by Griswold only internal to the factory, as they do not appear in the Griswold sales literature. Then more markings were added until most of the pans produced from the 1910s forward were extensively marked. The markings on a fully marked pan included: the trade number, GRISWOLD, ERIE PA. U. S. A., pan description (e.g., CORN OR WHEAT STICK PAN), pattern number, and a patent date or number on some. This was done to sell pans, without any thought for the modern day collector. Word of mouth has always been the best form of advertising. Successful cooks using Griswold pans that were marked Griswold proved to be a very effective sales force.

While some pans were produced throughout Griswold's history, others came and went based on user demands. Griswold placed the various products before the public. The best sellers endured while others were dropped. This created pans of varying rarity for the modern day collector.

Many of the early pans, primarily the bread pans and the wide band French roll pans, did not have hang holes or any features that would facilitate hanging. Apparently users liked to hang their cookware in the kitchen. This lead to many hang holes being drilled in the pans that didn't have them. It should be noted that all of the pans produced from the early 1920s do have features that facilitate hanging. Again Griswold responded to the desires of its customers.

While the cast iron was by far the most popular line of muffin pans, Griswold did use other materials to offer versatility to the users. Some pans were made of aluminum, some chrome plated, some nickel plated, some with a silver-like finish, and two had a porcelain finish. Also two muffin pans (No 10 Popover Pan and No 273 Corn Stick Pan) were produced with a hammered finish on the top surface. A No 34 Plett Pan was produced with a specially milled bottom surface for use on electric stoves. Griswold tried to be all things for all people in the production of muffin pans.

Chapter 2.
Collecting
Griswold Muffin
Pans

Variations

A variation as used in this book pertaining to Griswold muffin pans is defined as a pan that is distinct from others because of a difference in shape, markings, or the location of markings. On some pans there is a letter used in conjunction with the pattern number. This letter indicates a different series, but it is not considered a different variation if that is the only difference. The muffin pans that were made for long periods of time have many variations while those that were short lived may exist in only one variation.

There are 226 variations described in this book. However, there are probably several variations that are still unknown to the collecting community and that are waiting to be "found". All of the variations described herein are known to the collecting community.

Series

There are many series of Griswold muffin pans. Collecting all of the variations may be out of the reach of many collectors. However, collecting series of the muffin pans may provide interesting challenges and satisfaction. The French roll pans are an interesting series and make an excellent wall display. There are many series, including Turk head pans, wheat stick pans, Vienna roll pans, corn stick pans, corn or wheat stick pans, bread pans, hearts/star pans, and gem pans.

Some collectors collect only the most fully marked of each pan. Others collect only the significantly different shapes of the various pans. Griswold muffin pans provide the versatility and flexibility to satisfy every cast iron cookware collector.

Affordability

Griswold muffin pans range in value from $15 to $3000. The rarest pans are beyond the reach of the average collector. However, one should be able to acquire approximately one half of the variations for about $100 or less and approximately one third of them for about $50 or less. Collecting the 15 variations of the No 10 Popover Pan or the 15 variations of the No 22 Bread Stick Pan is affordable, enjoyable, and extremely challenging. Many times it is possible, by knowing how to identify the early pans, to obtain very expensive pans for a modest price. Griswold muffin pans or series of them are affordable for every collector of cast iron cookware.

Reproductions

Reproductions are not the detriment to cast iron cookware collectors that they are to many areas of antique collecting. There are reproductions of several Griswold muffin pans, namely the No 2 Vienna Roll Pan, No 27 and No 28 Wheat Stick Pans, No 262 Corn Stick Pan, and No 280 Corn or Wheat Stick Pan. There may be some others. These reproductions are, for the most part, rather crude and grainy, slightly smaller in size, and generally of poor quality. Even a novice collector should be able to distinguish between the originals and the reproductions. The reproductions currently known are not collectible and are considered of no value.

The Challenges for the Collector

The 226 variations of Griswold muffin pans range from the extremely common to a couple of pans that are illustrated in Griswold catalogs but are not presently in the collecting community. It is a challenge to get these pans out of attics and cupboards and into collections. Collecting Griswold muffin pans will try your patience, test your knowledge, and provide unlimited enjoyment.

Griswold Wide Band French Roll Pans -- top from left: No 11, No 17, bottom: No 15, No 16

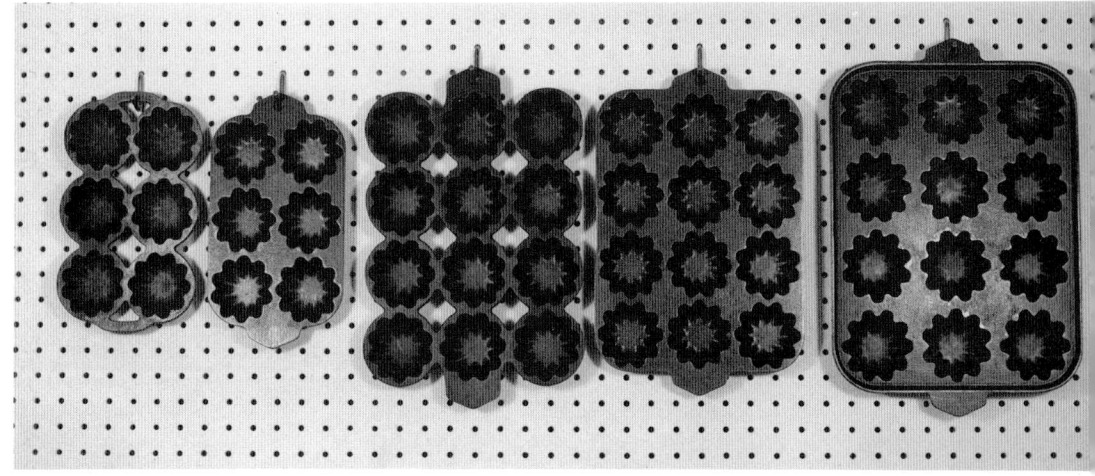

Griswold Turk Head Pans -- from left: No 13, No 130, No 14, No 140, No 240

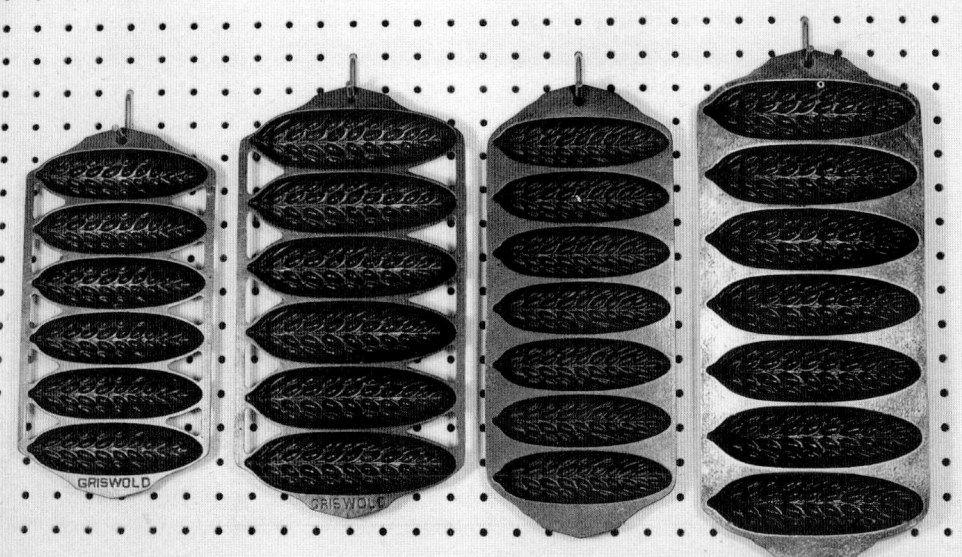

Griswold Wheat Stick Pans -- from left: No 27, No 28, No 2700, No 2800

Griswold Corn Stick Pans -- from left: No 262, No 273, No 283

Griswold Hearts/Star Pans -- from left: No 100, No 50

Chapter 3.
Variations of Griswold Cast Iron Muffin Pans

Summary

The following text provides detailed information on the 59 cast iron muffin pans, and the 207 variations of them, that were made and marketed by Griswold.

Pan No.	Description	P/N	No. of Variations
No 1	Vienna Roll Pan	955?	1
No 1	Gem Pan	940	3
No 2	Vienna Roll Pan	956	3
No 2	Gem Pan	941	4
No 3	Gem Pan	942	5
No 4	Vienna Roll Pan	957	4
No 5	Gem Pan	943	7
No 6	Gem Pan	944	6
No 6	Vienna Roll Pan	958	6
No 7	Gem Pan	945	3
No 8	Gem Pan	946	6
No 9	Golfball Pan (10 Cup)	947	3
No 9	Golfball Pan	947	6
No 10	Popover Pan	948	15
No 10	Popover Pan	949	2
No 10	Popover Pan (Hammered)	2070	1
No 11	French Roll Pan (H Pattern)	949?	2
No 11	French Roll Pan	950	11
No 12	Gem Pan	951	7
No 13	Turk Head Pan	640	1
No 14	Gem Pan	952	6
No 14	Turk Head Pan	641	1
No 15	French Roll Pan	6138	3
No 16	French Roll Pan	6139	5
No 17	French Roll Pan	6140	6
No 18	Popover Pan	6141	7
No 19	Golfball Pan	966	3
No 20	Turk Head Pan	953	8
No 21	Bread Stick Pan	961	1
No 22	Bread Stick Pan	954	15
No 23	Bread Stick Pan	955	2
No 24	Bread Pan	959	2
No 24	Bread Stick Pan	957	1
No 26	Bread Pan	960	2
No 26	Vienna Roll Pan	958	2
No 27	Wheat Stick Pan	638	4
No 28	Bread Pan	961?	1
No 28	Wheat Stick Pan	639	4
No 31	Danish Cake Pan	963	4
No 32	Danish Cake Pan	962	7
No 33	Munk Pan	2992	2
No 34	Plett Pan	2980	5
No 34	Plett Pan (Milled Bottom)	969	1
No 50	Hearts/Star Pan	959	1
No 100	Hearts/Star Pan	960	1
No 130	Turk Head Pan	634	1
No 140	Turk Head Pan	635	1
No 240	Turk Head Pan	631	1
No 262	Corn Stick Pan	625	2
No 270	Corn or Wheat Stick Pan	636	1
No 272	Corn or Wheat Stick Pan	629	2
No 273	Corn Stick Pan	930	1
No 273	Corn Stick Pan (Hammered)	2073	1
No 280	Corn or Wheat Stick Pan	637	1
No 282	Corn or Wheat Stick Pan	630	2
No 283	Corn Stick Pan	931	1
No 2700	Wheat Stick Pan	632	1
No 2800	Wheat Stick Pan	633	1
No -	Corn or Wheat Stick Pan	623	1

Dimensions for each of the pans are given in the following pages. These dimensions could vary from 1/16 to 1/8 of an inch on similar pans since there were differences from mold to mold.

A rarity number from 1 to 10 is assigned to each variation where 1 is the most common and 10 is the rarest. The rarity number can be described as; 1-2 very common, 3-4 common, 5-6 uncommon, 7-8 rare, and 9-10 very rare. The rarity number was determined by considering the availability of the pans to the collecting community in the judgment of the author. The rarity number is a relative number and was not analytically determined. Therefore, the rarity number should be used as an indicator and not an absolute.

Values are the most used, misused, and controversial part of any book on antiques and collectibles. The value range was obtained by considering the rarity and the desirability as well as recent transactions known to the author. The value range stated herein are the **retail values** for pans that **have been cleaned** (cooking residue removed) and are in **excellent condition** (no cracks, pitting, rust or warpage). The value is for pans as they were made. Casting flaws, unless extreme, would not significantly affect the value. Pans that have not been cleaned are valued at 25-30% less. The value of damaged pans would depend on the rarity, desirability, and the extent of the damage and would have to be considered on an individual basis.

The production dates of each pan are not accurately known. The approximate production dates have been determined primarily by information from the Griswold sales catalogs. As would be expected, the pans that were produced for longer periods of time have the greatest number of variations.

No 1 Vienna Roll Pan

P/N 955?
No. of cups: 1
Dimensions: 13 13/16" x 4 7/8"
Production Date: 1880s to 1890s
Rarity: 10
Value: $2500 to $3000

The No 1 Vienna Roll Pan is only known in one variation, which is without a P/N. If it were made with a P/N, it is believed that the P/N would be 955. This is because of the sequence of P/N's and the location of the No 1 Vienna Roll Pan in the 1890 Griswold catalog. This is a very rare and desirable pan.

NO 1 VIENNA ROLL PAN P/N 955?

NO 1 (955?) RARITY: 10

VIENNA ROLL PAN No 1

VIEW OF TOP SIDE

NOTE: DRAWING IS NOT TO SCALE

VIEW OF UNDERSIDE

Top view of No 1 Vienna Roll Pan

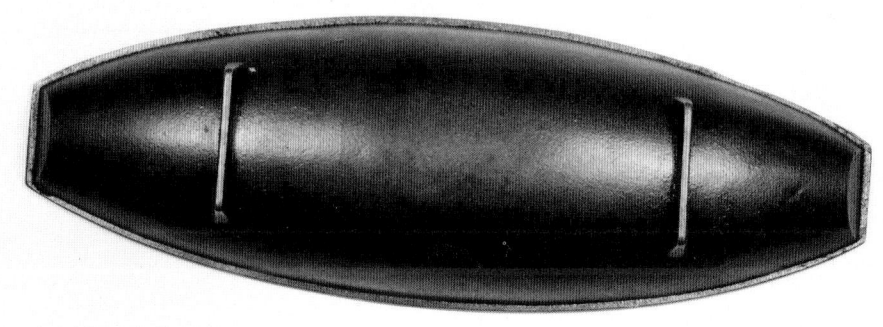

Underside of No 1 Vienna Roll Pan

No 1 Gem Pan

P/N 940
No. of cups: 11
Dimensions: 11 1/2" x 7 3/4"
Production Date: 1880s to 1920s
Variation 1: Rarity 4; Value: $90 to $110
Variation 2: Rarity 5; Value: $175 to $200
Variation 3: Rarity 6; Value: $300 to $325

The No 1 Gem Pan is very similar to the No 2 Gem Pan; however, the No 1 Gem Pan has square corners in the bottom of the cups whereas the No 2 Gem Pan has rounded corners. It is suspected there may be other variations of this pan that are not presently known to the collecting community.

Top view of Variation 3 of No 1 Gem Pan

Underside of Variation 2 of No 1 Gem Pan

Underside of Variation 3 of No 1 Gem Pan

NO 1 GEM PAN
P/N 940

VARIATION 1 RARITY: 4

(OPEN FRAME)   (VARIATION 1)

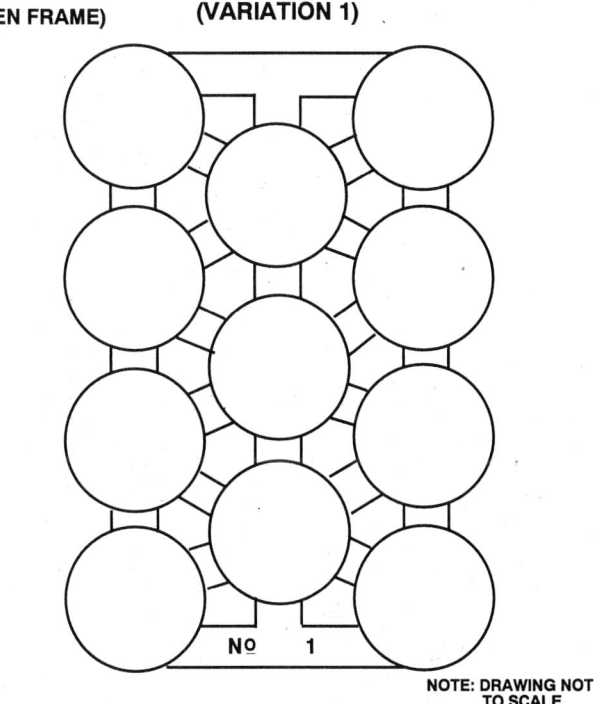

NO 1

NOTE: DRAWING NOT
TO SCALE

VIEW OF UNDERSIDE

NO 1 GEM PAN
P/N 940

VARIATION 3 RARITY: 6

(OPEN FRAME)   (VARIATION 3)

(RAISED LETTERS)

NO   1

GRISWOLD

ERIE, PA.,   U. S. A.

940

NOTE: DRAWING NOT
TO SCALE

VIEW OF UNDERSIDE

NO 1 GEM PAN
P/N 940

VARIATION 2 RARITY: 5

(OPEN FRAME)   (VARIATION 2)

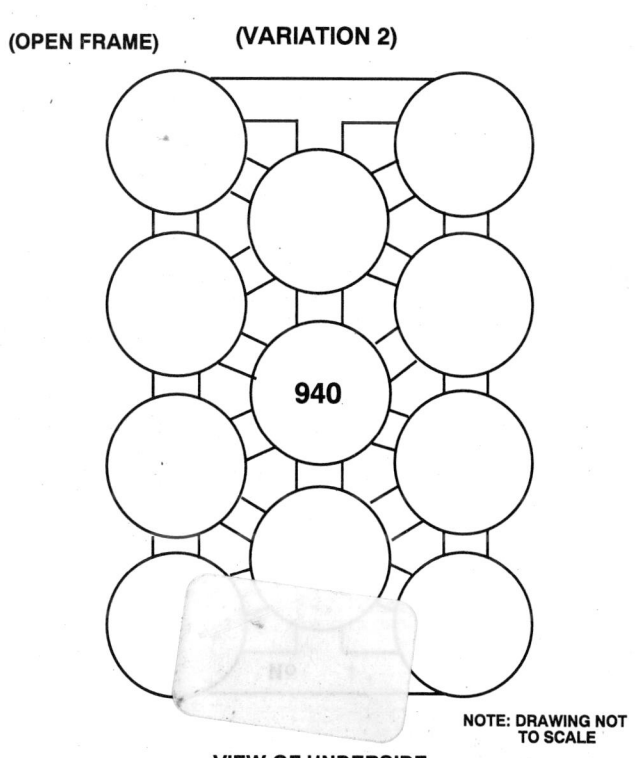

940

NOTE: DRAWING NOT
TO SCALE

VIEW OF UNDERSIDE

13

No 2 Vienna Roll Pan

P/N 956
No. of cups: 2
Dimensions: 12" x 7 1/2"
Production Date: 1880s to 1910s
Variation 1: Rarity 8; Value $700 to $900
Variation 2: Rarity 9; Value $1000 to $1200
Variation 3: Rarity 10; Value $2300 to $2600

The No 2 Vienna Roll Pan is an early pan that has VIENNA ROLL BREAD PAN written in raised letters on the inside of the cups. Variation 3 is marked with P/N 956 and does not have the lettering on the inside of the cups. Variation 3 is the rarest and most desirable of the No 2 Vienna Roll Pans.

Top view of Variation 2 of No 2 Vienna Roll Pan

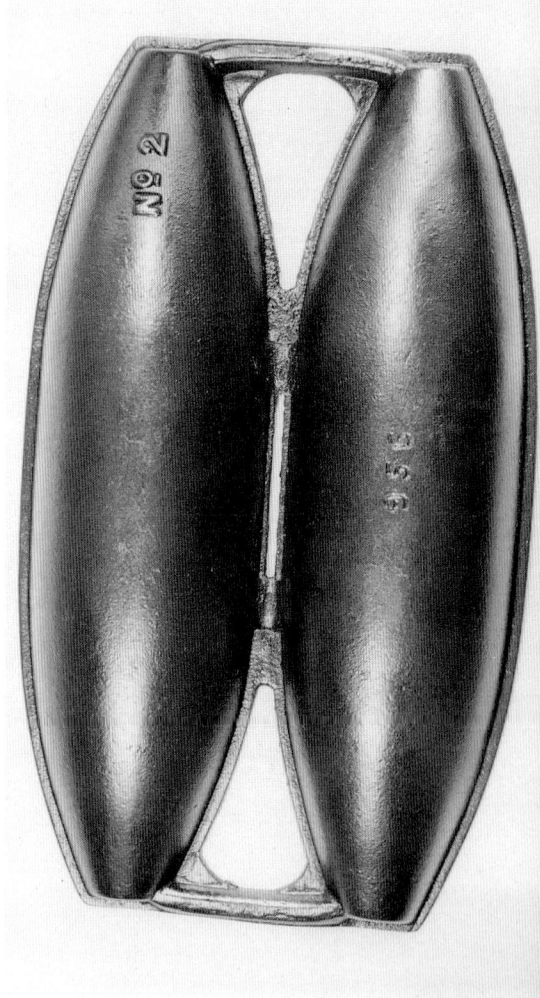

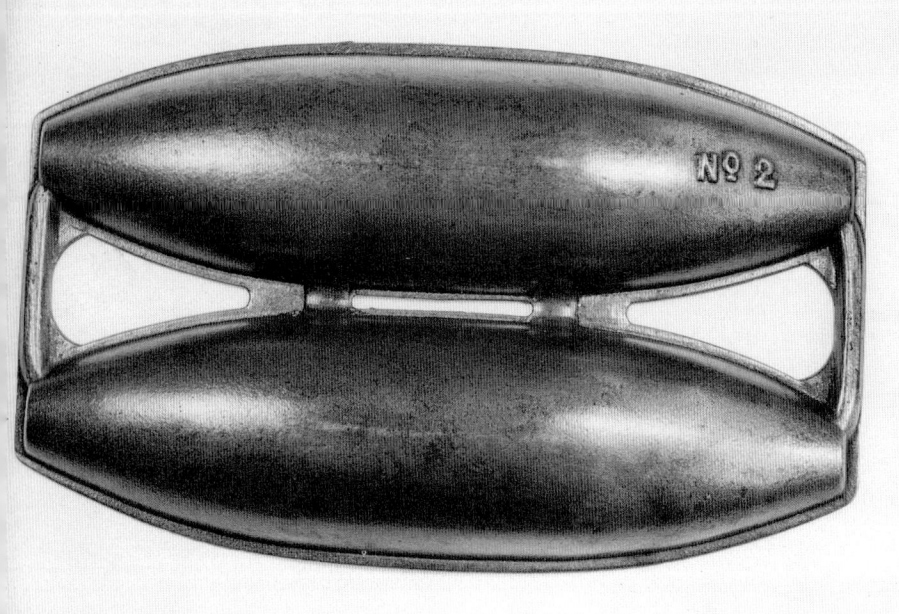

Underside of Variation 3 of No 2 Vienna Roll Pan

Underside of Variation 2 of No 2 Vienna Roll Pan

NO 2 VIENNA ROLL PAN
P/N 956

VARIATION 1 RARITY: 8

(OPEN FRAME)   (VARIATION 1)

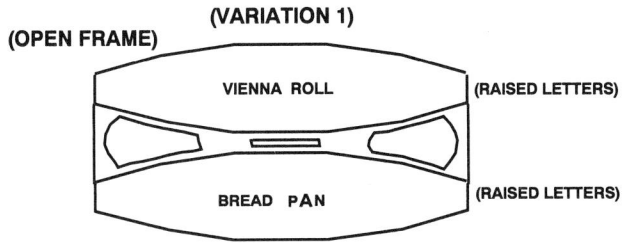

VIENNA ROLL   (RAISED LETTERS)

BREAD PAN   (RAISED LETTERS)

VIEW OF TOP SIDE

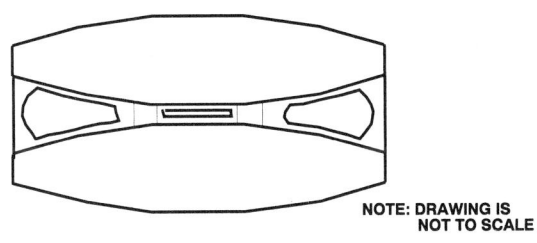

NOTE: DRAWING IS
NOT TO SCALE

VIEW OF UNDERSIDE

NO 2 VIENNA ROLL PAN
P/N 956

VARIATION 2 RARITY: 9

(OPEN FRAME)   (VARIATION 2)

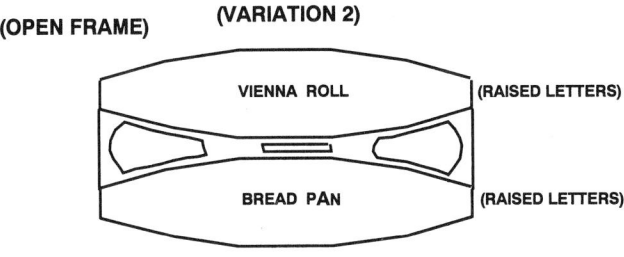

VIENNA ROLL   (RAISED LETTERS)

BREAD PAN   (RAISED LETTERS)

VIEW OF TOP SIDE

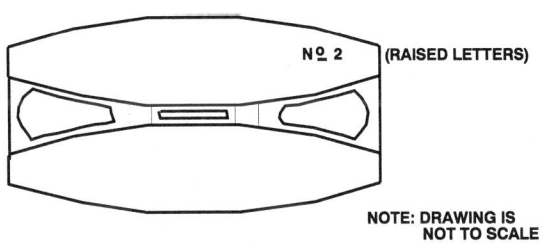

N⁰ 2   (RAISED LETTERS)

NOTE: DRAWING IS
NOT TO SCALE

VIEW OF UNDERSIDE

NO 2 VIENNA ROLL PAN
P/N 956

VARIATION 3 RARITY: 10

(OPEN FRAME)   (VARIATION 3)

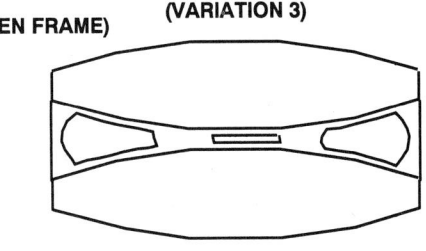

VIEW OF TOP SIDE

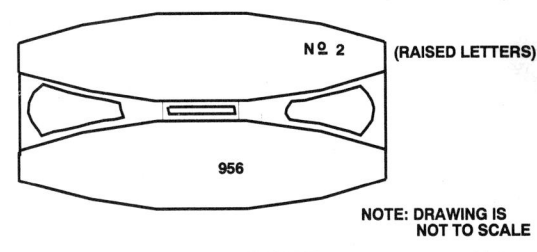

N⁰ 2   (RAISED LETTERS)

956

NOTE: DRAWING IS
NOT TO SCALE

VIEW OF UNDERSIDE

No 2 Gem Pan

P/N 941
No. of cups: 11
Dimensions: 12 1/2" x 8 1/2"
Production Date: 1880s to 1900s
Variation 1: Rarity 5; Value $90 to $110
Variation 2: Rarity 6; Value $175 to $200
Variation 3: Rarity 6; Value $150 to $175
Variation 4: Rarity 7; Value $300 to $350

    The No 2 Gem Pan is another early pan and is identified by the P/N 941. This pan has rounded corners on the bottom of the cups. This pan is of moderate rarity and the variation with the P/N is the most desirable.

Top view of Variation 4 of No 2 Gem Pan

Underside of Variation 2 of No 2 Gem Pan

Underside of Variation 4 of No 2 Gem Pan

NO 2 GEM PAN
P/N 941

VARIATION 1 RARITY: 5

(OPEN FRAME)   **(VARIATION 1)**

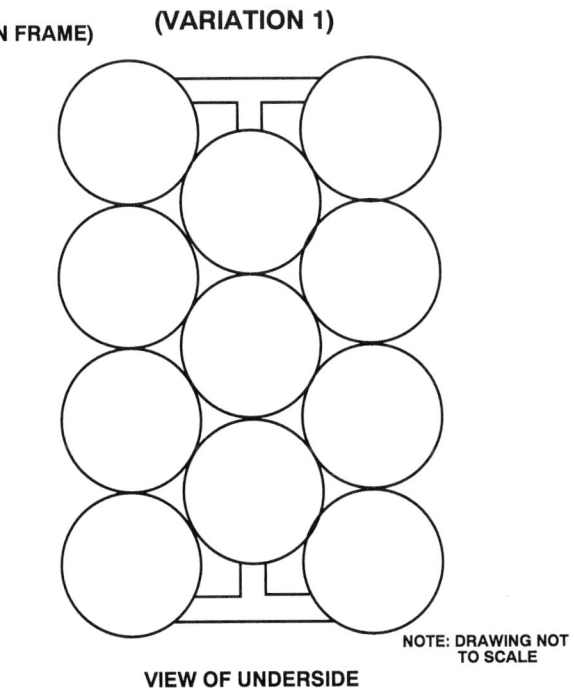

NOTE: DRAWING NOT
TO SCALE

VIEW OF UNDERSIDE

NOTE: THERE ARE NO MARKINGS ON THIS PAN. THE SIZE AND
QUALITY ARE IDENTICAL TO THE MARKED PANS.

NO 2 GEM PAN
P/N 941

VARIATION 3 RARITY: 6

(OPEN FRAME)   **(VARIATION 3)**

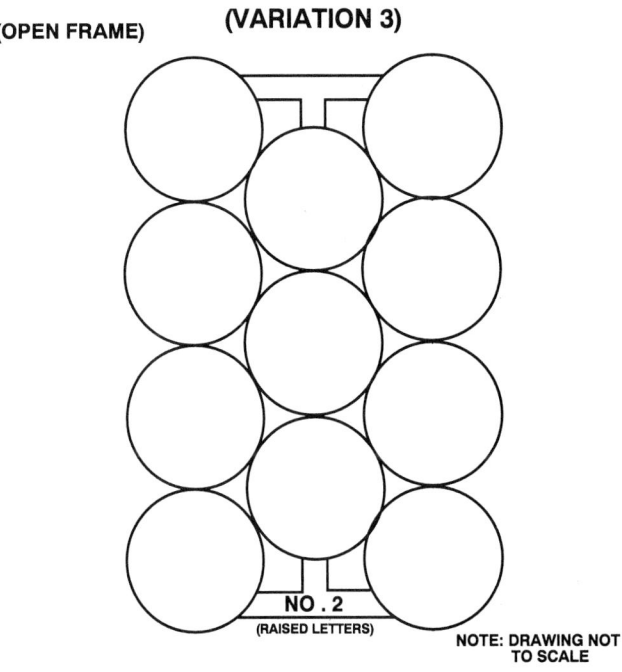

NO . 2
(RAISED LETTERS)   NOTE: DRAWING NOT
TO SCALE

VIEW OF UNDERSIDE

NOTE: THE UNDERSIDE OF THE HANDLES ARE ROUNDED

NO 2 GEM PAN
P/N 941

VARIATION 2 RARITY: 6

(OPEN FRAME)

(VARIATION 2)

N⍛ 2
(RAISED LETTERS)
NOTE: DRAWING NOT
TO SCALE

VIEW OF UNDERSIDE

NO 2 GEM PAN
P/N 941

VARIATION 4 RARITY: 7

(OPEN FRAME)   **(VARIATION 4)**

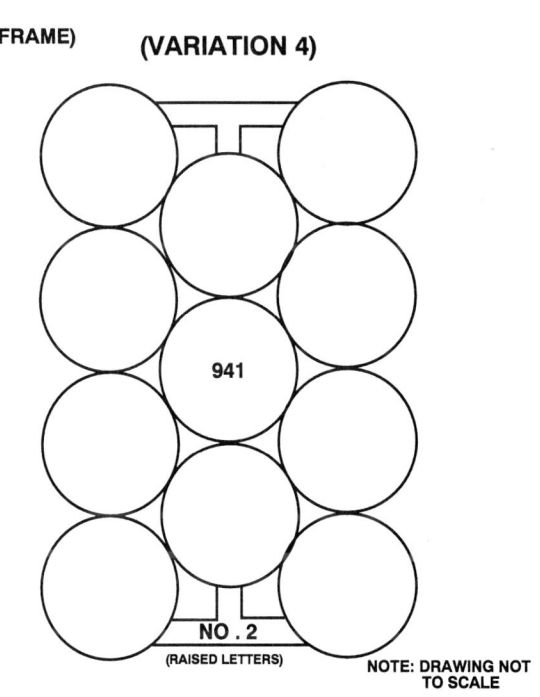

941

NO . 2
(RAISED LETTERS)   NOTE: DRAWING NOT
TO SCALE

VIEW OF UNDERSIDE

NOTE: THE UNDERSIDE OF THE HANDLES ARE ROUNDED

No 3 Gem Pan

P/N 942
No. of cups: 11
Dimensions: 12 1/2" x 8 1/2"
Production Date: 1880s to 1920s
Variation 1: Rarity 5; Value $115 to $135
Variation 2: Rarity 6; Value $140 to $160
Variation 3: Rarity 6; Value $250 to $300
Variation 4: Rarity 6; Value $450 to $500
Variation 5: Rarity 7; Value $550 to $600

The No 3 Gem Pan was made until the 1920s. There are 5 variations of this pan which range from pans with few marks to one with the slant logo with ERIE, PA U.S.A. As with most pans, the most fully marked pan is the most desirable and coveted by collectors.

Underside of Variation 1 of No 3 Gem Pan

NO 3 GEM PAN
P/N 942

VARIATION 1 RARITY: 5

(OPEN FRAME)   (VARIATION 1)

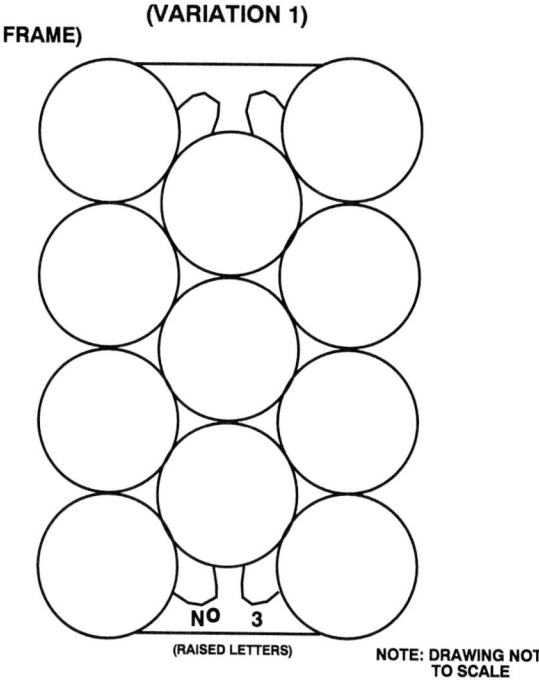

(RAISED LETTERS)   NOTE: DRAWING NOT TO SCALE

VIEW OF UNDERSIDE

NO 3 GEM PAN
P/N 942

VARIATION 2 RARITY: 6

(OPEN FRAME)   (VARIATION 2)

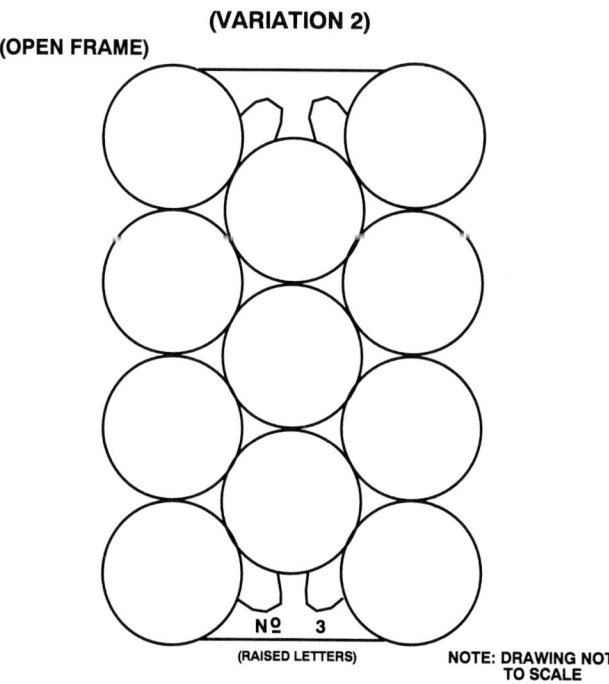

(RAISED LETTERS)   NOTE: DRAWING NOT TO SCALE

VIEW OF UNDERSIDE

NO 3 GEM PAN
P/N 942

VARIATION 3 RARITY: 6

(VARIATION 3)

(OPEN FRAME)

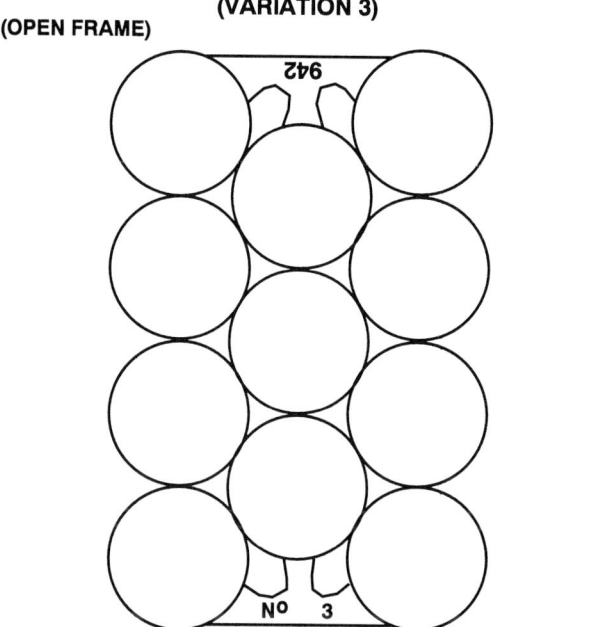

942

Nº 3

(RAISED LETTERS)

NOTE: DRAWING NOT TO SCALE

VIEW OF UNDERSIDE

Top view of Variation 4 of No 3 Gem Pan

NO 3 GEM PAN
P/N 942

VARIATION 4 RARITY: 6

(VARIATION 4)

(OPEN FRAME)

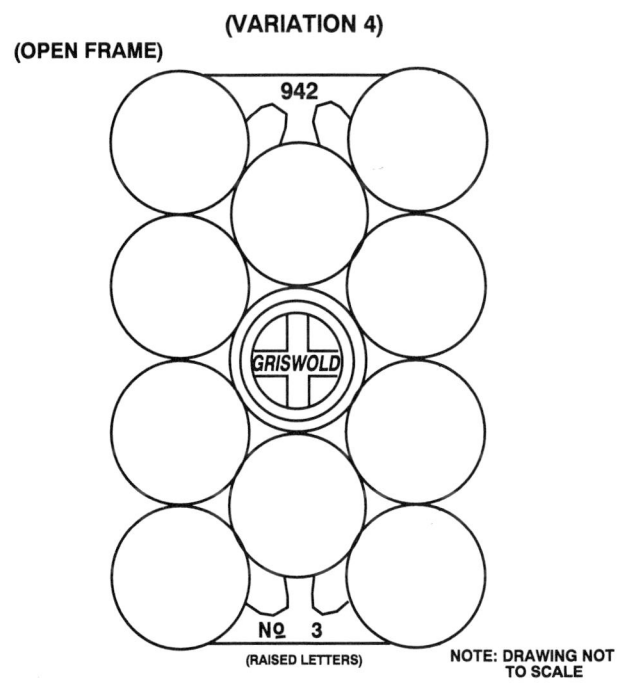

942

GRISWOLD

Nº 3

(RAISED LETTERS)

NOTE: DRAWING NOT TO SCALE

VIEW OF UNDERSIDE

Underside of Variation 5 of No 3 Gem Pan

NO 3 GEM PAN
P/N 942

VARIATION 5 RARITY: 7

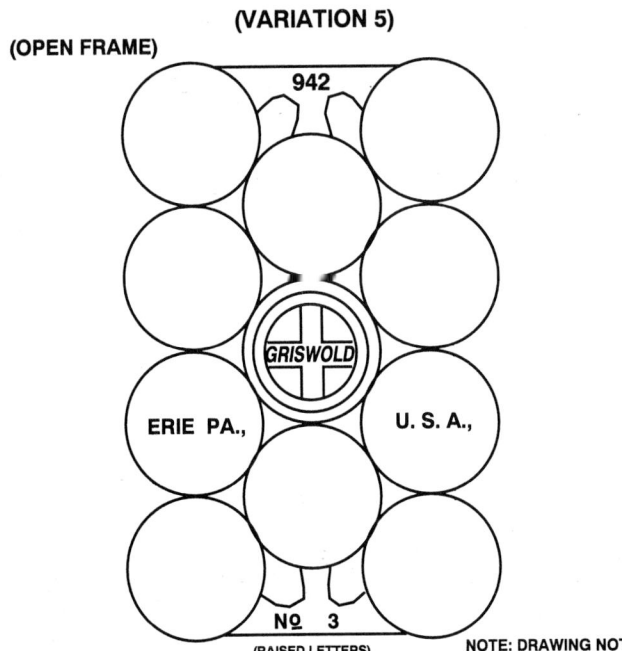

(OPEN FRAME)

(VARIATION 5)

942

GRISWOLD

ERIE PA.,   U. S. A.,

Nº 3

(RAISED LETTERS)

NOTE: DRAWING NOT TO SCALE

VIEW OF UNDERSIDE

No 4 Vienna Roll Pan

P/N 957
No. of cups: 4
Dimensions: 12 1/2" x 6 1/2"
Production Date: 1880s to 1910s
Variation 1: Rarity 10; Value $400 to $500
Variation 2: Rarity 10; Value $700 to $800
Variation 3: Rarity 10; Value $1000 to $1200
Variation 4: Rarity 10; Value $2500 to $3000

The No 4 Vienna Roll Pan is another early pan without many markings. There are variations of this pan with gate marks. Variation 4 is the most marked variation with a No 4 and 957 (the P/N). This variation is very rare, with only about 4 known in the collecting community.

NO 4 VIENNA ROLL PAN
P/N 957

VARIATION 1 RARITY: 10

(OPEN FRAME)   (VARIATION 1)

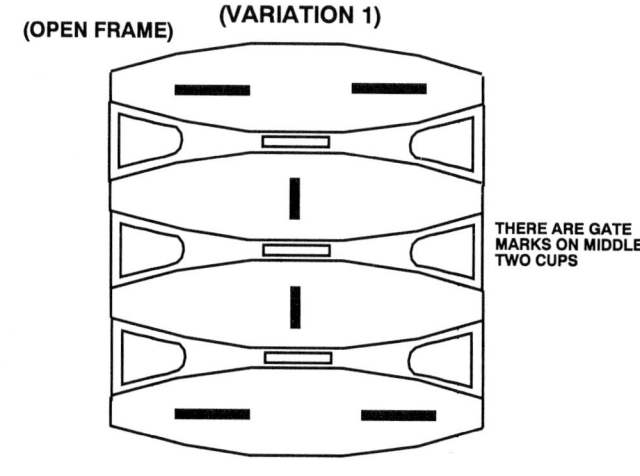

THERE ARE GATE MARKS ON MIDDLE TWO CUPS

NOTE: DRAWING IS NOT TO SCALE

VIEW OF UNDERSIDE

NOTE: THERE ARE NO MARKINGS ON THIS PAN, BUT THE DIMENSIONS AND QUALITY ARE SIMILAR TO THE MARKED NO 4 VIENNA ROLL PAN

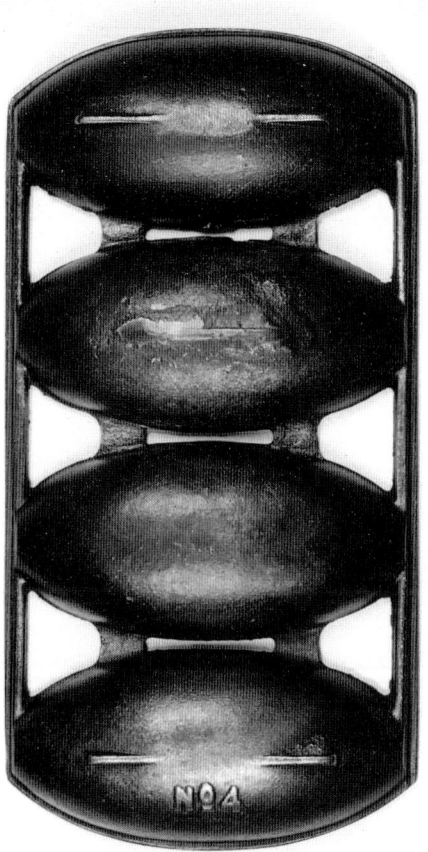

Underside of Variation 2 of No 4 Vienna Roll Pan

NO 4 VIENNA ROLL PAN
P/N 957

VARIATION 2 RARITY: 10

(VARIATION 2)

(OPEN FRAME)

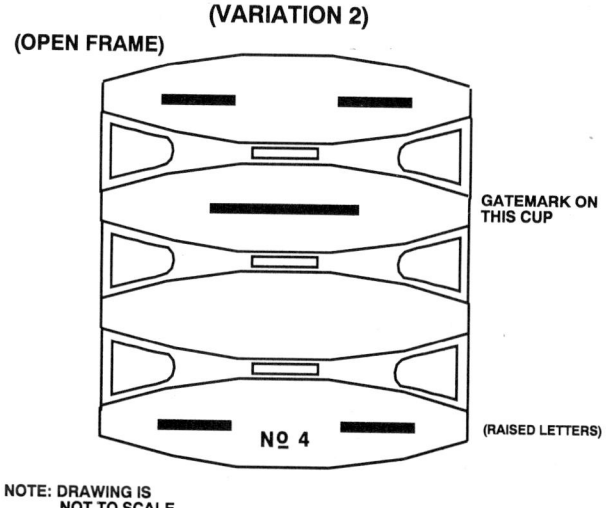

GATEMARK ON THIS CUP

NO 4

(RAISED LETTERS)

NOTE: DRAWING IS NOT TO SCALE

VIEW OF UNDERSIDE

Top view of Variation 3 of No 4 Vienna Roll Pan

NO 4 VIENNA ROLL PAN
P/N 957

VARIATION 3 RARITY: 10

(VARIATION 3)

(OPEN FRAME)

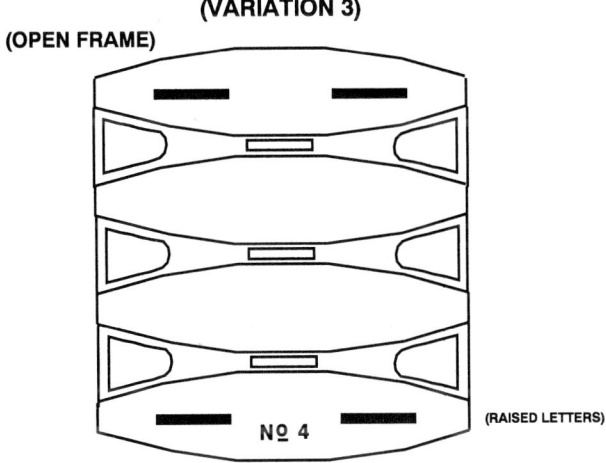

NO 4

(RAISED LETTERS)

NOTE: DRAWING IS NOT TO SCALE

VIEW OF UNDERSIDE

Underside of Variation 3 of No 4 Vienna Roll Pan

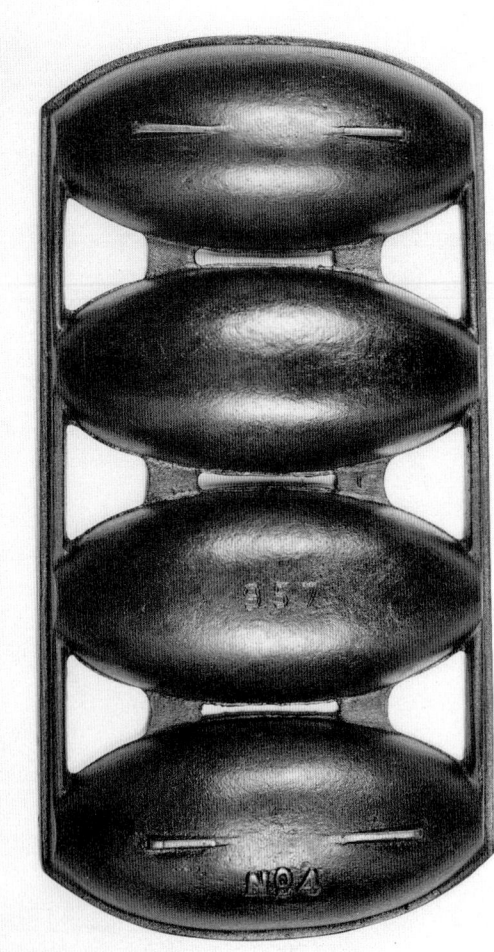

Underside of Variation 4 of No 4 Vienna Roll Pan

NO 4 VIENNA ROLL PAN
P/N 957

VARIATION 4 RARITY: 10

(OPEN FRAME)   **(VARIATION 4)**

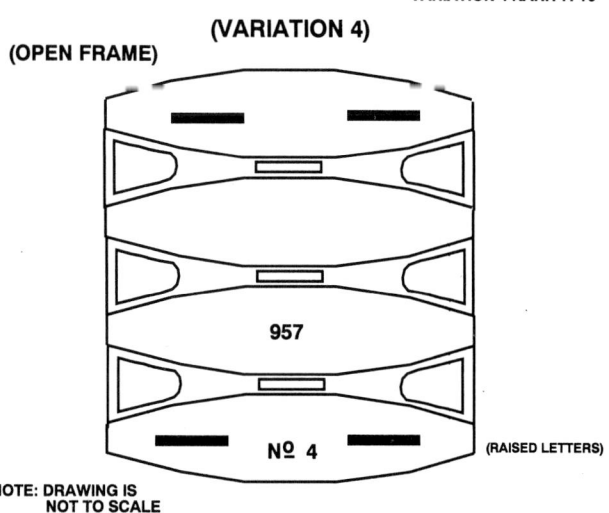

957

NO 4   (RAISED LETTERS)

NOTE: DRAWING IS
NOT TO SCALE

VIEW OF UNDERSIDE

No 5 Gem Pan

P/N 943
No. of cups: 8
Dimensions: 12" x 7 1/2"
Production Date: 1880s to 1920s
Variation 1: Rarity 5; Value $110 to $125
Variation 2: Rarity 7; Value $225 to $275
Variation 3: Rarity 5; Value $125 to $150
Variation 4: Rarity 5; Value $225 to $275
Variation 5: Rarity 7; Value $600 to $700
Variation 6: Rarity 8; Value $700 to $800
Variation 7: Rarity 10; Value $1200 to $1500

The No 5 Gem Pan is a very interesting pan. Variation 2 is only marked with 943 (the P/N) in raised letters in a lettering style not normally used by Griswold. Variations 3 and 4 are marked N 5. These are the only examples where "No" was not used to represent number. Griswold is very consistent and methodical ... except for the inconsistencies. There is only one example of Variation 7 presently known in the collecting community.

Top view of Variation 1 of No 5 Gem Pan

NO 5 GEM PAN
P/N 943

VARIATION 1 RARITY: 5

(VARIATION 1)

(OPEN FRAME)

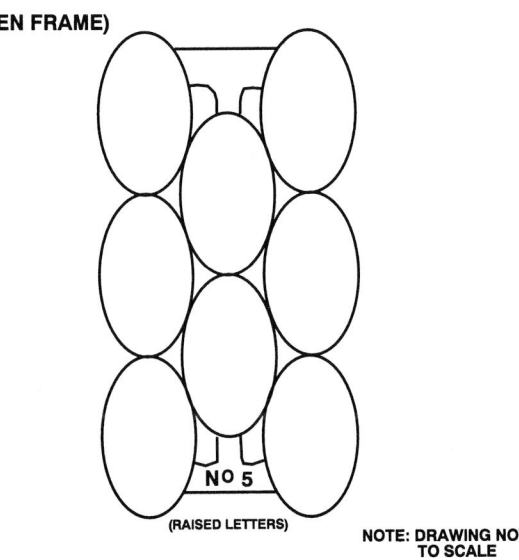

NO 5

(RAISED LETTERS)

NOTE: DRAWING NOT
TO SCALE

VIEW OF UNDERSIDE

Underside of Variation 2 of No 5 Gem Pan

NO 5 GEM PAN
P/N 943

VARIATION 2 RARITY: 7

(VARIATION 2)

(OPEN FRAME)

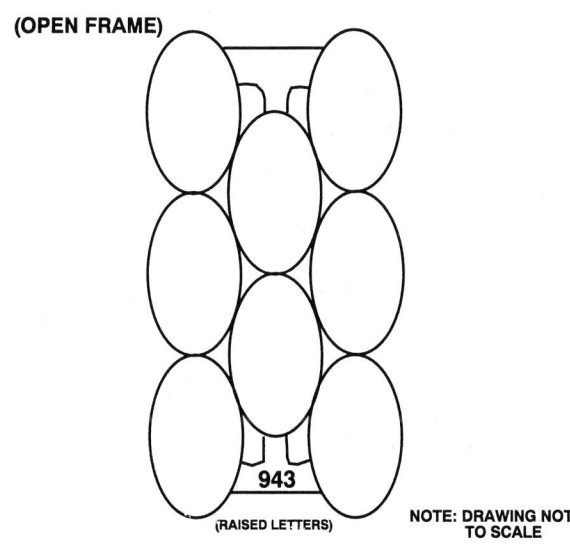

943

(RAISED LETTERS)

NOTE: DRAWING NOT
TO SCALE

VIEW OF UNDERSIDE

NO 5 GEM PAN
P/N 943

VARIATION 3 RARITY: 5

(VARIATION 3)

(OPEN FRAME)

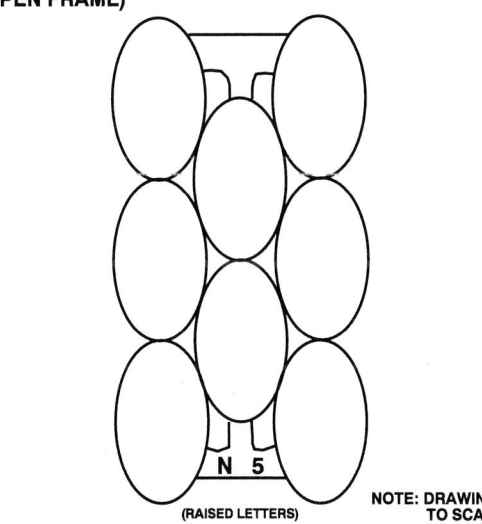

N 5

(RAISED LETTERS)

NOTE: DRAWING NOT
TO SCALE

VIEW OF UNDERSIDE

Underside of Variation 4 of No 5 Gem Pan

NO 5 GEM PAN
P/N 943

VARIATION 4 RARITY: 5

(VARIATION 4)
(OPEN FRAME)

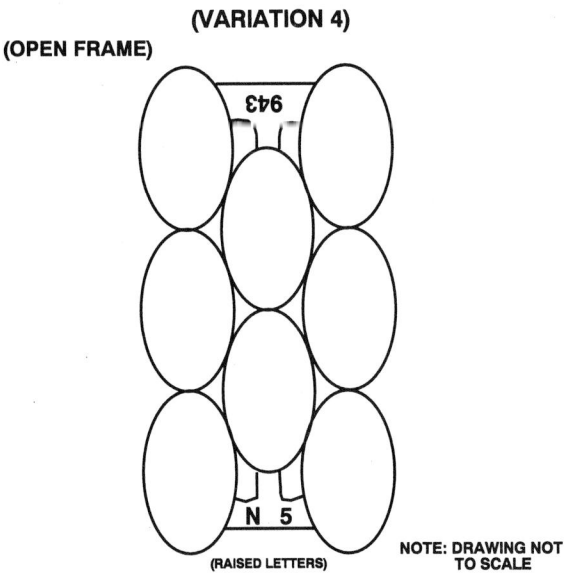

(RAISED LETTERS)

NOTE: DRAWING NOT TO SCALE

VIEW OF UNDERSIDE

NO 5 GEM PAN
P/N 943

VARIATION 5 RARITY: 7

(VARIATION 5)
(OPEN FRAME)

NOTE: DRAWING NOT TO SCALE

(RAISED LETTERS)

VIEW OF UNDERSIDE

Underside of Variation 6 of No 5 Gem Pan

NO 5 GEM PAN
P/N 943

VARIATION 6 RARITY: 8

(VARIATION 6)

(OPEN FRAME)

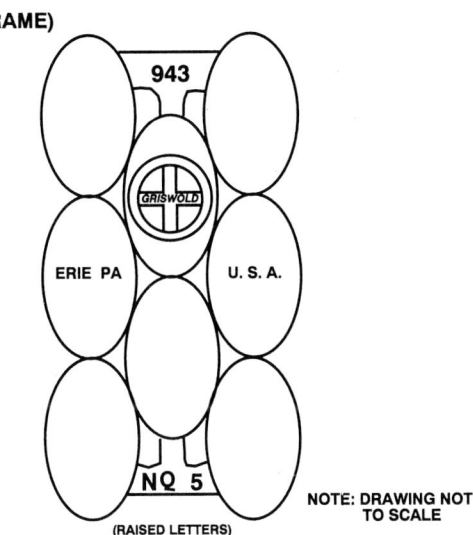

VIEW OF UNDERSIDE

NO 5 GEM PAN
P/N 943

VARIATION 7 RARITY: 10

(VARIATION 7)

(OPEN FRAME)

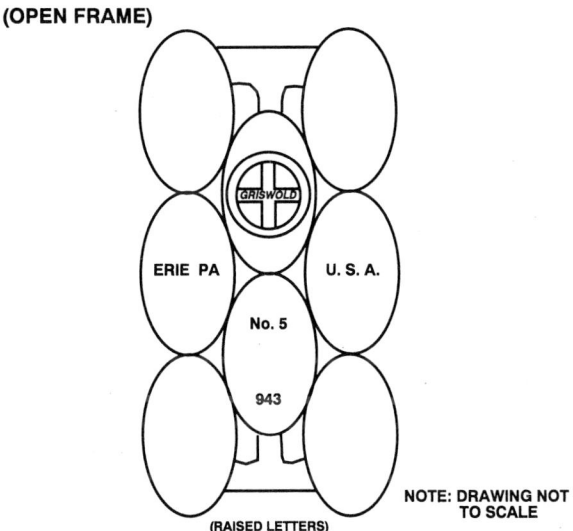

VIEW OF UNDERSIDE

No 6 Gem Pan

P/N 944
No. of cups: 12
Dimensions: 13" x 7 1/2"
Production Date: 1880s to 1920s
Variation 1: Rarity 6; Value $150 to $175
Variation 2: Rarity 5; Value $125 to $150
Variation 3: Rarity 6; Value $200 to $225
Variation 4: Rarity 6; Value $225 to $250
Variation 5: Rarity 10; Value $1400 to $1600
Variation 6: Rarity 7; Value $550 to $650

The No 6 Gem Pan was made for a long period of time. Variation 5 (marked with a slant logo) was recently discovered by the collecting community. There are only 3 or 4 examples of this pan presently known, making this the rarest of the No 6 Gem Pan variations. Variation 6 is the latest pan and the most fully marked variation.

NO 6 GEM PAN
P/N 944

VARIATION 1 RARITY: 6

(OPEN FRAME) **(VARIATION 1)**

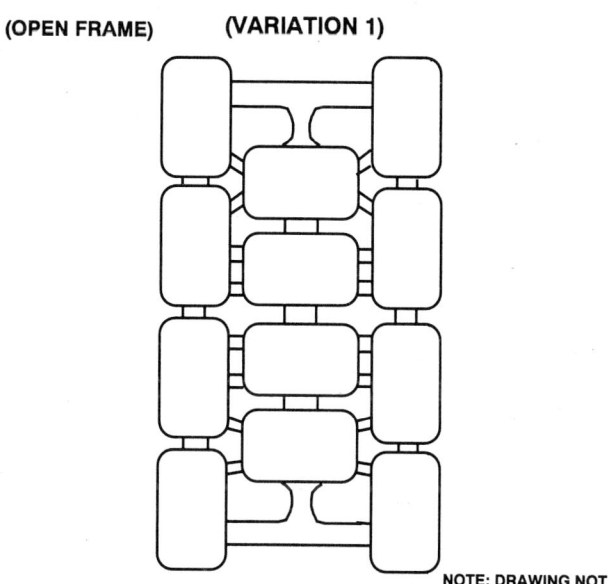

VIEW OF UNDERSIDE

NOTE: THERE ARE NO MARKINGS ON THIS PAN. THE WORKMANSHIP AND QUALITY ARE IDENTICAL TO THE EARLY MARKED PANS.

NO 6 GEM PAN
P/N 944

(OPEN FRAME) **(VARIATION 2)**

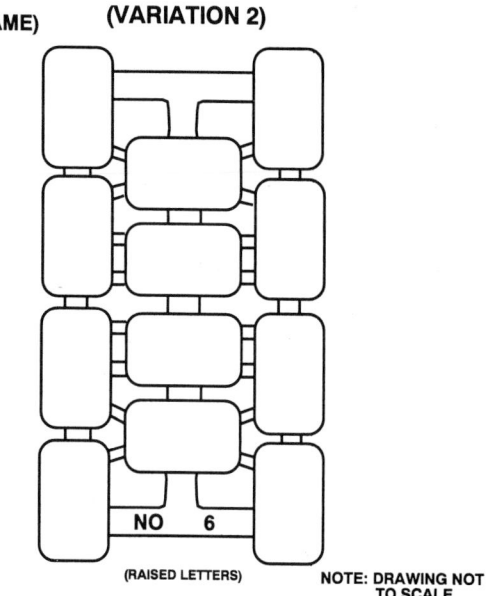

NO 6

(RAISED LETTERS) **NOTE: DRAWING NOT TO SCALE**

VIEW OF UNDERSIDE

NO 6 GEM PAN
P/N 944

(OPEN FRAME) **(VARIATION 3)**

NO 6

(RAISED LETTERS) **NOTE: DRAWING NOT TO SCALE**

VIEW OF UNDERSIDE

Top view of Variation 4 of No 6 Gem Pan

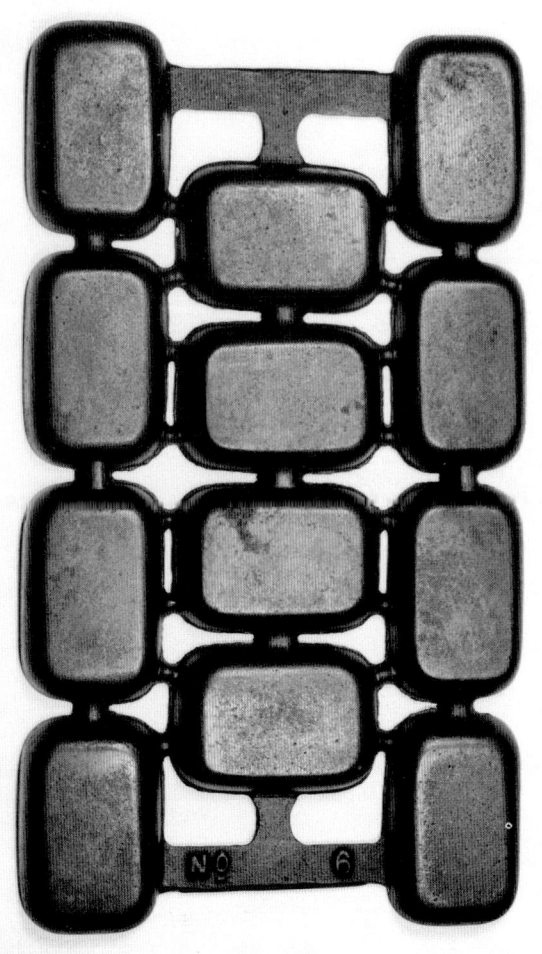

Underside of Variation 3 of No 6 Gem Pan

Underside of Variation 4 of No 6 Gem Pan

Underside of Variation 5 of No 6 Gem Pan

NO 6 GEM PAN
P/N 944

VARIATION 4 RARITY: 6

(OPEN FRAME)   (VARIATION 4)

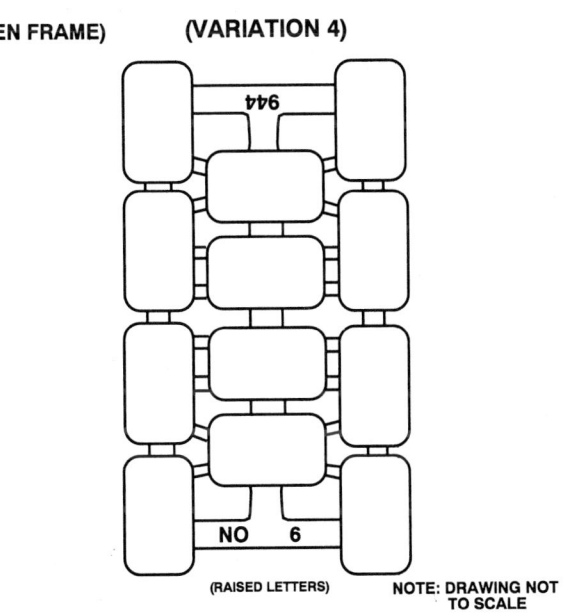

(RAISED LETTERS)   NOTE: DRAWING NOT TO SCALE

VIEW OF UNDERSIDE

NO 6 GEM PAN
P/N 944

VARIATION 5 RARITY: 10

(OPEN FRAME)   (VARIATION 5)

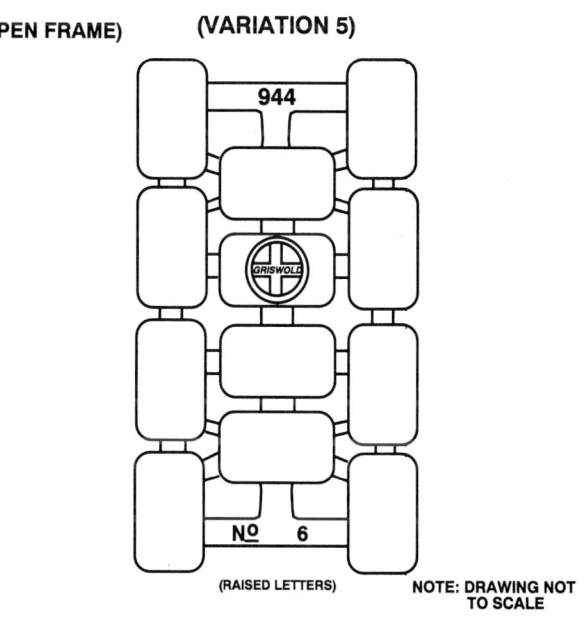

(RAISED LETTERS)   NOTE: DRAWING NOT TO SCALE

VIEW OF UNDERSIDE

Top view of Variation 6 of No 6 Gem Pan

NO 6 GEM PAN
P/N 944

VARIATION 6 RARITY: 7

(OPEN FRAME) **(VARIATION 6)**

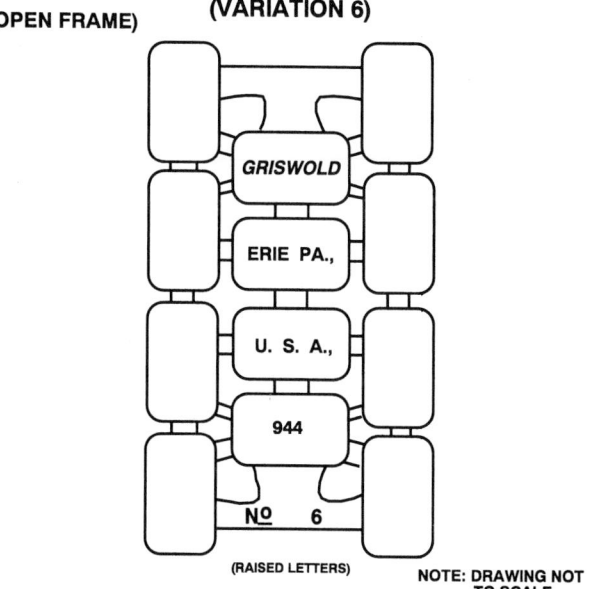

GRISWOLD

ERIE PA.,

U. S. A.,

944

N⁰   6

(RAISED LETTERS)   **NOTE: DRAWING NOT
TO SCALE**

VIEW OF UNDERSIDE

Underside of Variation 6 of No 6 Gem Pan

No 6 Vienna Roll Pan

P/N 958
No. of cups: 6
Dimensions: 12 1/2" x 6 1/2"
Production Date: 1880s to 1910s
Variation 1: Rarity 5; Value $200 to $250
Variation 2: Rarity 3; Value $75 to $100
Variation 3: Rarity 4; Value $100 to $125
Variation 4: Rarity 5; Value $175 to $200
Variation 5: Rarity 5; Value $225 to $275
Variation 6: Rarity 5; Value $250 to $300

The No 6 Vienna Roll Pan is a very interesting pan. Variation 1 is one of only two Griswold pans presently known to have both a gate mark and the P/N on the same pan. The No 6 was changed to No 26 in the 1910s, apparently to avoid confusion with the No 6 Gem Pan. The No 6 Vienna Roll Pan is a fairly common pan.

NO 6 VIENNA ROLL PAN
P/N 958

VARIATION 1 RARITY: 5

(VARIATION 1)

(OPEN FRAME)

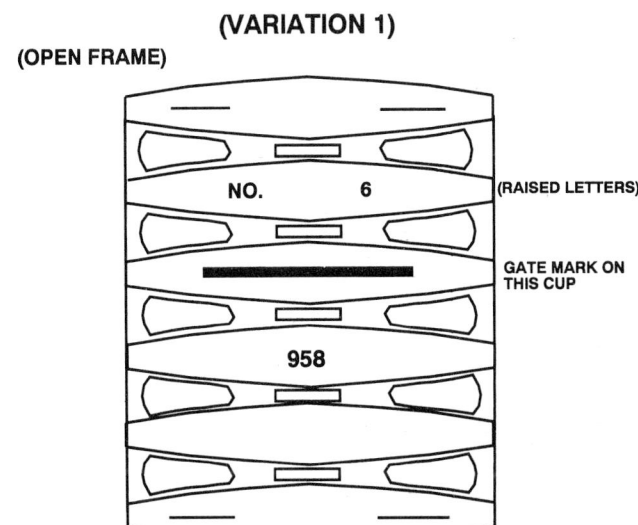

NO. 6 (RAISED LETTERS)

GATE MARK ON THIS CUP

958

NOTE: DRAWING IS NOT TO SCALE

VIEW OF UNDERSIDE

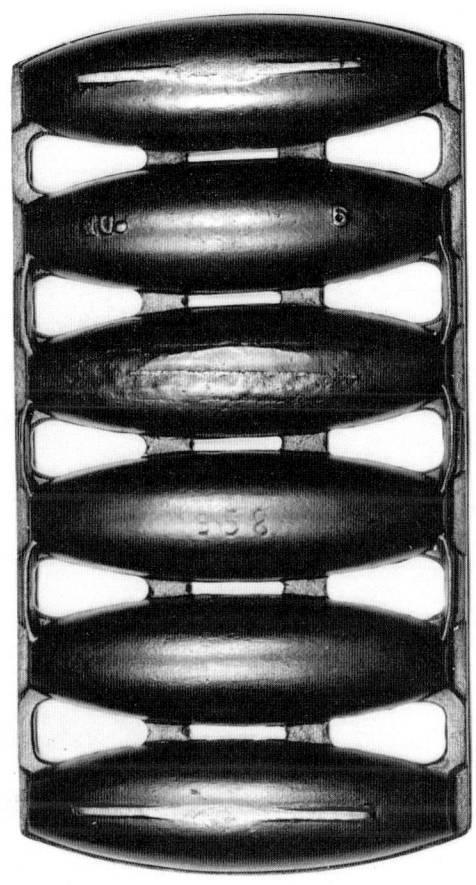

Underside of Variation 1 of No 6 Vienna Roll Pan

NO 6 VIENNA ROLL PAN
P/N 958

VARIATION 2 RARITY: 3

(VARIATION 2)

(OPEN FRAME)

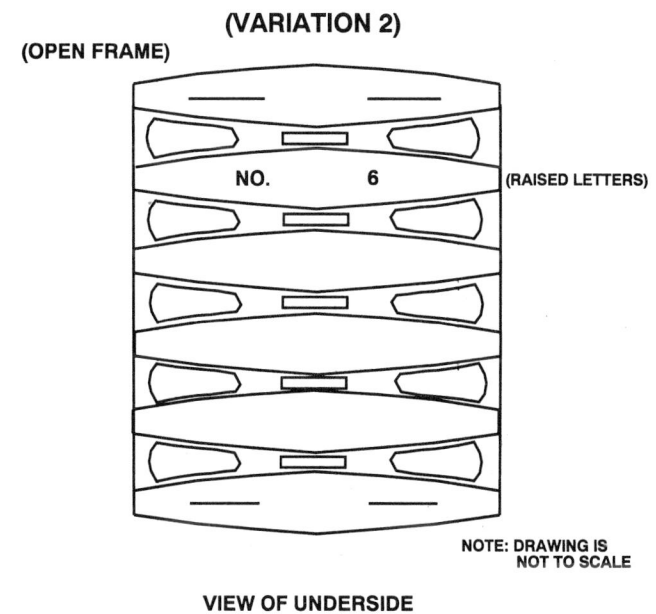

NO. 6 (RAISED LETTERS)

NOTE: DRAWING IS NOT TO SCALE

VIEW OF UNDERSIDE

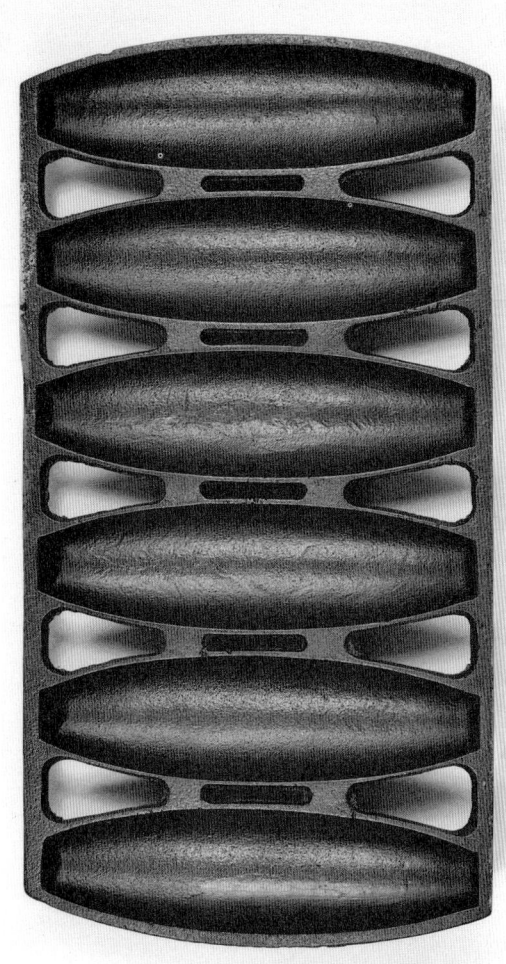

Top view of Variation 3 of No 6 Vienna Roll Pan

NO 6 VIENNA ROLL PAN
P/N 958

VARIATION 3 RARITY: 4

(VARIATION 3)

(OPEN FRAME)

NO.   6   (RAISED LETTERS)

958

NOTE: DRAWING IS
NOT TO SCALE

VIEW OF UNDERSIDE

Top view of Variation 4 of No 6 Vienna Roll Pan

NO 6 VIENNA ROLL PAN
P/N 958

VARIATION 4 RARITY: 5

(OPEN FRAME)   ### (VARIATION 4)

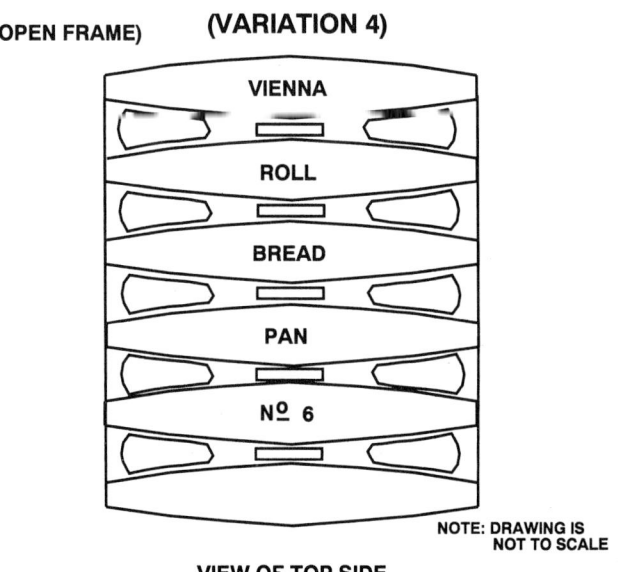

VIENNA

ROLL

BREAD

PAN

Nº 6

NOTE: DRAWING IS
NOT TO SCALE

VIEW OF TOP SIDE

NOTE: ALL LETTERING IS IN RAISED LETTERS
NO MARKINGS ON UNDERSIDE

Underside of Variation 5 of No 6 Vienna Roll Pan

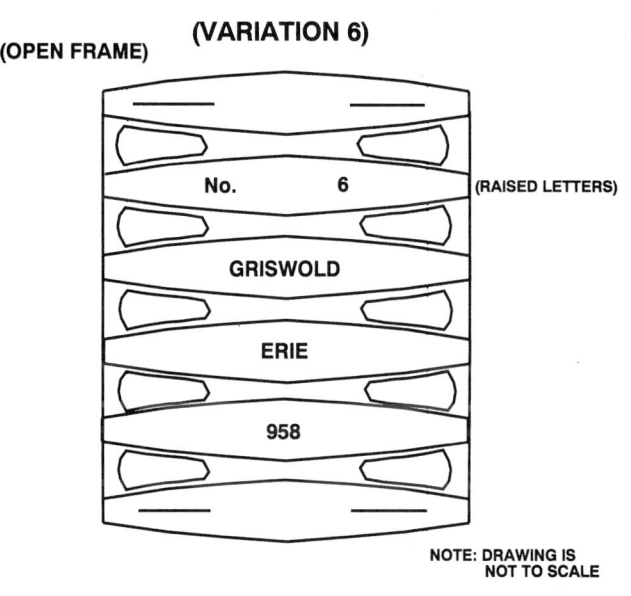

Undeside of Variation 6 of No 6 Vienna Roll Pan

NO 6 VIENNA ROLL PAN
P/N 958

VARIATION 5 RARITY: 5

NO 6 VIENNA ROLL PAN
P/N 958

VARIATION 6 RARITY: 5

(OPEN FRAME)   **(VARIATION 5)**

(OPEN FRAME)   **(VARIATION 6)**

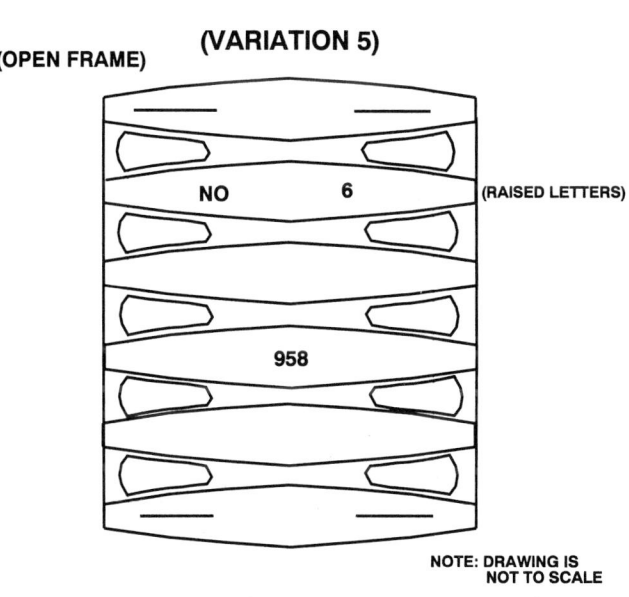

NO   6   (RAISED LETTERS)

958

NOTE: DRAWING IS
NOT TO SCALE

VIEW OF UNDERSIDE

No.   6   (RAISED LETTERS)

GRISWOLD

ERIE

958

NOTE: DRAWING IS
NOT TO SCALE

VIEW OF UNDERSIDE

No 7 Gem Pan

P/N 945
No. of cups: 8
Dimensions: 11 3/4" x 7 5/8"
Production Date: 1880s to 1900s
Variation 1: Rarity 7; Value $175 to $225
Variation 2: Rarity 7; Value $175 to $225
Variation 3: Rarity 8; Value $700 to $800
    The No 7 Gem Pan was only made until the early 1900s.
Variation 3 (marked with No 7 and P/N 945) is the rarest
and most coveted by collectors.

Underside of Variation 2 of No 7 Gem Pan

NO 7 GEM PAN
P/N 945

VARIATION 1 RARITY: 7

(OPEN FRAME)   (VARIATION 1)

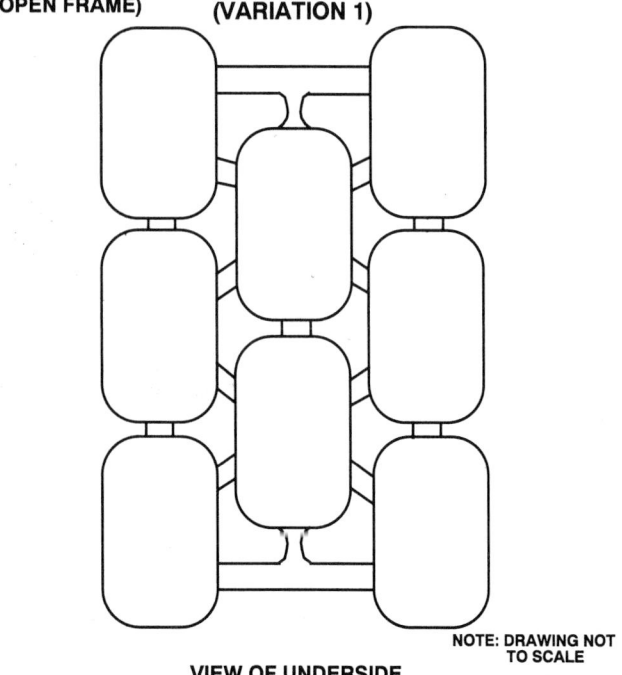

NOTE: DRAWING NOT TO SCALE

VIEW OF UNDERSIDE

NOTE: THERE ARE NO MARKINGS ON THIS PAN. THE WORKMANSHIP AND
QUALITY ARE IDENTICAL TO THE EARLY MARKED PANS.

NO 7 GEM PAN
P/N 945

VARIATION 2 RARITY: 7

(OPEN FRAME)   (VARIATION 2)

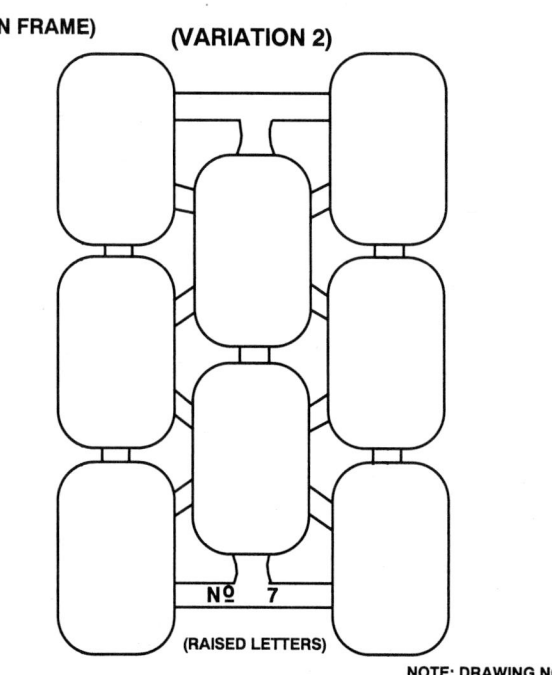

(RAISED LETTERS)

NOTE: DRAWING NOT TO SCALE

VIEW OF UNDERSIDE

Top view of Variation 3 of No 7 Gem Pan

NO 7 GEM PAN
P/N 945

(OPEN FRAME) **(VARIATION 3)**

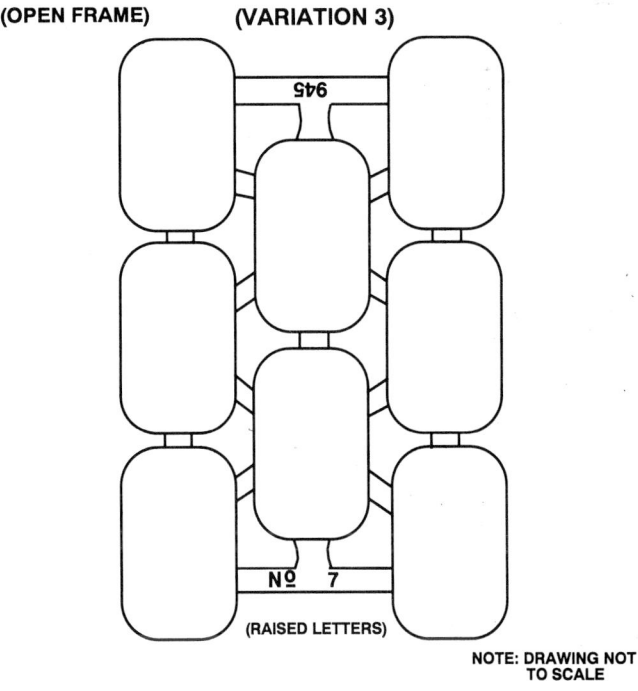

(RAISED LETTERS)

NOTE: DRAWING NOT
TO SCALE

VIEW OF UNDERSIDE

Underside of Variation 3 of No 7 Gem Pan

No 8 Gem Pan

P/N 946
No. of cups: 8
Dimensions: Wide Band 12 3/4" x 6 7/8"; Narrow Band 12
    3/4" x 6 1/4"
Production Date: 1880s to 1940s
Variation 1: Rarity 3; Value $50 to $75
Variation 2: Rarity 3; Value $75 to $100
Variation 3: Rarity 3; Value $75 to $100
Variation 4: Rarity 3; Value $75 to $100
Variation 5: Rarity 4; Value $200 to $250
Variation 6: Rarity 4; Value $200 to $250

    The No 8 Gem Pan was made in two different shapes,
the early wide band and the late version with no center
band. The early pans are the most common and the late
pans are the most desired by collectors.

NO 8 GEM PAN
P/N 946

VARIATION 1 RARITY: 3

(VARIATION 1)

(OPEN FRAME)

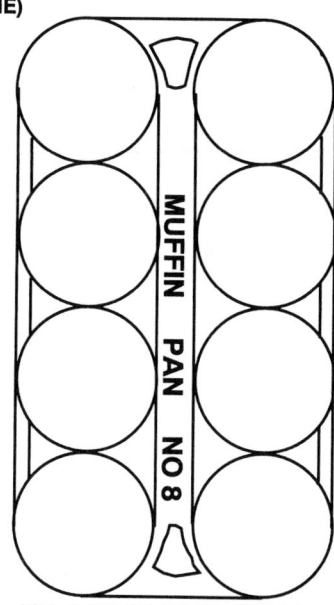

NOTE: MUFFIN PAN NO 8 IS IN RAISED LETTERS

NOTE: DRAWING NOT
TO SCALE

VIEW OF UNDERSIDE

Underside of Variation 2 of No 8 Gem Pan

Underside of Variation 1 of No 8 Gem Pan

34

NO 8 GEM PAN
P/N 946

VARIATION 2 RARITY: 3

(OPEN FRAME)   **(VARIATION 2)**

NO. 8 MUFFIN PAN NO. 8

NOTE: NO. 8 MUFFIN PAN NO. 8 IS IN RAISED LETTERS

NOTE: DRAWING NOT TO SCALE

VIEW OF UNDERSIDE

NO 8 GEM PAN
P/N 946

VARIATION 3 RARITY: 3

(OPEN FRAME)   **(VARIATION 3)**

NO. 8 MUFFIN PAN NO. 8

946

NOTE: NO. 8 MUFFIN PAN NO. 8 IS IN RAISED LETTERS

NOTE: DRAWING NOT TO SCALE

VIEW OF UNDERSIDE

Top view of Variation 3 of No 8 Gem Pan

NO 8 GEM PAN
P/N 946

VARIATION 4 RARITY: 3

(VARIATION 4)

(OPEN FRAME)   (RAISED LETTERS)

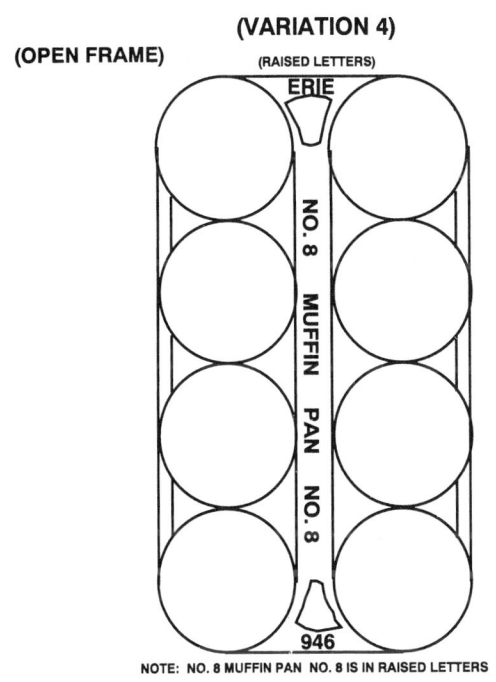

ERIE

NO. 8 MUFFIN PAN NO. 8

946

NOTE: NO. 8 MUFFIN PAN NO. 8 IS IN RAISED LETTERS

NOTE: DRAWING NOT TO SCALE

VIEW OF UNDERSIDE

NO 8 GEM PAN
P/N 946

VARIATION 5 RARITY: 4

(OPEN FRAME)   (VARIATION 5)

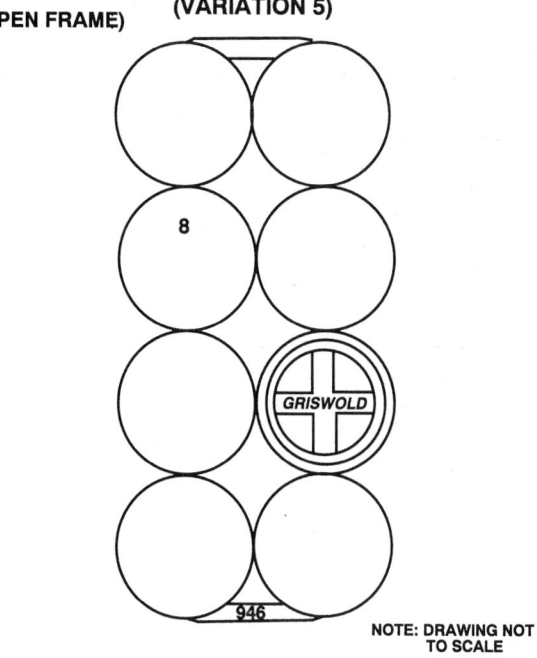

NOTE: DRAWING NOT TO SCALE

VIEW OF UNDERSIDE

Top view of Variation 6 of No 8 Gem Pan

Underside of Variation 6 of No 8 Gem Pan

NO 8 GEM PAN
P/N 946

VARIATION 6 RARITY: 4

(VARIATION 6)

(OPEN FRAME)   (RAISED LETTERS)
NO 8

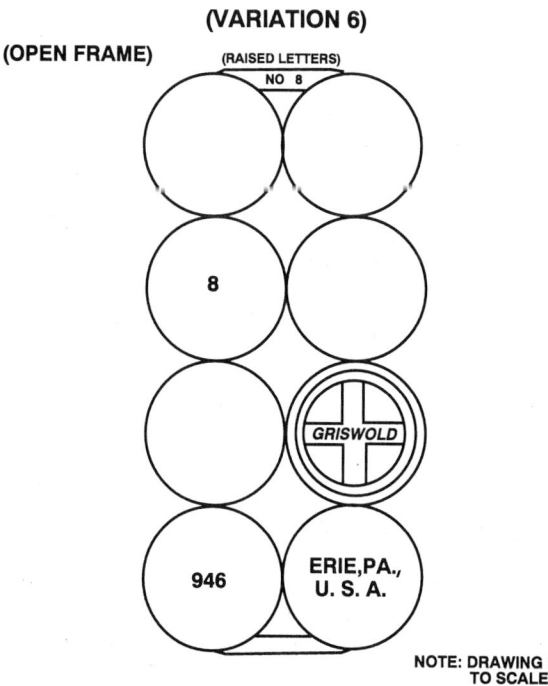

NOTE: DRAWING NOT TO SCALE

VIEW OF UNDERSIDE

No 9 Golfball Pan (10 Cup)

P/N 947
No. of cups: 10
Dimensions: 9 1/2" x 7"
Production Date: 1880s
Variation 1: Rarity 7; Value $200 to $250
Variation 2: Rarity 6; Value $250 to $300
Variation 3: Rarity 10; Value $1400 to $1600

    The No 9 Golfball Pan (10 Cup) does not appear in any known Griswold literature. Its identification as a Griswold pan is based on the P/N 947. This pan was made in the 1870s and 1880s. The 1890 Griswold catalog pictures the No 9 Golfball Pan as a 12 cup pan. Some of the early 10 cup pans have a tab-like feature on top of the handles. This feature is a byproduct of the casting process that was used but there is no known explanation of it. The No 9 Golfball Pan (10 cup) is of moderate rarity. There is presently only one example of Variation 3 known in the collecting community.

NO 9 GOLFBALL PAN (10 CUP)
P/N 947

(OPEN FRAME)

VARIATION 1 RARITY: 7

(VARIATION 1)

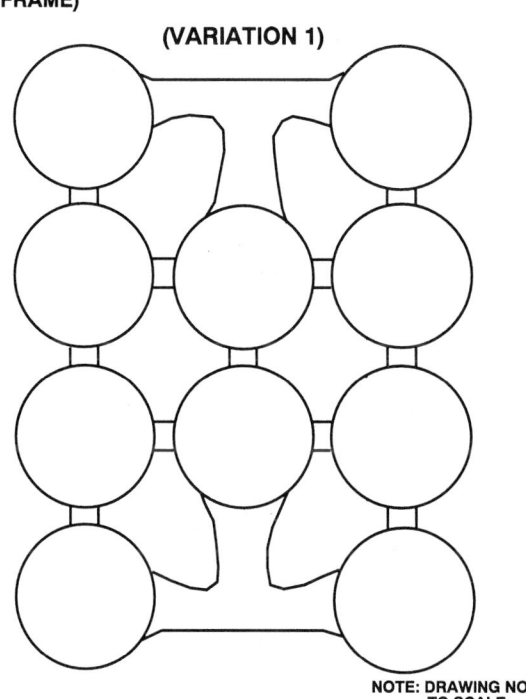

NOTE: DRAWING NOT TO SCALE

VIEW OF UNDERSIDE

NOTE: THERE ARE NO MARKINGS ON THIS PAN. THE WORKMANSHIP AND QUALITY ARE SIMILAR TO THE CORRESPONDING MARKED PAN

Top view of Variation 2 of No 9 Golfball Pan (10 Cup)

NO 9 GOLFBALL PAN (10 CUP)
P/N 947

VARIATION 2 RARITY: 6

(OPEN FRAME)

(VARIATION 2)

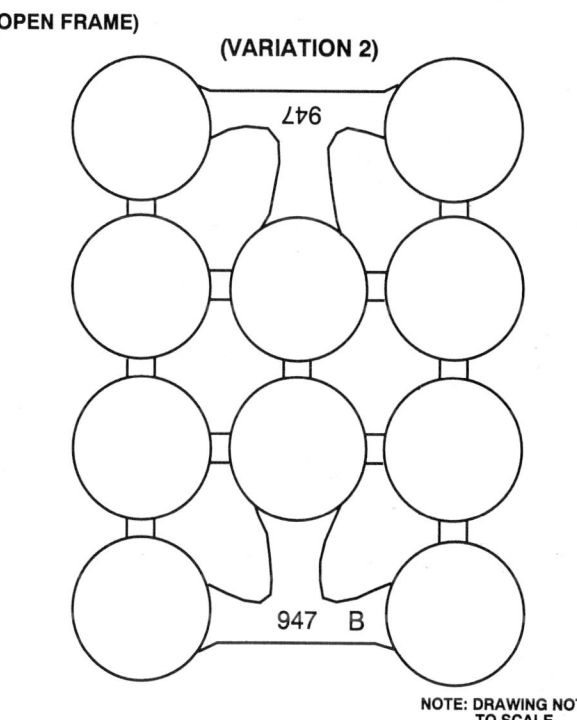

947

947   B

NOTE: DRAWING NOT TO SCALE

VIEW OF UNDERSIDE

NOTE: THERE ARE SOME EXAMPLES OF THIS VARIATION WITHOUT THE LETTER B AND SMALL DIFFERENCES IN THE SPACING OF THE P/N's

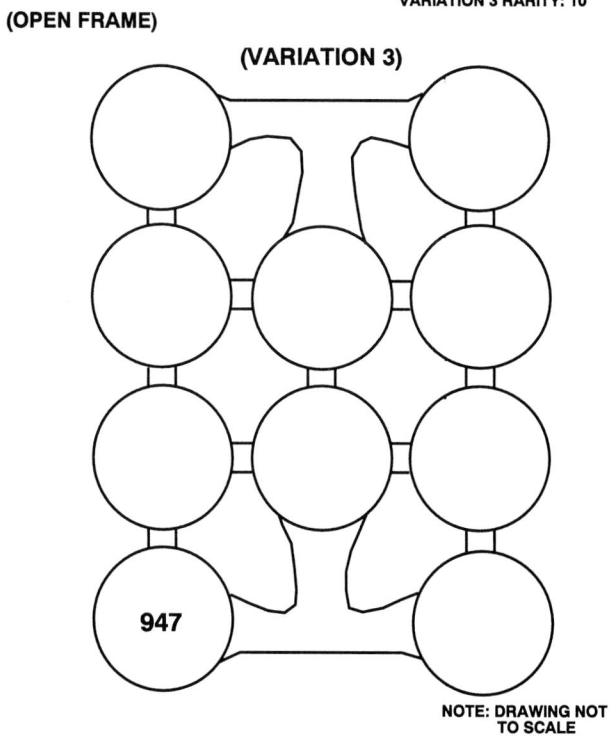

NO 9 GOLFBALL PAN (10 CUP)
P/N 947

(OPEN FRAME)

(VARIATION 3)

947

NOTE: DRAWING NOT
TO SCALE

VIEW OF UNDERSIDE

Underside of Variation 2 of No 9 Golfball Pan (10 Cup)

Top view of Variation 3 of No 9 Golfball Pan (10 Cup)

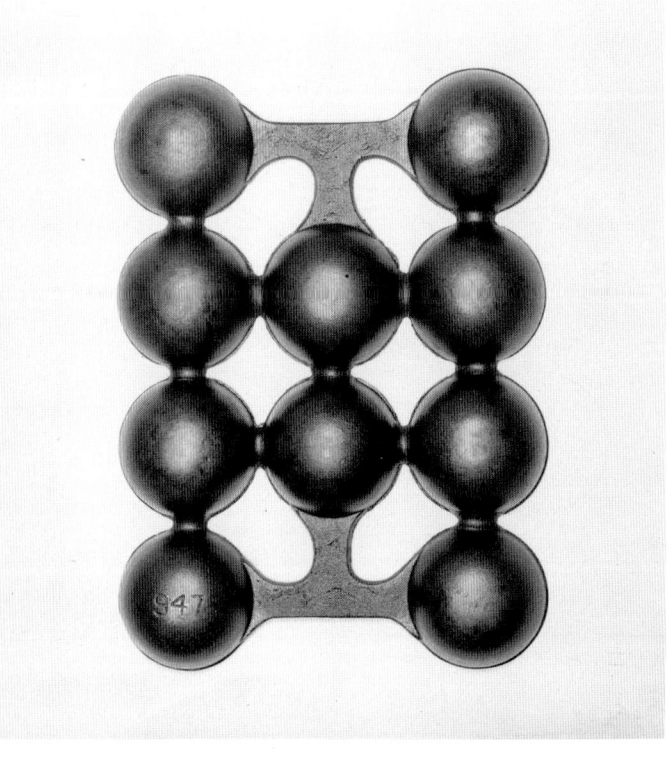

Underside of Variation 3 of No 9 Golfball Pan (10 cup)

No 9 Golfball Pan

P/N 947
No. of cups: 12
Dimensions: 10 3/8" x 7"
Production Date: 1890s to 1950s
Variation 1: Rarity 4; Value $100 to $125
Variation 2: Rarity 4; Value $100 to $125
Variation 3: Rarity 4; Value $100 to $125
Variation 4: Rarity 3; Value $75 to $100
Variation 5: Rarity 5; Value $150 to $175
Variation 6: Rarity 4; Value $150 to $175

    The No 9 Golfball Pan was made from the 1890s to the 1950s and is a common pan. Variation 6 is rather unusual as it has markings on the underside of all 12 cups. Variation 6 is the most desired variation. Variation 4 is the most common variation.

NO 9 GOLFBALL PAN
P/N 947

VARIATION 1 RARITY: 4

(OPEN FRAME) (VARIATION 1)

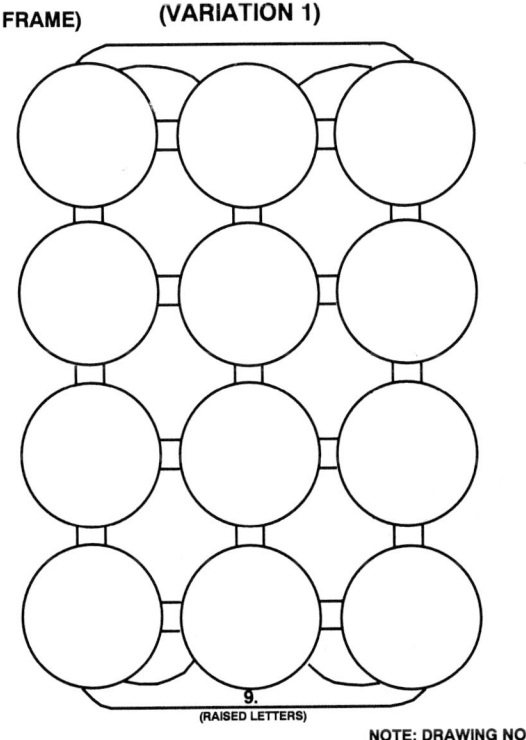

9.
(RAISED LETTERS)

NOTE: DRAWING NOT TO SCALE

VIEW OF UNDERSIDE

NO 9 GOLFBALL PAN
P/N 947

VARIATION 2 RARITY: 4

(OPEN FRAME) (VARIATION 2)

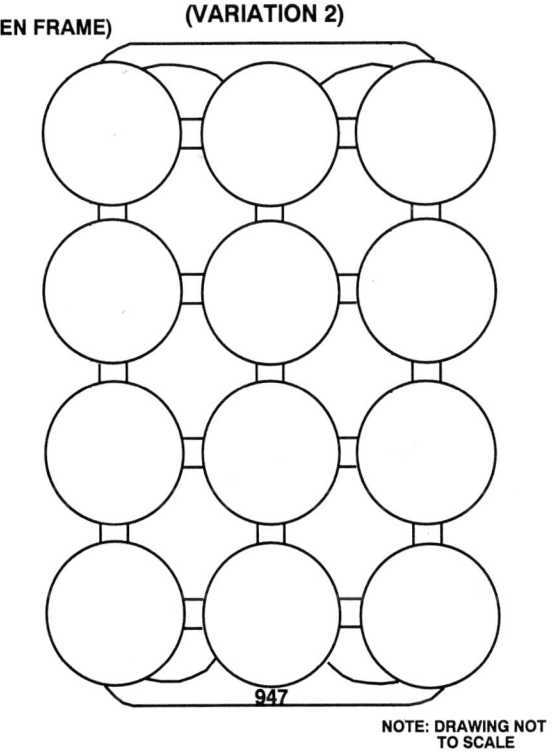

947

NOTE: DRAWING NOT TO SCALE

VIEW OF UNDERSIDE

Underside of Variation 3 of No 9 Golfball Pan

Top view of Variation 4 of No 9 Golfball Pan

NO 9 GOLFBALL PAN
P/N 947

VARIATION 3 RARITY: 4

(OPEN FRAME)   **(VARIATION 3)**

947

9.
(RAISED LETTERS)

NOTE: DRAWING NOT
TO SCALE

VIEW OF UNDERSIDE

NO 9 GOLFBALL PAN
P/N 947

VARIATION 4 RARITY: 3

(OPEN FRAME)   **(VARIATION 4)**

947

947

NOTE: DRAWING NOT
TO SCALE

VIEW OF UNDERSIDE

Underside of Variation 4 of No 9 Golfball Pan

NO 9 GOLFBALL PAN
P/N 947

VARIATION 5 RARITY: 5

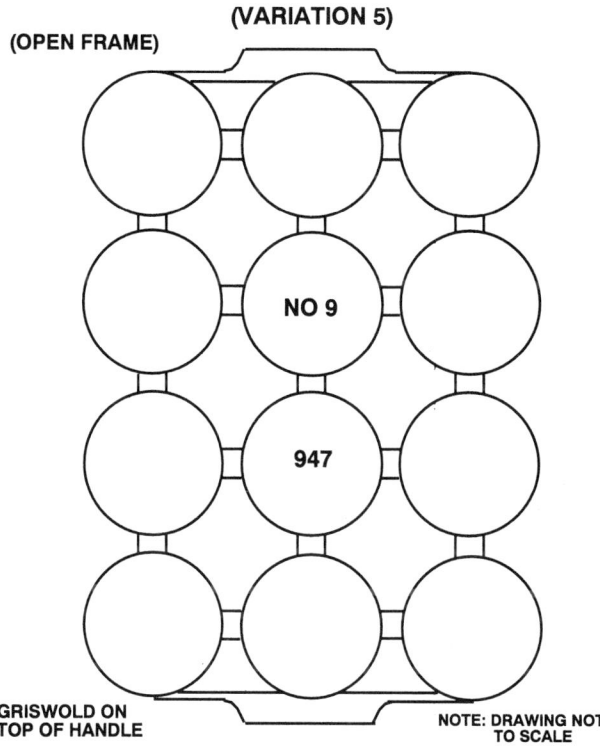

(OPEN FRAME) **(VARIATION 5)**

NO 9

947

GRISWOLD ON TOP OF HANDLE

NOTE: DRAWING NOT TO SCALE

VIEW OF UNDERSIDE

Top view of Variation 6 of No 9 Golfball Pan

Underside of Variation 6 of No 9 Golfball Pan

NO 9 GOLFBALL PAN
P/N 947

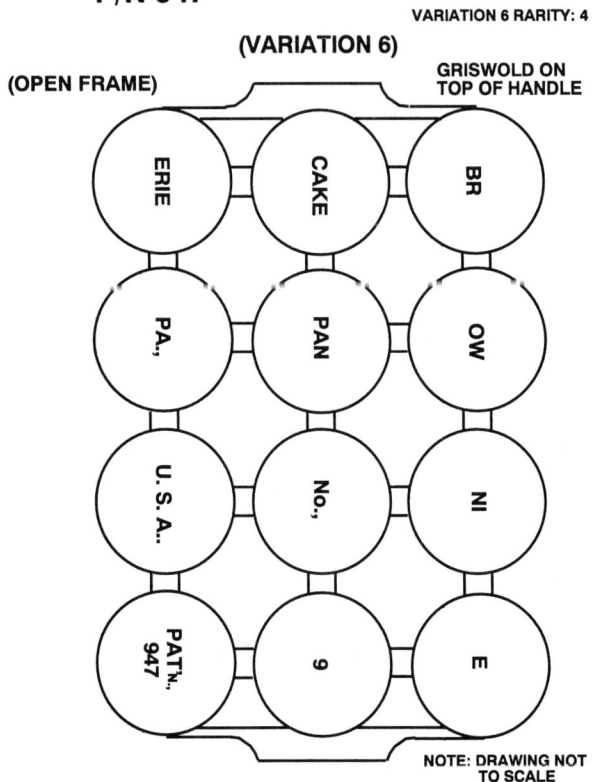

VARIATION 6 RARITY: 4

(VARIATION 6)

(OPEN FRAME)

GRISWOLD ON
TOP OF HANDLE

ERIE	CAKE	BR
PA.,	PAN	OW
U.S.A.	No.,	NI
PATN., 947	9	E

NOTE: DRAWING NOT
TO SCALE

VIEW OF UNDERSIDE

No 10 Popover Pan

P/N 948
No. of cups: 11
Dimensions: 11 1/8" x 7 5/8"
Production Date: 1880s to 1950s
Variation 1: Rarity 3; Value $75 to $100
Variation 2: Rarity 2; Value $50 to $75
Variation 3: Rarity 4; Value $125 to $150
Variation 4: Rarity 1; Value $20 to $40
Variation 5: Rarity 4; Value $125 to $150
Variation 6: Rarity 1; Value $20 to $40
Variation 7: Rarity 3; Value $50 to $75
Variation 8: Rarity 3; Value $50 to $75
Variation 9: Rarity 3; Value $50 to $75
Variation 10: Rarity 2; Value $50 to $70
Variation 11: Rarity 1; Value $30 to $50
Variation 12: Rarity 1; Value $25 to $40
Variation 13: Rarity 1; Value $25 to $40
Variation 14: Rarity 1; Value $25 to $40
Variation 15: Rarity 3; Value $100 to $125

The No 10 Popover Pan is one of the most common pans and was made throughout Griswold's long history. Variation 1 has a rather distinctive tab-like features on the top of the handles. These are from the casting process that was used but there is no known explanation for them. Variation 5 is an interesting and uncommon variation with the markings on top of the handles. Variation 15 was made for the U. S. Navy. The many variations of the No 10 Popover Pan present a real challenge for any collector.

Top view of Variation 1 of No 10 Popover Pan

NO 10 POPOVER PAN
P/N 948

VARIATION 1 RARITY: 3

(OPEN FRAME)

(VARIATION 1)

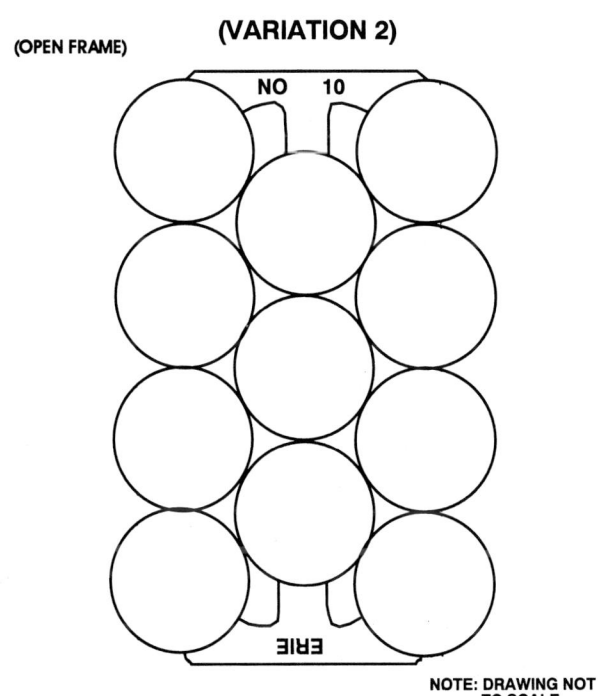

NOTE: DRAWING NOT
TO SCALE

VIEW OF UNDERSIDE

NOTE: THERE ARE TAB LIKE FEATURES ON TOP OF THE HANDLES THAT
APPARENTLY WERE PART OF THE VERY EARLY CASTING PROCESS.

NOTE: THE LETTERING IS VERY WEAK ON THIS VARIATION

NO 10 POPOVER PAN
P/N 948

VARIATION 2 RARITY: 2

(OPEN FRAME)

(VARIATION 2)

NO   10

NOTE: DRAWING NOT
TO SCALE

VIEW OF UNDERSIDE

NO 10 POPOVER PAN
P/N 948

VARIATION 3 RARITY: 4

(OPEN FRAME)

(VARIATION 3)

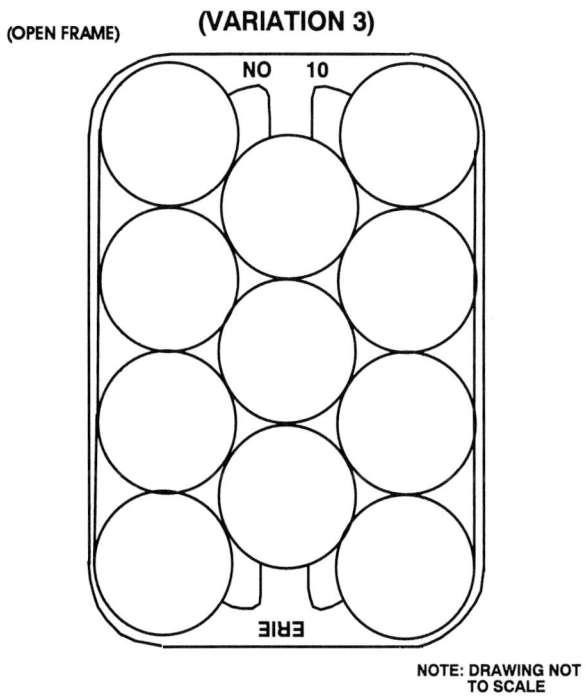

NOTE: DRAWING NOT
TO SCALE

VIEW OF UNDERSIDE

NO 10 POPOVER PAN
P/N 948

VARIATION 4 RARITY: 1

(OPEN FRAME)

(VARIATION 4)

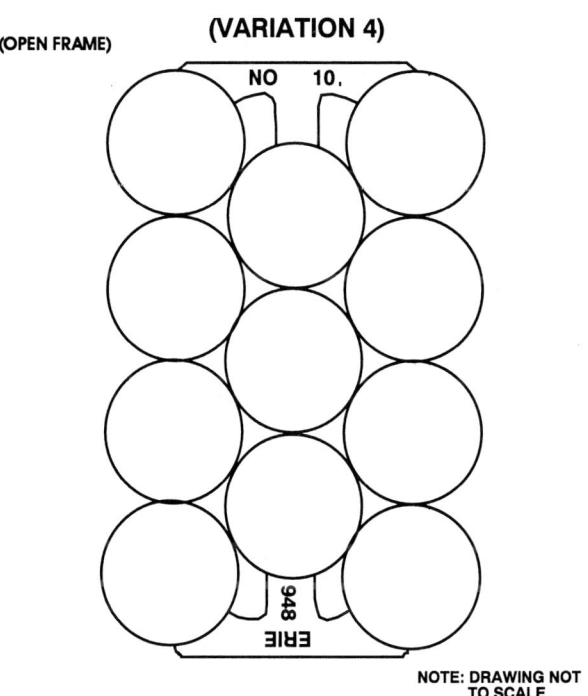

NOTE: DRAWING NOT
TO SCALE

VIEW OF UNDERSIDE

Top view of Variation 5 of No 10 Popover Pan

NO 10 POPOVER PAN
P/N 948

VARIATION 5 RARITY: 4

(OPEN FRAME) **(VARIATION 5)**

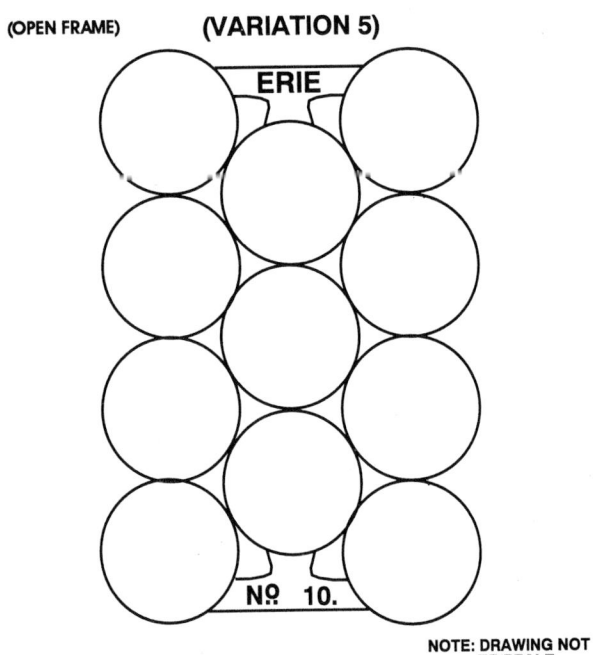

ERIE

Nº 10.

NOTE: DRAWING NOT
TO SCALE

VIEW OF TOP SIDE

NO 10 POPOVER PAN
P/N 948

VARIATION 6 RARITY: 1

(VARIATION 6)

(OPEN FRAME)

(RAISED LETTERS)

NO   01

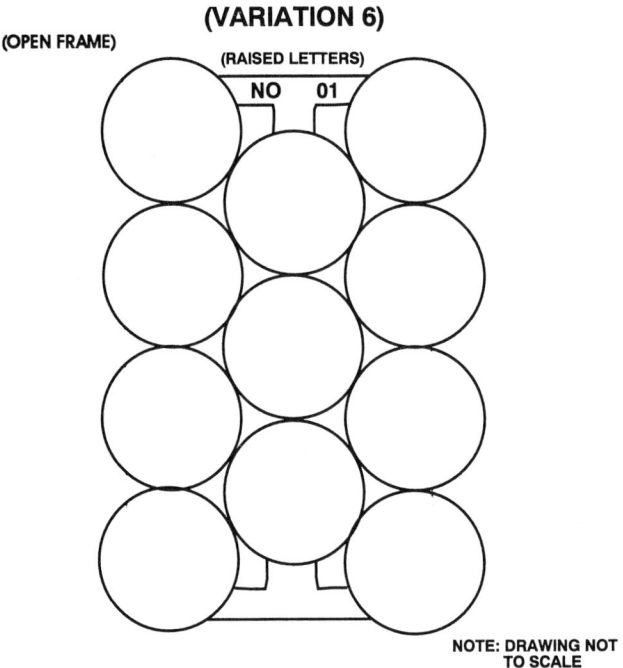

NOTE: DRAWING NOT
TO SCALE

VIEW OF UNDERSIDE

NOTE: THE UNDERSIDE OF HANDLES ARE ROUNDED.

Top view of Variation 7 of No 10 Popover Pan

44

NO 10 POPOVER PAN
P/N 948

VARIATION 7 RARITY: 3

(VARIATION 7)

(OPEN FRAME)

(RAISED LETTERS)

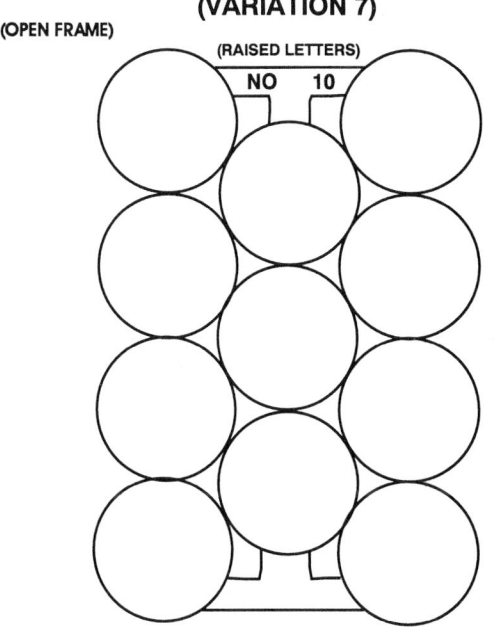

NOTE: DRAWING NOT
TO SCALE

VIEW OF UNDERSIDE

NOTE: THE UNDERSIDE OF HANDLES ARE ROUNDED.
NOTE: THIS VARIATION EXISTS WITH DIFFERENT SIZE LETTERING.

NO 10 POPOVER PAN
P/N 948

VARIATION 8 RARITY: 3

(VARIATION 8)

(OPEN FRAME)

(RAISED LETTERS)

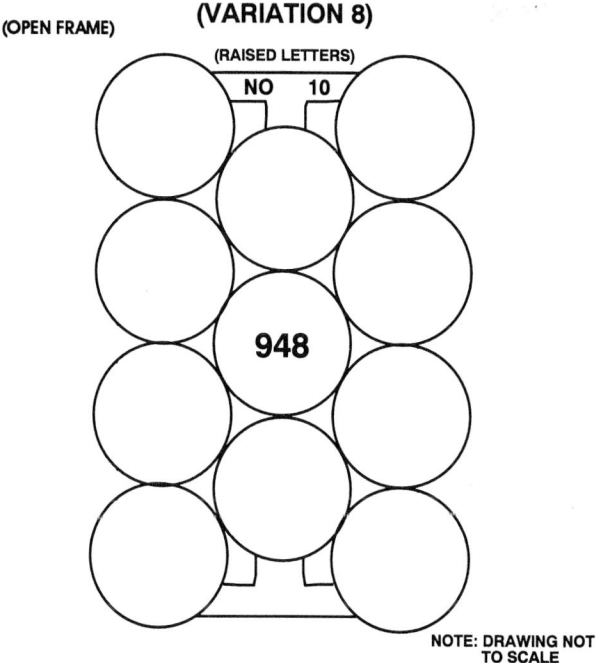

NOTE: DRAWING NOT
TO SCALE

VIEW OF UNDERSIDE

NOTE: THE UNDERSIDE OF HANDLES ARE ROUNDED

Underside of Variation 8 of No 10 Popover Pan

45

Underside of Variation 9 of No 10 Popover Pan

Underside of Variation 10 of No 10 Popover Pan

NO 10 POPOVER PAN
P/N 948

VARIATION 9 RARITY: 3

NO 10 POPOVER PAN
P/N 948

VARIATION 10 RARITY: 2

(OPEN FRAME)

(VARIATION 9)

(RAISED LETTERS)

NO 10

948

NOTE: DRAWING NOT
TO SCALE

VIEW OF UNDERSIDE

NOTE: THE UNDERSIDE OF HANDLES ARE ROUNDED.

(OPEN FRAME)

(VARIATION 10)

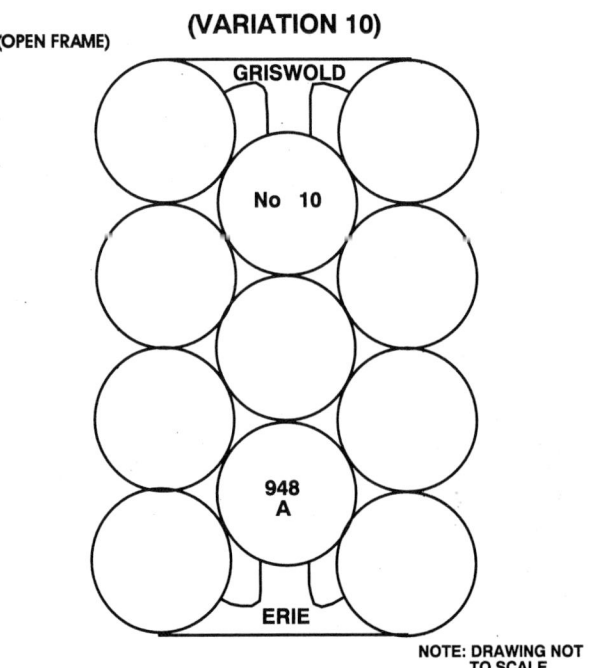

GRISWOLD

No 10

948
A

ERIE

NOTE: DRAWING NOT
TO SCALE

VIEW OF UNDERSIDE

46

NO 10 POPOVER PAN
P/N 948

VARIATION 11 RARITY: 1

(OPEN FRAME)   **(VARIATION 11)**

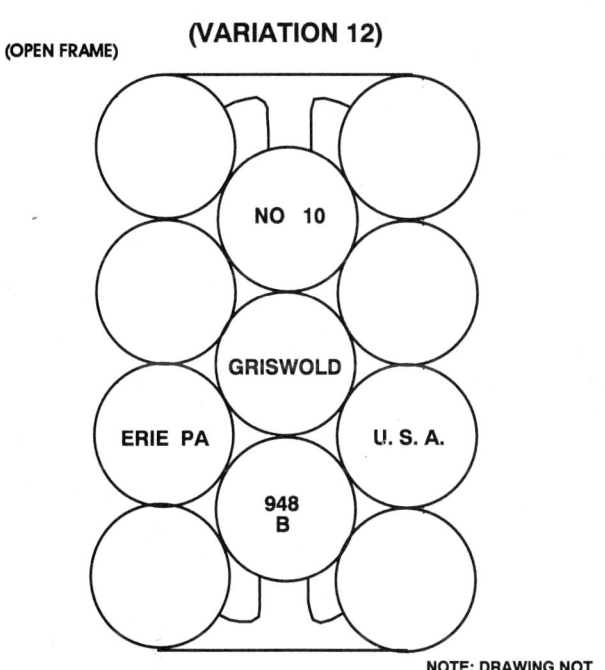

NOTE: DRAWING NOT
TO SCALE

VIEW OF UNDERSIDE

NO 10 POPOVER PAN
P/N 948

VARIATION 13 RARITY: 1

(OPEN FRAME)   **(VARIATION 13)**

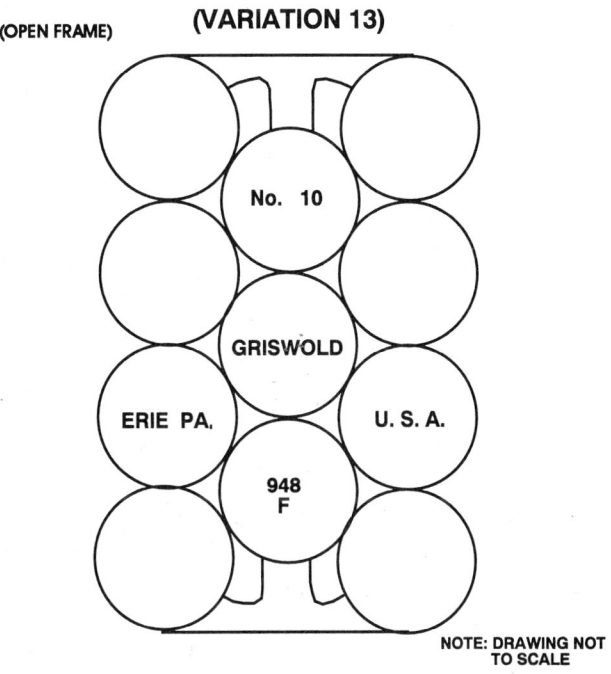

NOTE: DRAWING NOT
TO SCALE

VIEW OF UNDERSIDE

NO 10 POPOVER PAN
P/N 948

VARIATION 12 RARITY: 1

(OPEN FRAME)   **(VARIATION 12)**

NOTE: DRAWING NOT
TO SCALE

VIEW OF UNDERSIDE

NOTE: THERE ARE MINOR VARIATIONS ON THE STYLE, SIZE, AND SPACING
OF THE LETTERING ON THIS PAN.

NO 10 POPOVER PAN
P/N 948

VARIATION 14 RARITY: 1

(SOLID FRAME)   **(VARIATION 14)**

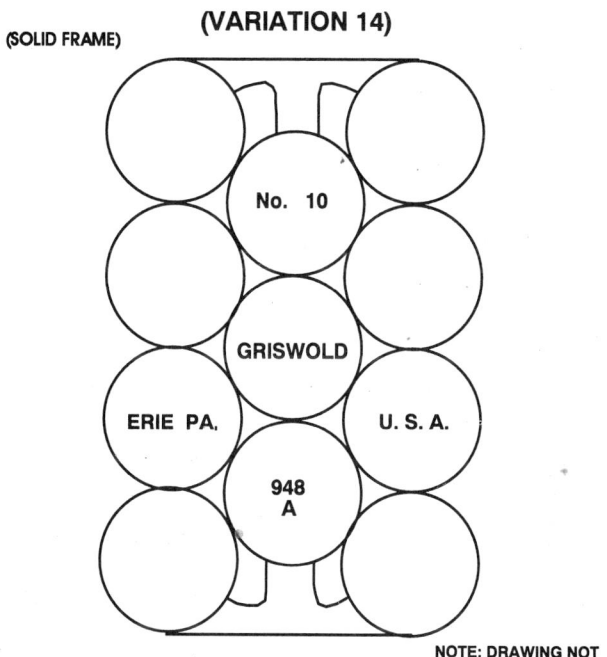

NOTE: DRAWING NOT
TO SCALE

VIEW OF UNDERSIDE

NO 10 POPOVER PAN
P/N 948

(VARIATION 15)

(SOLID FRAME)

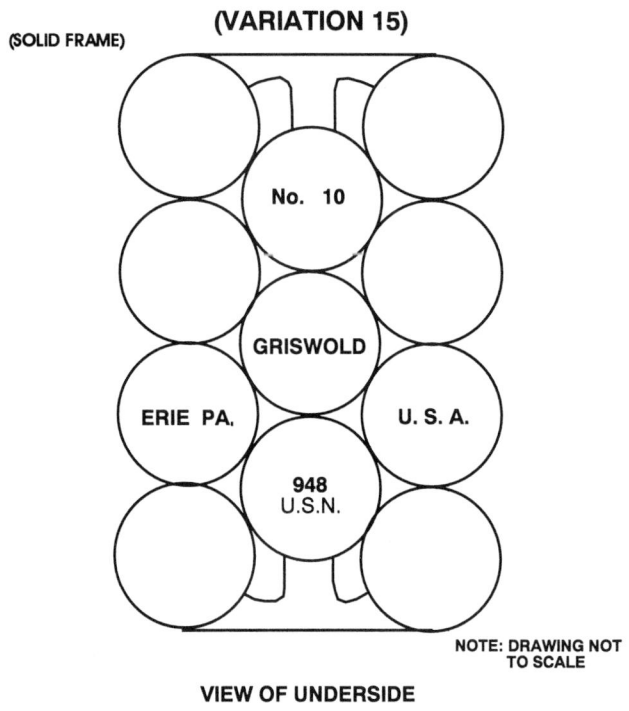

No. 10

GRISWOLD

ERIE PA.　　　U. S. A.

948
U.S.N.

NOTE: DRAWING NOT
TO SCALE

VIEW OF UNDERSIDE

Top view of Variation 15 of No 10 Popover Pan

Underside of Variation 15 of No 10 Popover
Pan

No 10 Popover Pan (P/N 949)

P/N 949
No. of cups: 11
Dimensions: 11 1/8" x 7 3/4"
Production Date: 1950s
Variation 1: Rarity 1; Value $20 to $40
Variation 2: Rarity 1; Value $20 to $40

The No 10 Popover Pan (P/N 949) is common and was made in the 1950s. It has shallower cups than the No 10 Popover Pan marked P/N 948.

NO 10 POPOVER PAN
P/N 949

VARIATION 1 RARITY: 1

(OPEN FRAME) **(VARIATION 1)**

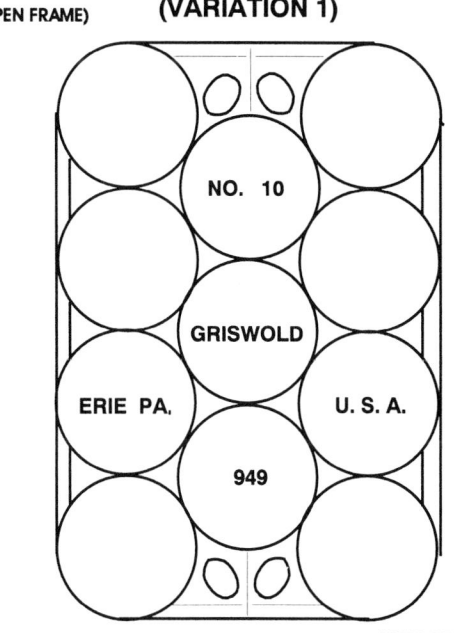

NOTE: DRAWING NOT
TO SCALE

VIEW OF UNDERSIDE

Underside of Variation 2 of No 10 Popover Pan (P/N 949)

Top view of Variation 2 of No 10 Popover Pan (P/N 949)

NO 10 POPOVER PAN
P/N 949

VARIATION 2 RARITY: 1

(SOLID FRAME) **(VARIATION 2)**

NOTE: DRAWING NOT
TO SCALE

VIEW OF UNDERSIDE

No 10 Popover Pan (Hammered)

P/N 2070
No. of cups: 11
Dimensions: 11 1/8" x 7 5/8"
Production Date: 1940s
Rarity: 6
Value: $200 to $250

The No 10 Popover Pan (P/N 2070) was part of a special hammered set of cookware produced by Griswold. The hammered effect was cast into the pan. This pan is uncommon.

NO 10 POPOVER PAN (HAMMERED) P/N 2070

NO 10 (2070) RARITY: 6

(SOLID FRAME)

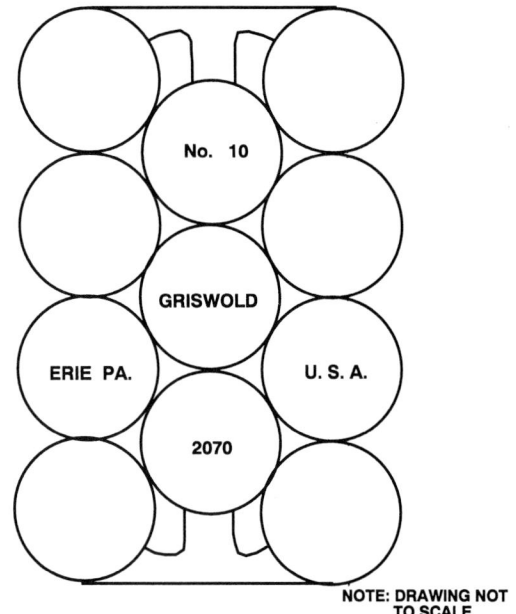

NOTE: DRAWING NOT TO SCALE

VIEW OF UNDERSIDE
NOTE: THE TOP SURFACE OF THIS PAN IS HAMMERED

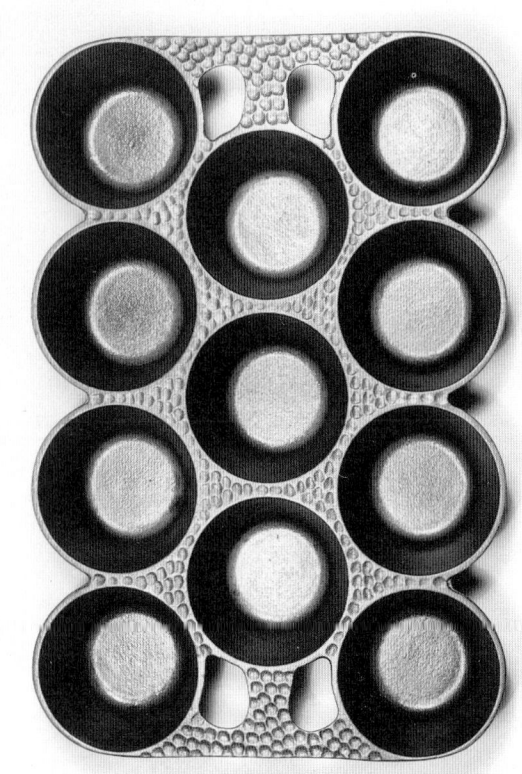

Top view of No 10 popover Pan (Hammered)

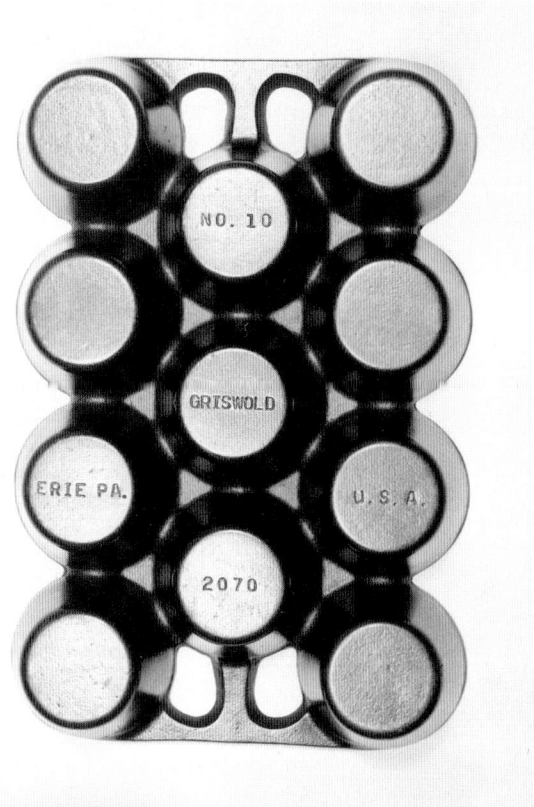

Underside of No 10 Popover Pan (Hammered)

No 11 French Roll Pan (H Pattern)

P/N 949?
No. of cups: 12
Dimensions: 12 1/2" x 7 3/4"
Production Date: 1890s
Variation 1: Rarity 10; Value $900 to $1100
Variation 2: Rarity 10; Value $900 to $1100

    The No 11 French Roll Pan (H Pattern) is only known in a totally unmarked form. Its existence is based on an illustration in the 1890 Griswold catalog. Based on the sequence in the 1890 catalog, this pan would have 949 for a pattern number if it was made with a pattern number. This is a very rare pan; however, it does not have great appeal to collectors because it is totally unmarked.

**NO 11 FRENCH ROLL PAN (H PATTERN)
P/N 949?**

VARIATION 1 RARITY: 10

(VARIATION 1)

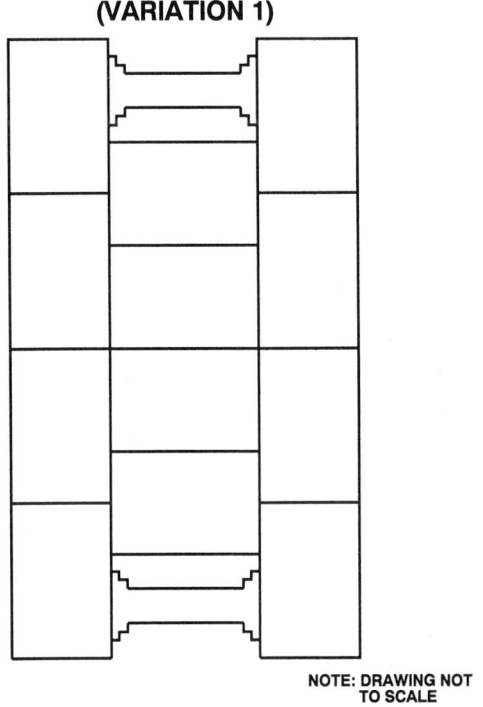

NOTE: DRAWING NOT TO SCALE

VIEW OF TOP SIDE

NOTE: THERE ARE NO MARKINGS ON THIS PAN

Underside of Variation 1 of No 11 French Roll Pan (H Pattern)

Top view of Variation 2 of No 11 French Roll Pan (H Pattern)

NO 11 FRENCH ROLL PAN (H PATTERN)
P/N 949?

VARIATION 2 RARITY: 10

(VARIATION 2)

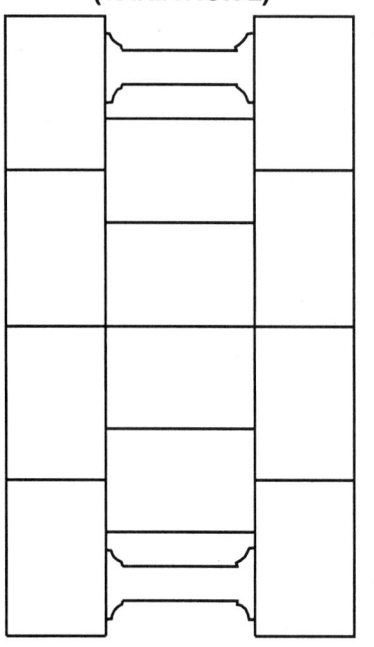

NOTE: DRAWING NOT
TO SCALE

VIEW OF TOP SIDE

NOTE: THERE ARE NO MARKINGS ON THIS PAN

Underside of Variation 2 of No 11 French Roll Pan (H Pattern)

52

No 11 French Roll Pan

P/N 950
No. of cups: 12
Dimensions: 12 7/8" x 6 1/8"; Wide Band 12 5/8" x 6 5/8"
Production Date: 1880s to 1950s
Variation 1: Rarity 2; Value $70 to $90
Variation 2: Rarity 2; Value $50 to $70
Variation 3: Rarity 2; Value $50 to $70
Variation 4: Rarity 2; Value $60 to $80
Variation 5: Rarity 3; Value $80 to $100
Variation 6: Rarity 3; Value $90 to $110
Variation 7: Rarity 1; Value $30 to $50
Variation 8: Rarity 2; Value $60 to $80
Variation 9: Rarity 1; Value $30 to $50
Variation 10: Rarity 2; Value $50 to $70
Variation 11: Rarity 1; Value $30 to $50

    The No 11 French Roll Pan was made in three different styles: the New England Style (NES), the wide band, and the late narrow band. Variation 5 is an example of an error made by Griswold. It is marked N E S oN 11 instead of N E S No 11. The No 11 French Roll Pan is common although the many variations provide considerable challenge to the collector.

Underside of Variation 1 of No 11 French Roll Pan, New England Style

NO 11 FRENCH ROLL PAN, NEW ENGLAND STYLE P/N 950

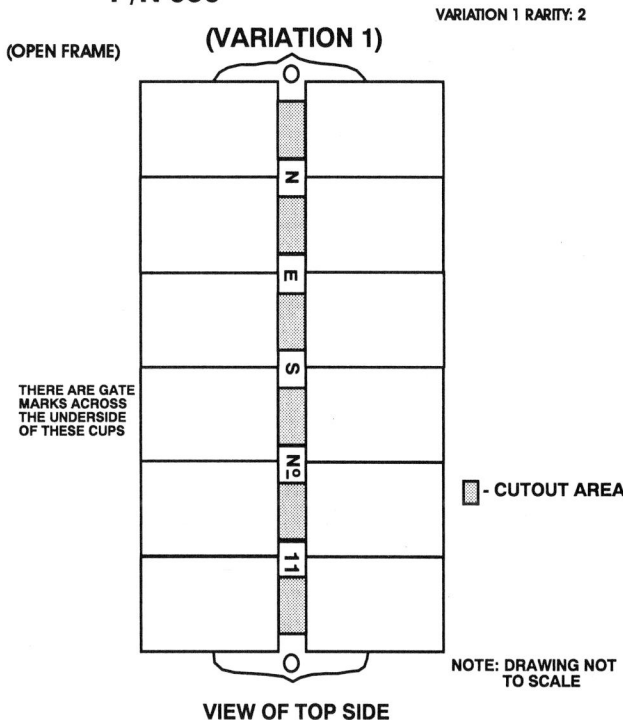

NO 11 FRENCH ROLL PAN, NEW ENGLAND STYLE P/N 950

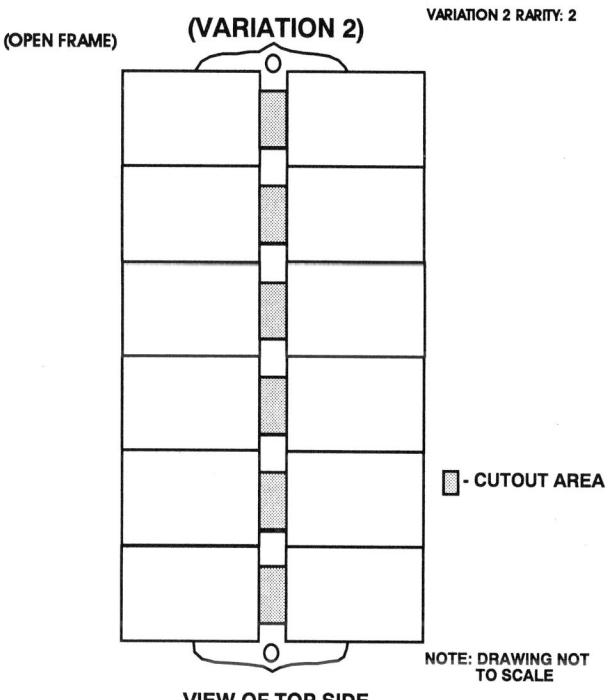

NOTE: THERE ARE NO MARKINGS ON THIS PAN. THE WORKMANSHIP AND QUALITY ARE SIMILAR TO THE EARLY N. E. S. PANS.

NO 11 FRENCH ROLL PAN, NEW ENGLAND STYLE P/N 950

(VARIATION 3)

VARIATION 3 RARITY: 2

(OPEN FRAME)

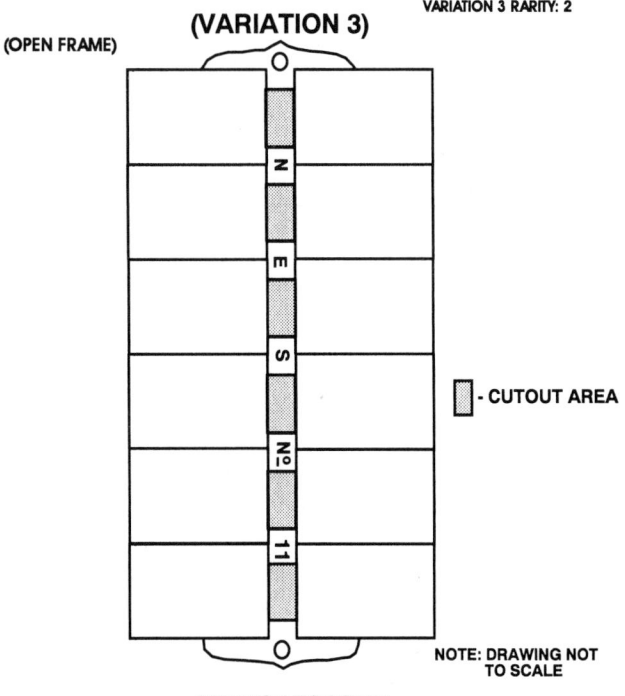

☐ - CUTOUT AREA

NOTE: DRAWING NOT TO SCALE

VIEW OF TOP SIDE

(THERE ARE NO MARKINGS ON UNDERSIDE)

NO 11 FRENCH ROLL PAN, NEW ENGLAND STYLE P/N 950

(VARIATION 4)

VARIATION 4 RARITY: 2

(OPEN FRAME)

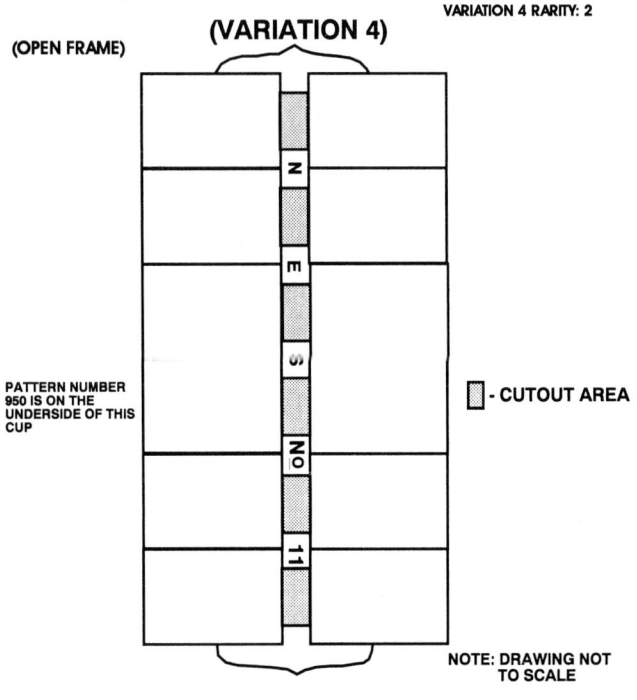

PATTERN NUMBER 950 IS ON THE UNDERSIDE OF THIS CUP

☐ - CUTOUT AREA

NOTE: DRAWING NOT TO SCALE

VIEW OF TOP SIDE

NOTE: ON SOME EXAMPLES OF THIS PAN PORTIONS OF THE LETTERING ON TOP OF THE CENTER BAND MAY BE VERY WEAK (OR MISSING).

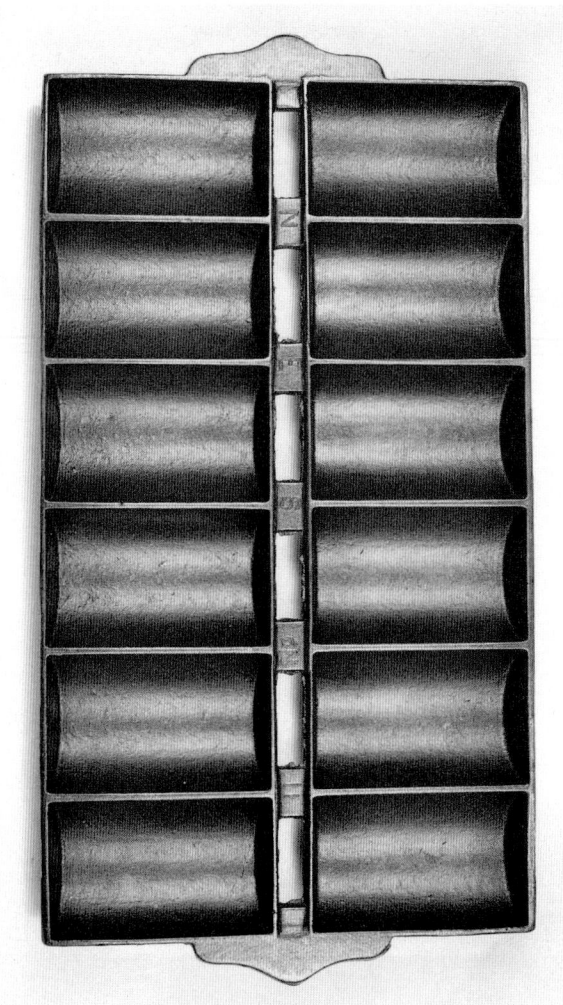

Top view of Variation 5 of No 11 French Roll Pan, New England Style

NO 11 FRENCH ROLL PAN, NEW ENGLAND STYLE P/N 950

(VARIATION 5)

VARIATION 5 RARITY: 3

(OPEN FRAME)

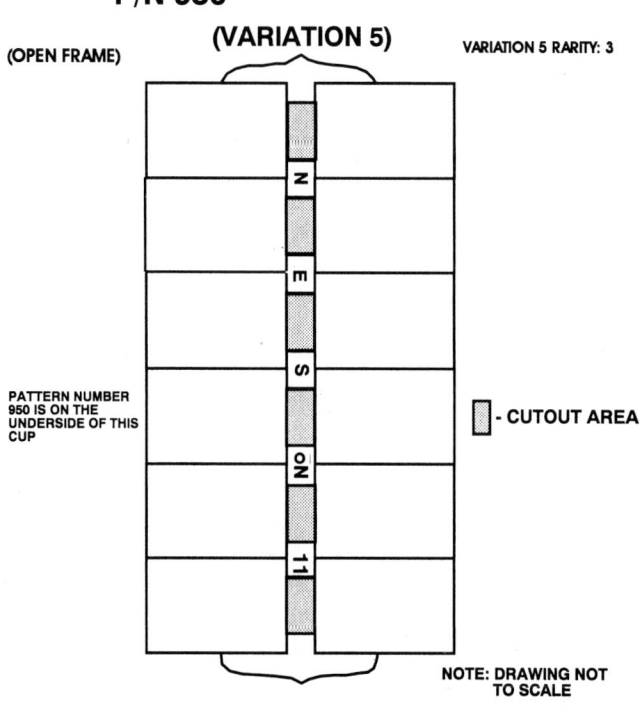

PATTERN NUMBER 950 IS ON THE UNDERSIDE OF THIS CUP

☐ - CUTOUT AREA

NOTE: DRAWING NOT TO SCALE

VIEW OF TOP SIDE

54

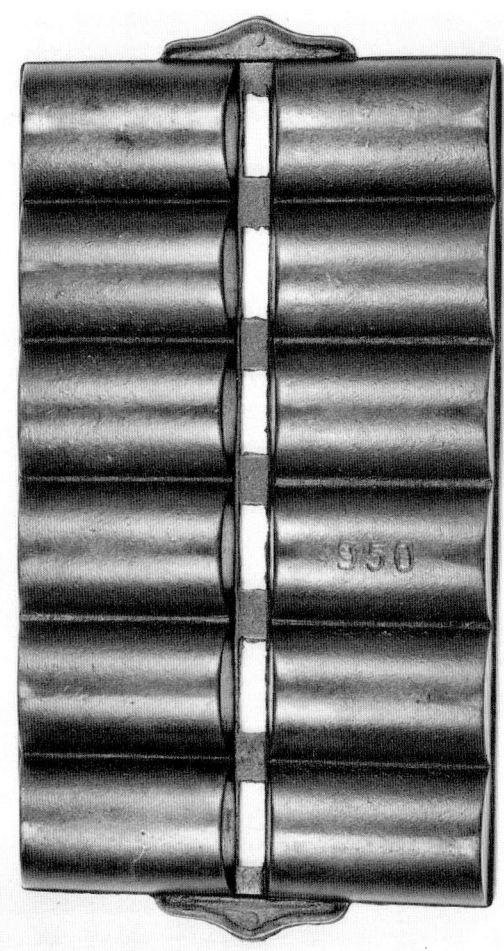

Underside of Variation 5 of No 11 French Roll Pan, New England Style

NO 11 FRENCH ROLL PAN
P/N 950

VARIATION 6 RARITY: 3

(VARIATION 6)

(SOLID FRAME)

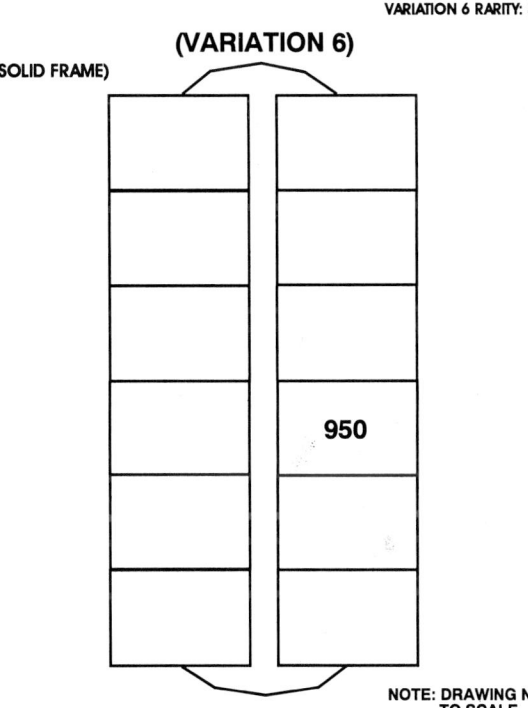

950

NOTE: DRAWING NOT
TO SCALE

VIEW OF UNDERSIDE

Top view of Variation 7 of No 11 French Roll Pan

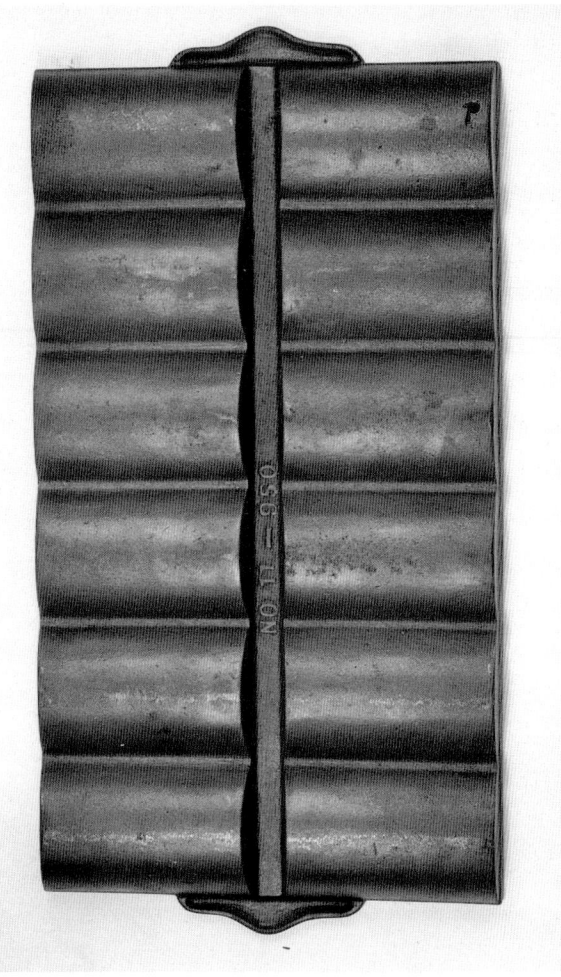

Underside of Variation 7 of No 11 French Roll Pan

NO 11 FRENCH ROLL PAN
P/N 950

VARIATION 7 RARITY: 1

(VARIATION 7)

(SOLID FRAME)

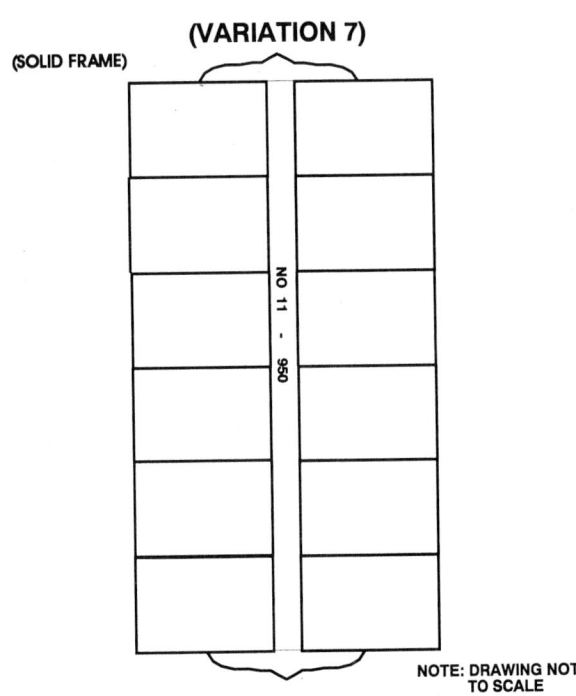

NO 11 - 950

NOTE: DRAWING NOT
TO SCALE

VIEW OF UNDERSIDE

NOTE: NO 11 - 950 IS IN RAISED LETTERS

Top view of Variation 8 of No 11 French Roll Pan

NO 11 FRENCH ROLL PAN
P/N 950

VARIATION 8 RARITY: 2

(VARIATION 8)

(SOLID FRAME)

GRISWOLD MFG CO ERIE PA U S A 950

GRISWOLD NO 11
IS IMPRINTED ON
TOP OF WIDE
BAND

NOTE: DRAWING NOT
TO SCALE

VIEW OF UNDERSIDE

NOTE: GRISWOLD MFG CO ERIE PA U S A IS IN RAISED LETTERS

Underside of Variation 8 of No 11 French Roll Pan

Top view of Variation 10 of No 11 French Roll Pan

NO 11 FRENCH ROLL PAN
P/N 950

VARIATION 9 RARITY: 1

NO 11 FRENCH ROLL PAN
P/N 950

VARIATION 10 RARITY: 2

(VARIATION 9)

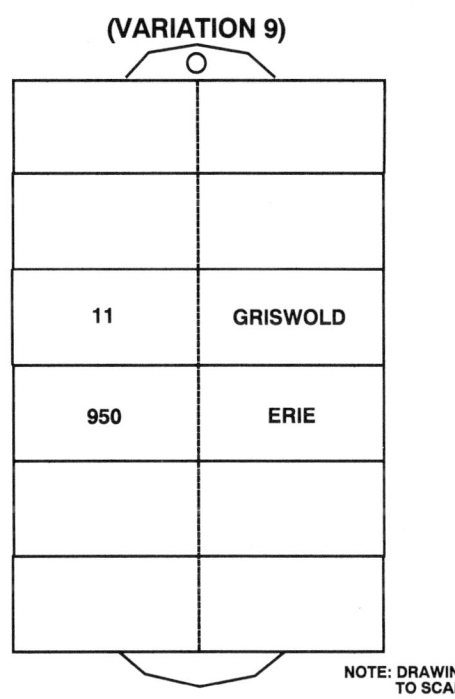

11	GRISWOLD
950	ERIE

NOTE: DRAWING NOT TO SCALE

VIEW OF UNDERSIDE

(VARIATION 10)

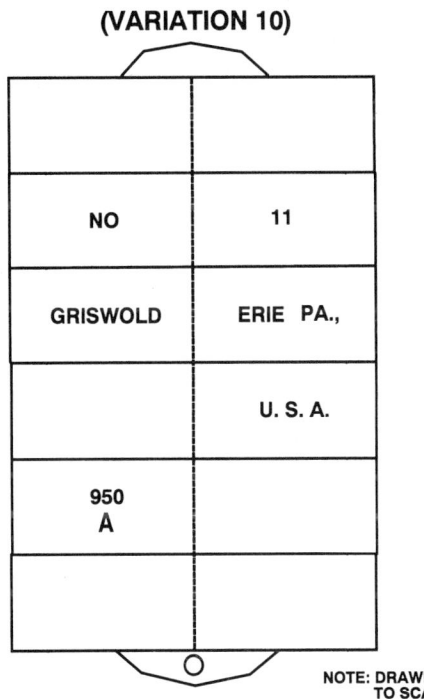

NO	11
GRISWOLD	ERIE PA.,
	U. S. A.
950 A	

NOTE: DRAWING NOT TO SCALE

VIEW OF UNDERSIDE

Top view of Variation 11 of No 11 French Roll Pan

NO 11 FRENCH ROLL PAN
P/N 950

(VARIATION 11)

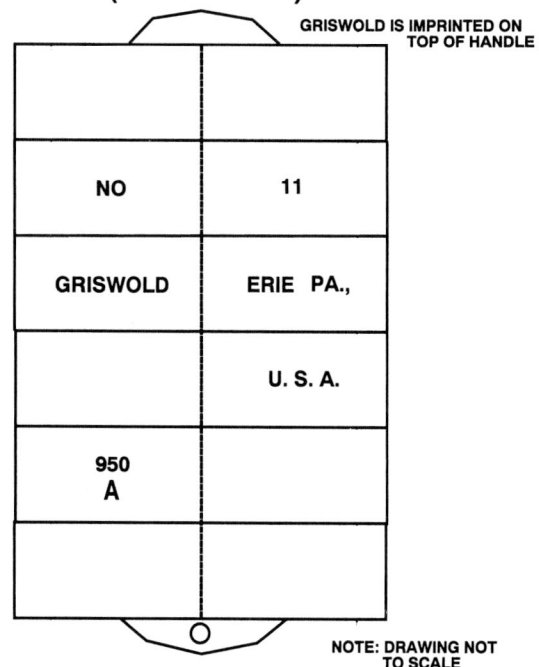

GRISWOLD IS IMPRINTED ON
TOP OF HANDLE

NO	11
GRISWOLD	ERIE PA.,
	U. S. A.
950 A	

NOTE: DRAWING NOT
TO SCALE

VIEW OF UNDERSIDE

Underside of Variation 11 of No 11 French Roll Pan

No 12 Gem Pan

P/N 951
No. of cups: 11
Dimensions: 11" x 7 1/4"
Production Date: 1880s to 1940s
Variation 1: Rarity 7; Value $200 to $250
Variation 2: Rarity 7; Value $250 to $300
Variation 3: Rarity 7; Value $275 to $325
Variation 4: Rarity 8; Value $600 to $650
Variation 5: Rarity 8; Value $600 to $700
Variation 6: Rarity 8; Value $600 to $700
Variation 7: Rarity 8; Value $600 to $700

    The No 12 Gem Pan was produced in two different shapes. The early pans had square corners while on the late pans the corners were rounded. The early pans are the most common. The No 12 Gem Pan is a rather dainty pan and is an excellent pan to display on a kitchen wall.

NO 12 GEM PAN
P/N 951

VARIATION 1 RARITY: 7

(OPEN FRAME)   (VARIATION 1)

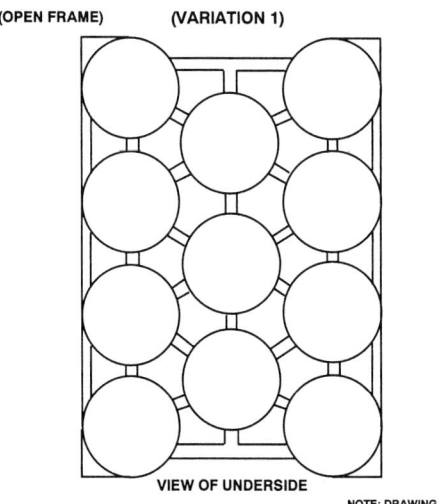

VIEW OF UNDERSIDE

NOTE: DRAWING NOT TO SCALE

NOTE: THERE ARE NO MARKINGS ON THIS PAN. THE WORKMANSHIP AND QUALITY ARE IDENTICAL TO THE EARLY MARKED PANS.
NOTE: THE UNDERSIDE OF HANDLES ARE ROUNDED.

Top view of Variation 3 of No 12 Gem Pan

NO 12 GEM PAN
P/N 951

VARIATION 2 RARITY: 7

(OPEN FRAME)   (VARIATION 2)

NO 12
(RAISED LETTERS)

NOTE: DRAWING NOT TO SCALE

VIEW OF UNDERSIDE

NOTE: THE UNDERSIDE OF HANDLES ARE ROUNDED.

NO 12 GEM PAN
P/N 951

VARIATION 3 RARITY: 7

(OPEN FRAME)   (VARIATION 3)

951

NO 12
(RAISED LETTERS)

VIEW OF UNDERSIDE   NOTE: DRAWING NOT TO SCALE

NOTE: THE UNDERSIDE OF HANDLES ARE ROUNDED.

Underside of Variation 3 of No 12 Gem Pan

Underside of Variation 4 of No 12 Gem Pan

NO 12 GEM PAN
P/N 951

VARIATION 4 RARITY: 8

(OPEN FRAME)   **(VARIATION 4)**

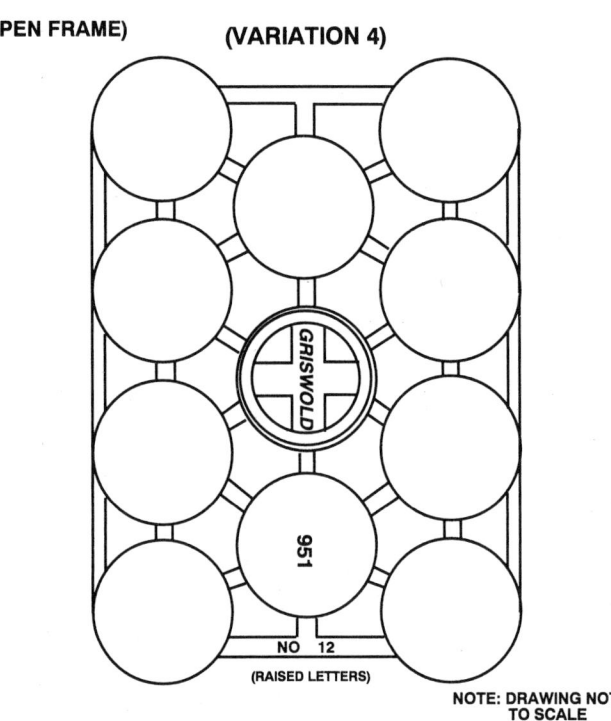

GRISWOLD

951

NO   12

(RAISED LETTERS)

NOTE: DRAWING NOT TO SCALE

VIEW OF UNDERSIDE

NOTE: THE UNDERSIDE OF HANDLES ARE ROUNDED

Top view of Variation 4 of No 12 Gem Pan

60

NO 12 GEM PAN
P/N 951

VARIATION 5 RARITY: 8

(OPEN FRAME)   (VARIATION 5)

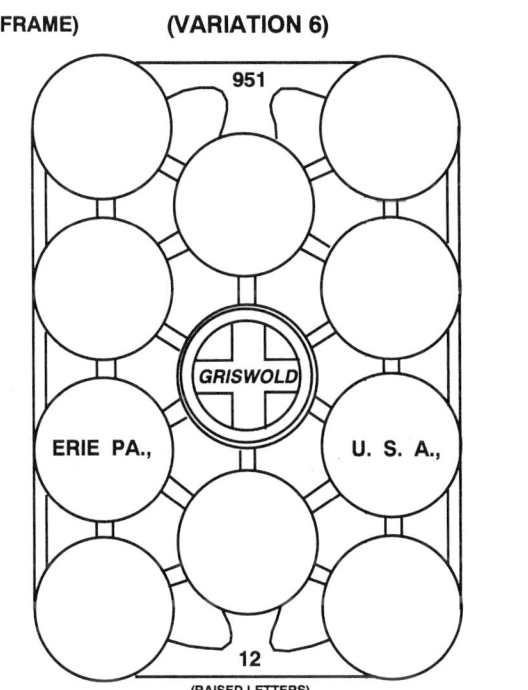

951

GRISWOLD

12

(RAISED LETTERS)   NOTE: DRAWING NOT
                                      TO SCALE

VIEW OF UNDERSIDE

NO 12 GEM PAN
P/N 951

VARIATION 6 RARITY: 8

(OPEN FRAME)   (VARIATION 6)

951

GRISWOLD

ERIE PA.,   U. S. A.,

12

(RAISED LETTERS)

NOTE: DRAWING NOT
TO SCALE

VIEW OF UNDERSIDE

Top view of Variation 7 of No 12 Gem Pan

Underside of Variation 7 of No 12 Gem Pan

NO 12 GEM PAN
P/N 951

VARIATION 7 RARITY: 8

(OPEN FRAME)   **(VARIATION 7)**

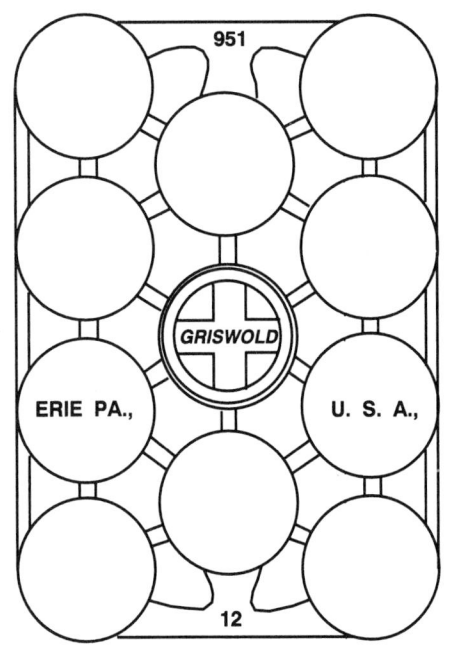

951

GRISWOLD

ERIE PA.,   U. S. A.,

12

NOTE: DRAWING NOT
TO SCALE

VIEW OF UNDERSIDE

No 13 Turk Head Pan

P/N 640
No. of cups: 6
Dimensions: 9 3/8" x 5 3/4"
Production Date: 1920s
Rarity: 10
Value: $1600 to $1800

    The No 13 Turk Head Pan is a small 6 cup pan. It is marked on the underside of all 6 cups with the curved GRISWOLD being unique to the No 13 and No 14 Turk Head Pans. This is a very rare and desirable pan.

Top view of No 13 Turk Head Pan

Underside of No 13 Turk Head Pan

No 14 Gem Pan

P/N 952
No. of cups: 12
Dimensions: 12 1/2" x 6 5/8"
Production Date: 1880s to 1900s
Variation 1: Rarity 9; Value $500 to $700
Variation 2: Rarity 9; Value $500 to $700
Variation 3: Rarity 8; Value $700 to $900
Variation 4: Rarity 9; Value $900 to $1100
Variation 5: Rarity 10; Value $1500 to $1700
Variation 6: Rarity 10; Value $1500 to $1700

The No 14 Gem Pan is a very early pan that was made both with an open frame and a solid frame. The open frame pan has cutouts between the cups and the solid frame pan does not. None of the variations of this pan were made with hang holes. Many of the No 14 Gem Pans have had holes drilled in them by the owner to facilitate hanging on a wall. All of the No 14 Gem Pans are uncommon. Variations 5 and 6 (marked with P/N 952) are very rare.

NO 13 TURK HEAD PAN
P/N 640

NO 13 (640) RARITY: 10

(OPEN FRAME)

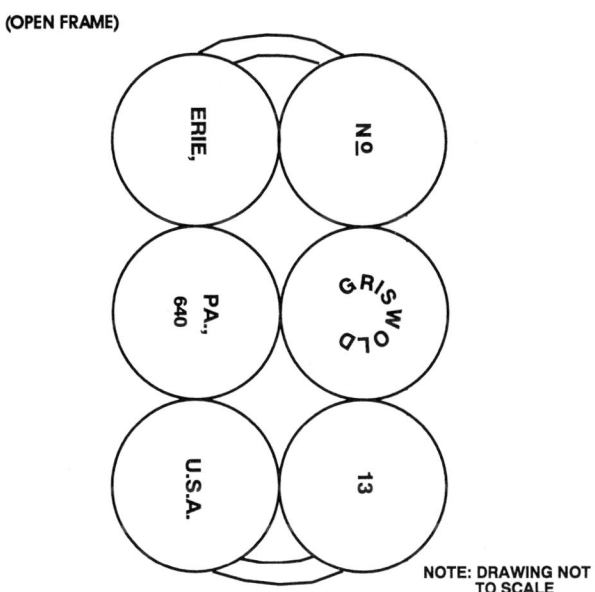

NOTE: DRAWING NOT TO SCALE

VIEW OF UNDERSIDE

NO 14 GEM PAN
P/N 952

VARIATION 1 RARITY: 9

(VARIATION 1)

(SOLID FRAME)

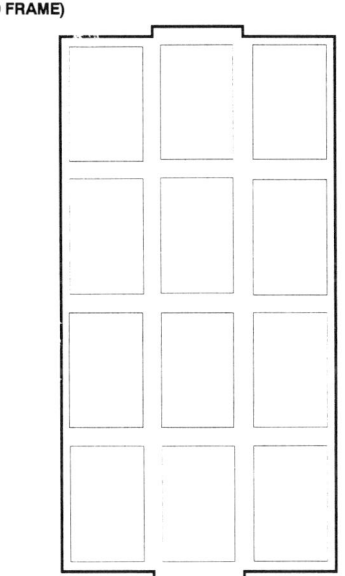

NOTE: DRAWING NOT TO SCALE

VIEW OF UNDERSIDE

NOTE: THERE ARE NO MARKINGS ON THIS PAN. THE WORKMANSHIP AND QUALITY ARE IDENTICAL TO THE MARKED PANS.

Top view of Variation 2 of No 14 Gem Pan

Underside of Variation 2 of No 14 Gem Pan

NO 14 GEM PAN
P/N 952

VARIATION 2 RARITY: 9

(VARIATION 2)

(OPEN FRAME)

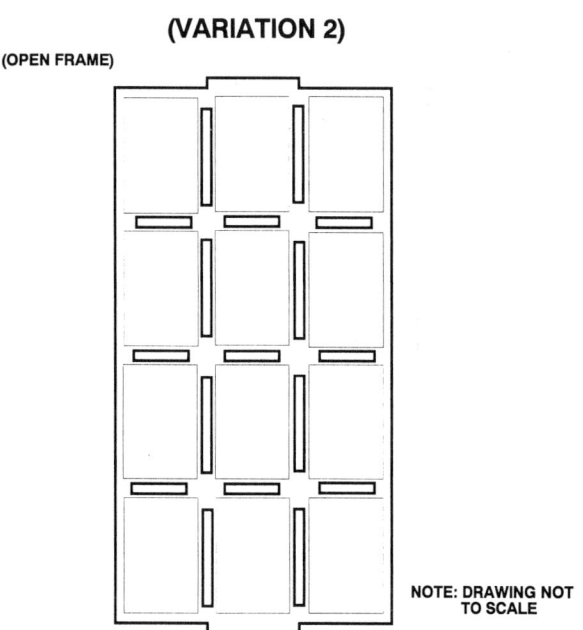

NOTE: DRAWING NOT TO SCALE

VIEW OF UNDERSIDE
NOTE: THERE ARE NO MARKINGS ON THIS PAN. THE WORKMANSHIP AND QUALITY ARE IDENTICAL TO THE MARKED PANS.

NO 14 GEM PAN
P/N 952

VARIATION 3 RARITY: 8

(VARIATION 3)

(OPEN FRAME)

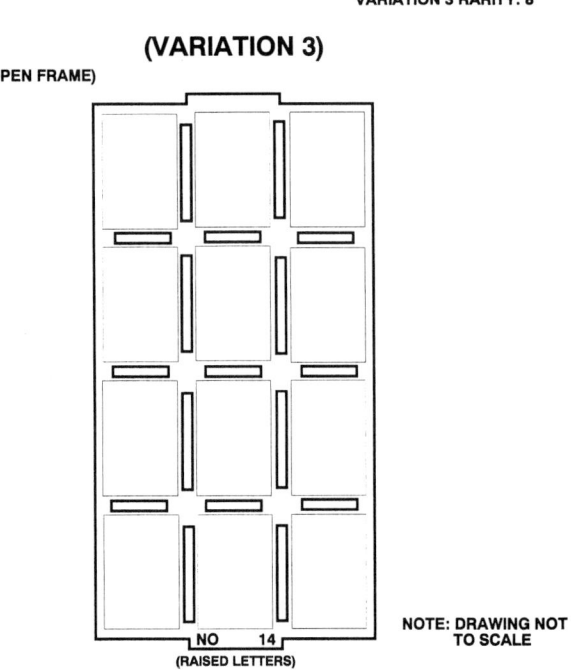

NO   14
(RAISED LETTERS)

NOTE: DRAWING NOT TO SCALE

VIEW OF UNDERSIDE

Underside of Variation 4 of No 14 Gem Pan

NO 14 GEM PAN
P/N 952

VARIATION 4 RARITY: 9

(VARIATION 4)

(OPEN FRAME)

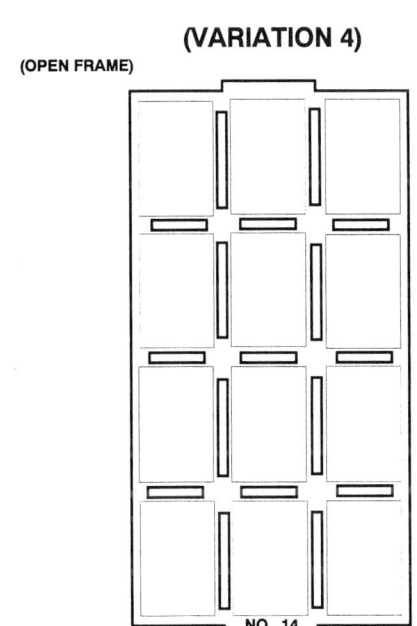

NO. 14
(RAISED LETTERS)

NOTE: DRAWING NOT
TO SCALE

VIEW OF UNDERSIDE

Underside of Variation 5 of No 14 Gem Pan. The hang hole was drilled by someone other than Griswold.

Top view of Variation 5 of No 14 Gem Pan. The hang hole was drilled by someone other than Griswold.

NO 14 GEM PAN
P/N 952

VARIATION 5 RARITY: 10

(VARIATION 5)

(SOLID FRAME)

952

NO. 14
(RAISED LETTERS)

NOTE: DRAWING NOT
TO SCALE

VIEW OF UNDERSIDE

NO 14 GEM PAN
P/N 952

VARIATION 6 RARITY: 10

(VARIATION 6)

(OPEN FRAME)

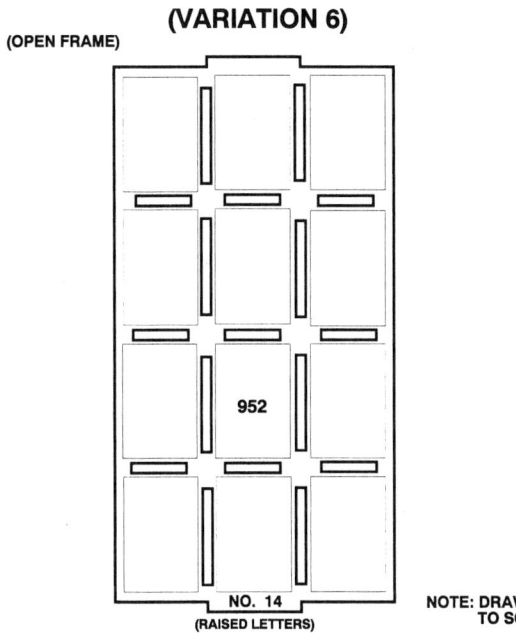

952

NO. 14
(RAISED LETTERS)

NOTE: DRAWING NOT
TO SCALE

VIEW OF UNDERSIDE

No 14 Turk Head Pan

P/N 641
No. of cups: 12
Dimensions: 13 1/8" x 8 3/8"
Production Date: 1920s
Rarity: 9
Value $1000 to $1100

    The No 14 Turk Head Pan along with the No 13 Turk Head Pan form one of several half pan/full pan sets that Griswold made. The markings are similar to the No 13 Turk Head Pan. The No 14 Turk Head Pan is rare but not as rare as the No 13 Turk Head Pan.

Underside of No 14 Turk Head Pan

Top view of No 14 Turk Head Pan

NO 14 TURK HEAD PAN
P/N 641

NO 14 (641) RARITY: 9

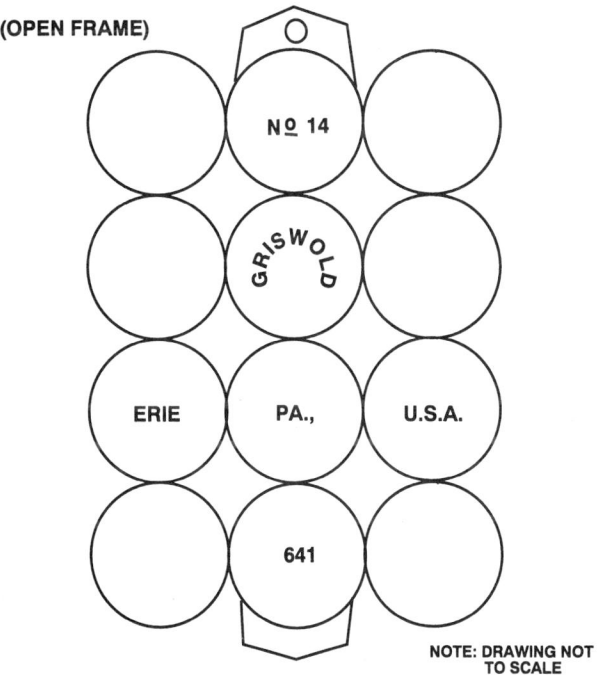

(OPEN FRAME)

NO 14

GRISWOLD

ERIE   PA.,   U.S.A.

641

NOTE: DRAWING NOT TO SCALE

VIEW OF UNDERSIDE

No 15 French Roll Pan

P/N 6138
No. of cups: 12
Dimensions: 14 3/8" x 7 1/2"; Wide Band 14 1/4" x 8"
Production Date: 1910s to 1940s
Variation 1: Rarity 8; Value $450 to $550
Variation 2: Rarity 7; Value $300 to $350
Variation 3: Rarity 6; Value $225 to $275

The No 15 French Roll Pan is a 12 cup pan. It is similar to the No 11 French Roll Pan but it has cups that are larger in size. The No 15, No 16, No 17, and No 18 pans have P/N's 6138, 6139, 6140, and 6141 respectively. Many of the Griswold pattern numbers are in logical sequences. However, these pattern numbers are mysterious and add to the intrigue of collecting Griswold.

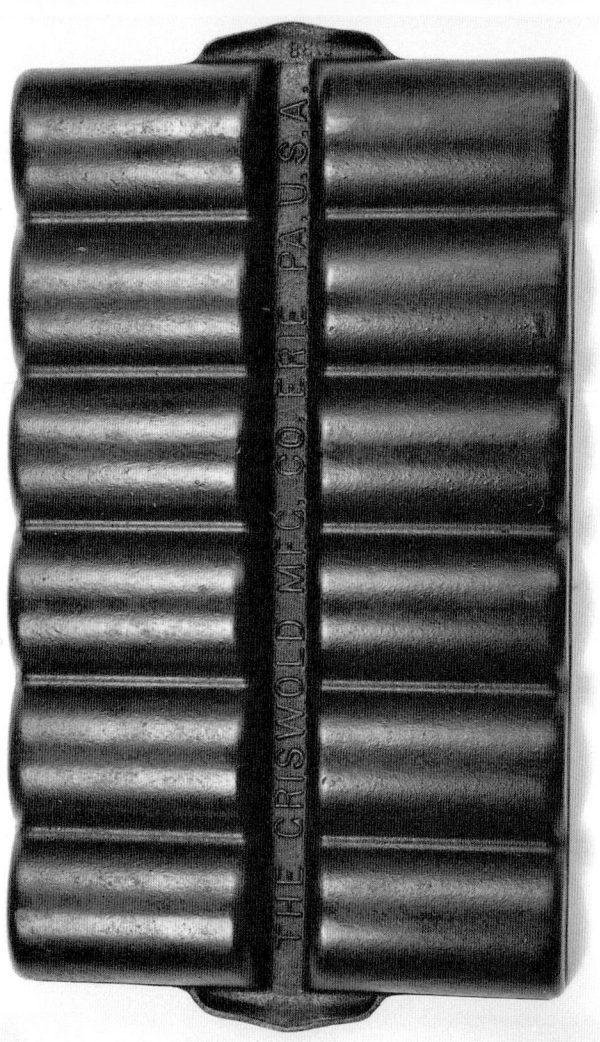

Underside of Variation 1 of No 15 French Roll Pan

Top view of Variation 1 of No 15 French Roll Pan

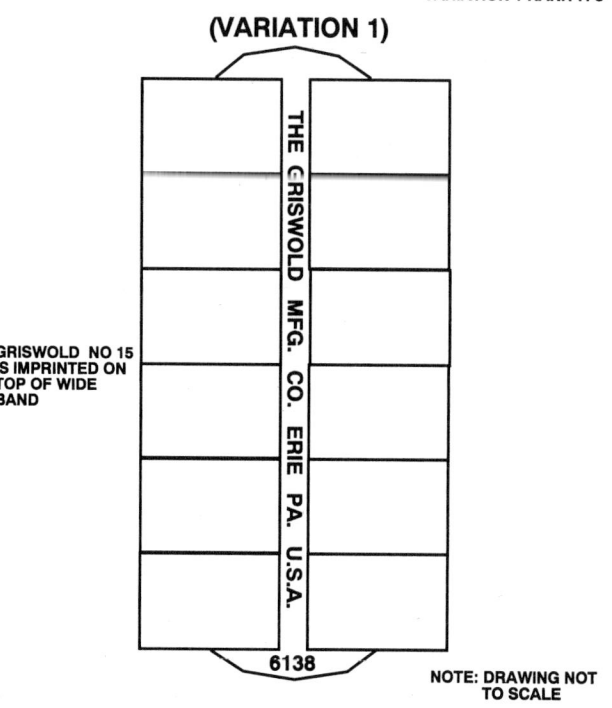

NO 15 FRENCH ROLL PAN
P/N 6138

VARIATION 1 RARITY: 8

(VARIATION 1)

THE GRISWOLD MFG. CO. ERIE PA. U.S.A.

GRISWOLD NO 15 IS IMPRINTED ON TOP OF WIDE BAND

6138

NOTE: DRAWING NOT TO SCALE

VIEW OF UNDERSIDE

NOTE: THE GRISWOLD MFG. CO. ERIE PA. U.S.A. IS IN RAISED LETTERS

NO 15 FRENCH ROLL PAN
P/N 6138

VARIATION 2 RARITY: 7

(VARIATION 2)

15	GRISWOLD
6138	ERIE

NOTE: DRAWING NOT
TO SCALE

VIEW OF UNDERSIDE

Underside of Variation 3 of No 15 French Roll Pan

NO 15 FRENCH ROLL PAN
P/N 6138

VARIATION 3 RARITY: 6

(VARIATION 3)

GRISWOLD IS IMPRINTED ON
TOP OF HANDLE

NO	15
GRISWOLD	ERIE PA.,
	U. S. A.,
6138	

NOTE: DRAWING NOT
TO SCALE

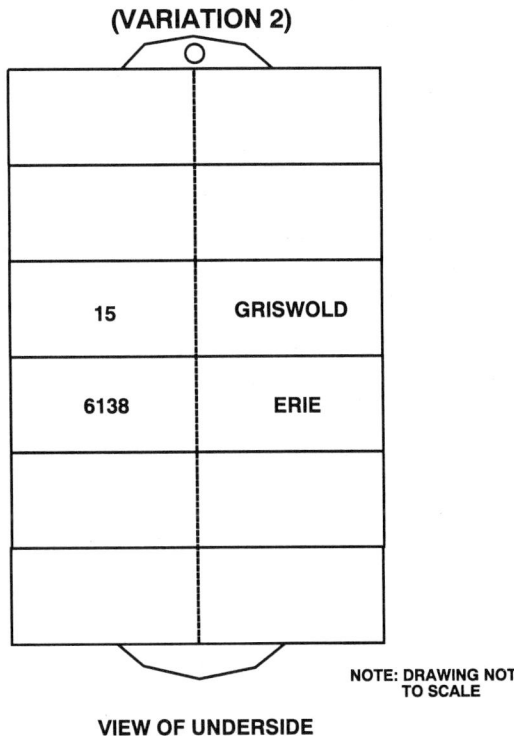

Top view of Variation 3 of No 15 French Roll Pan

VIEW OF UNDERSIDE

No 16 French Roll Pan

P/N 6139
No. of cups: 6
Dimensions: 8 5/8" x 6 3/4"; Wide Band 9 1/8" x 6 1/2"
Production Date: 1910s to 1940s
Variation 1: Rarity 10; Value $2500 to $3000
Variation 2: Rarity 8; Value $550 to $650
Variation 3: Rarity 8; Value $450 to $550
Variation 4: Rarity 8; Value $450 to $550
Variation 5: Rarity 8; Value $450 to $550

    The No 16 French Roll Pan forms another half pan/ full pan set with the No 15 French Roll Pan in both the wide band and narrow band variations. The No 16 wide band (Variation 1) is a very rare and desirable pan.

Underside of Variation 1 of No 16 French Roll Pan

Top view of Variation 1 of No 16 French Roll Pan

NO 16 FRENCH ROLL PAN
P/N 6139

VARIATION 1 RARITY: 10

(VARIATION 1)

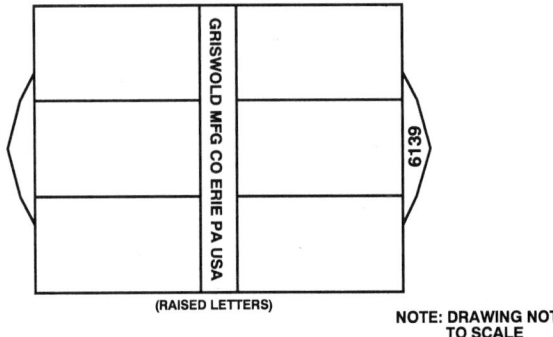

(RAISED LETTERS)

NOTE: DRAWING NOT TO SCALE

VIEW OF UNDERSIDE

NOTE: GRISWOLD No 16 IS IMPRINTED ON TOP OF CENTER BAND

NO 16 FRENCH ROLL PAN
P/N 6139

VARIATION 2 RARITY: 8

(VARIATION 2)

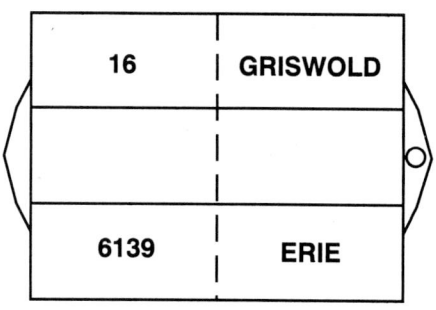

NOTE: DRAWING NOT TO SCALE

VIEW OF UNDERSIDE

70

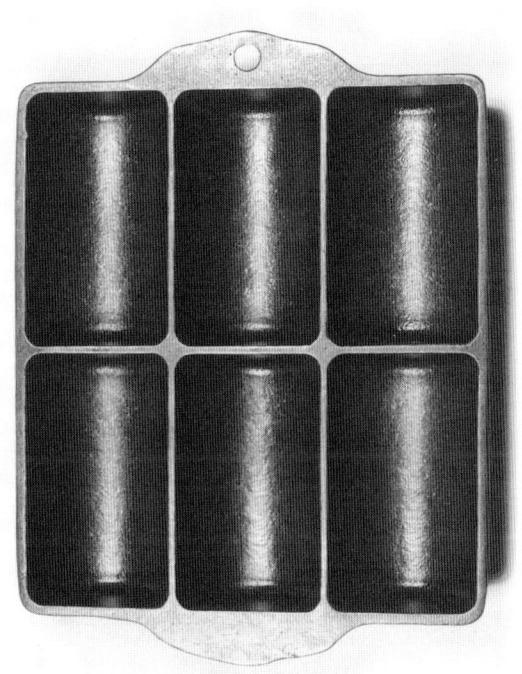

NO 16 FRENCH ROLL PAN
P/N 6139

VARIATION 4 RARITY: 8

(VARIATION 4)

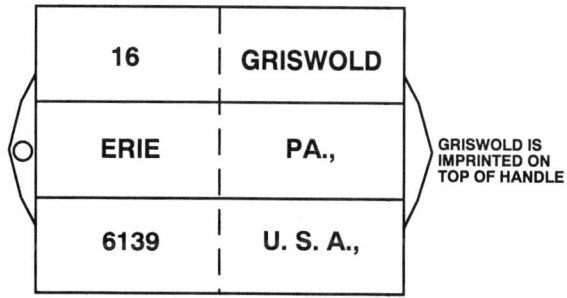

16	GRISWOLD
ERIE	PA.,
6139	U. S. A.,

GRISWOLD IS
IMPRINTED ON
TOP OF HANDLE

NOTE: DRAWING NOT
TO SCALE

VIEW OF UNDERSIDE

Top view of Variation 3 of No 16 French Roll Pan

NO 16 FRENCH ROLL PAN
P/N 6139

VARIATION 3 RARITY: 8

(VARIATION 3)

16	GRISWOLD
ERIE	PA.,
6139	U. S. A.,

NOTE: DRAWING NOT
TO SCALE

VIEW OF UNDERSIDE

Top view of Variation 5 of No 16 French Roll Pan

Underside of Variation 5 of No 16 French Roll Pan

NO 16 FRENCH ROLL PAN
P/N 6139

VARIATION 5 RARITY: 8

(VARIATION 5)

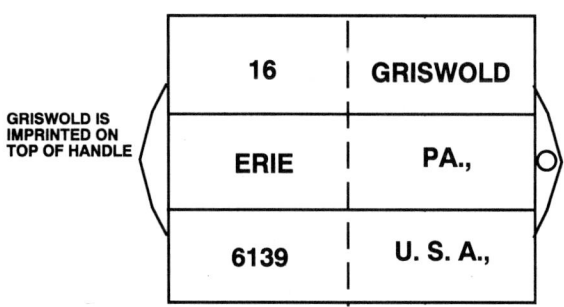

	16	GRISWOLD
GRISWOLD IS IMPRINTED ON TOP OF HANDLE	ERIE	PA.,
	6139	U. S. A.,

NOTE: DRAWING NOT TO SCALE

VIEW OF UNDERSIDE

No 17 French Roll Pan

P/N 6140
No. of cups: 6
Dimensions: 7 1/2" x 6"; Wide Band 7 7/8" x 5 3/4"
Production Date: 1910s to 1940s
Variation 1: Rarity 8; Value $500 to $600
Variation 2: Rarity 5; Value $175 to $200
Variation 3: Rarity 5; Value $200 to $225
Variation 4: Rarity 5; Value $200 to $225
Variation 5: Rarity 5; Value $175 to $200
Variation 6: Rarity 5; Value $175 to $200

The No 17 French Roll Pan is the half pan version of the No 11 French Roll Pan. There are many parallels among the variations of the No 11, No 15, No 16, and No 17 French Roll Pans. There are several sets that could be assembled from these four pans. The No 17 French Roll Pan is rather common except for its wide band variant (Variation 1).

Top view of Variation 1 of No 17 French Roll Pan

Underside of Variation 1 of No 17 French Roll Pan

NO 17 FRENCH ROLL PAN
P/N 6140

VARIATION 1 RARITY: 8

(VARIATION 1)

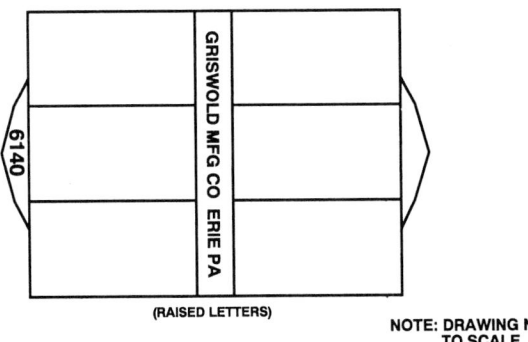

(RAISED LETTERS)

NOTE: DRAWING NOT TO SCALE

VIEW OF UNDERSIDE

NOTE: GRISWOLD No 17 IS IMPRINTED ON TOP OF CENTER BAND

Underside of Variation 2 of No 17 French Roll Pan

NO 17 FRENCH ROLL PAN
P/N 6140

VARIATION 2 RARITY: 5

(VARIATION 2)

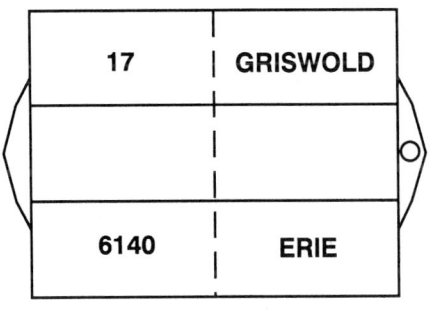

17	GRISWOLD
6140	ERIE

NOTE: DRAWING NOT TO SCALE

VIEW OF UNDERSIDE

Top view of Variation 2 of No 17 French Roll Pan

NO 17 FRENCH ROLL PAN
P/N 6140

VARIATION 3 RARITY: 5

(VARIATION 3)

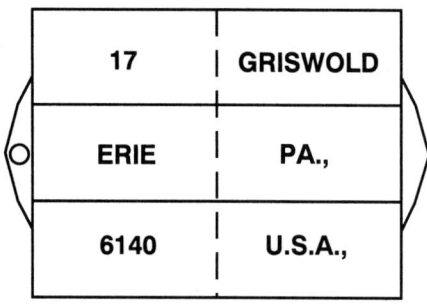

NOTE: DRAWING NOT
TO SCALE

VIEW OF UNDERSIDE

NO 17 FRENCH ROLL PAN
P/N 6140

VARIATION 5 RARITY: 5

(VARIATION 5)

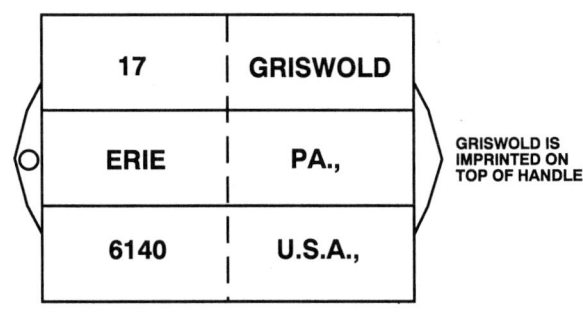

GRISWOLD IS
IMPRINTED ON
TOP OF HANDLE

NOTE: DRAWING NOT
TO SCALE

VIEW OF UNDERSIDE

NO 17 FRENCH ROLL PAN
P/N 6140

VARIATION 4 RARITY: 5

(VARIATION 4)

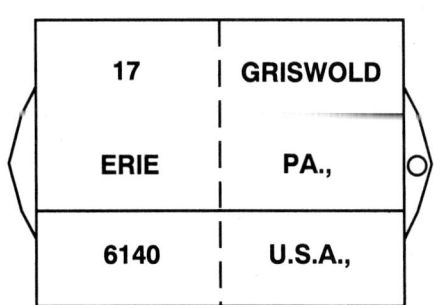

NOTE: DRAWING NOT
TO SCALE

VIEW OF UNDERSIDE

NO 17 FRENCH ROLL PAN
P/N 6140

VARIATION 6 RARITY: 5

(VARIATION 6)

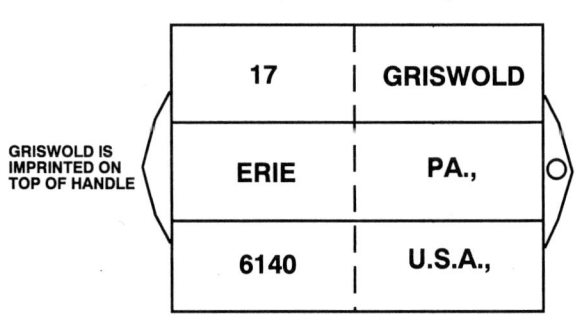

GRISWOLD IS
IMPRINTED ON
TOP OF HANDLE

NOTE: DRAWING NOT
TO SCALE

VIEW OF UNDERSIDE

Top view of Variation 6 of No 17 French Roll Pan

Underside of Variation 6 of No 17 French Roll Pan

No 18 Popover Pan

P/N 6141
No. of cups: 6
Dimensions: 8 5/8" x 5 1/2"; Late 9 1/4" x 5 1/2"
Production Date: 1910s to 1940s
Variation 1: Rarity 3; Value $115 to $135
Variation 2: Rarity 3; Value $115 to $135
Variation 3: Rarity 3; Value $90 to $110
Variation 4: Rarity 3; Value $90 to $110
Variation 5: Rarity 3; Value $70 to $90
Variation 6: Rarity 3; Value $80 to $100
Variation 7: Rarity 2; Value $50 to $70

The No 18 Popover Pan is the half pan version of the popular No 10 Popover Pan. The No 18 Popover Pan was made in three different shapes. The No 18 Popover Pan is a common pan and is easily obtainable.

Underside of Variation 1 of No 18 popover Pan

NO 18 POPOVER PAN
P/N 6141

VARIATION 1 RARITY: 3

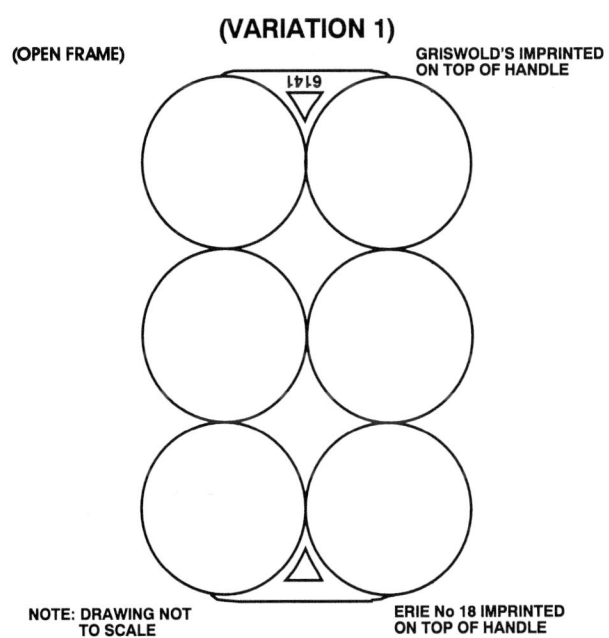

(VARIATION 1)

(OPEN FRAME)

GRISWOLD'S IMPRINTED ON TOP OF HANDLE

6141

NOTE: DRAWING NOT TO SCALE

ERIE No 18 IMPRINTED ON TOP OF HANDLE

VIEW OF UNDERSIDE

NO 18 POPOVER PAN
P/N 6141

(VARIATION 2)

(OPEN FRAME)

GRISWOLD'S IMPRINTED
ON TOP OF HANDLE

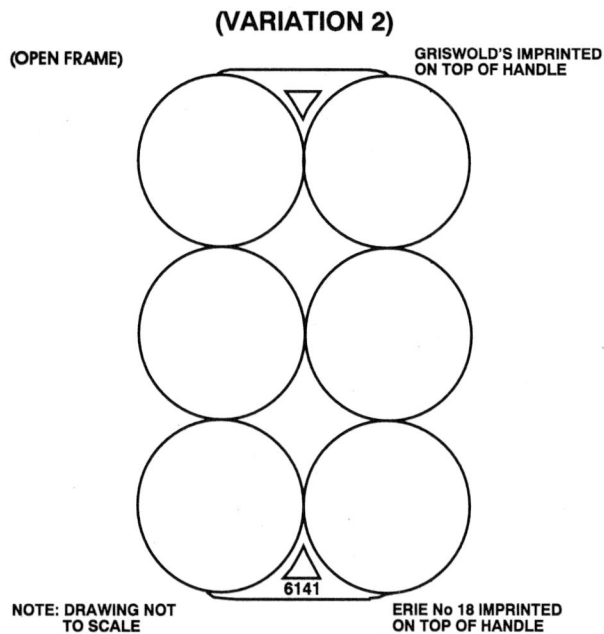

6141

NOTE: DRAWING NOT
TO SCALE

ERIE No 18 IMPRINTED
ON TOP OF HANDLE

VIEW OF UNDERSIDE

NO 18 POPOVER PAN
P/N 6141

(VARIATION 3)

(OPEN FRAME)

GRISWOLD'S IMPRINTED
ON TOP OF HANDLE

6141

NOTE: DRAWING NOT
TO SCALE

ERIE No 18 IMPRINTED
ON TOP OF HANDLE

VIEW OF UNDERSIDE

Top view of Variation 3 of No 18 Popover Pan

Underside of Variation 4 of No 18 Popover Pan

NO 18 POPOVER PAN
P/N 6141

VARIATION 4 RARITY: 3

(VARIATION 4)

(OPEN FRAME)

GRISWOLD'S IMPRINTED
ON TOP OF HANDLE

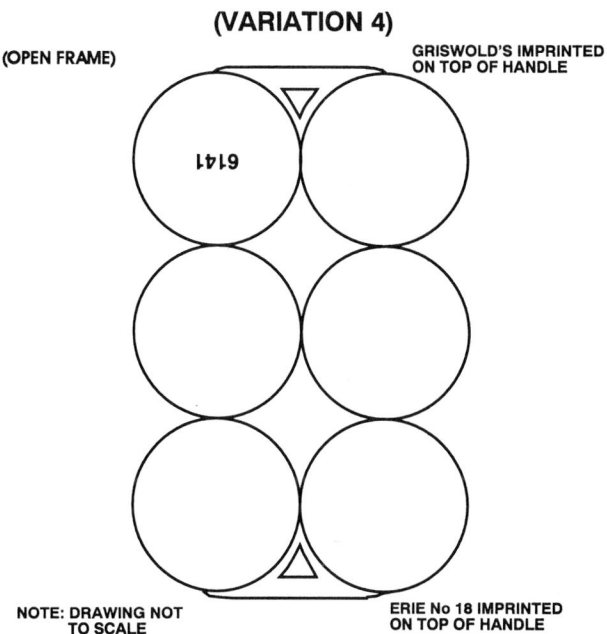

6141

NOTE: DRAWING NOT
TO SCALE

ERIE No 18 IMPRINTED
ON TOP OF HANDLE

VIEW OF UNDERSIDE

Underside of Variation 5 of No 18 Popover Pan

NO 18 POPOVER PAN
P/N 6141

VARIATION 5 RARITY: 3

(VARIATION 5)

(OPEN FRAME)

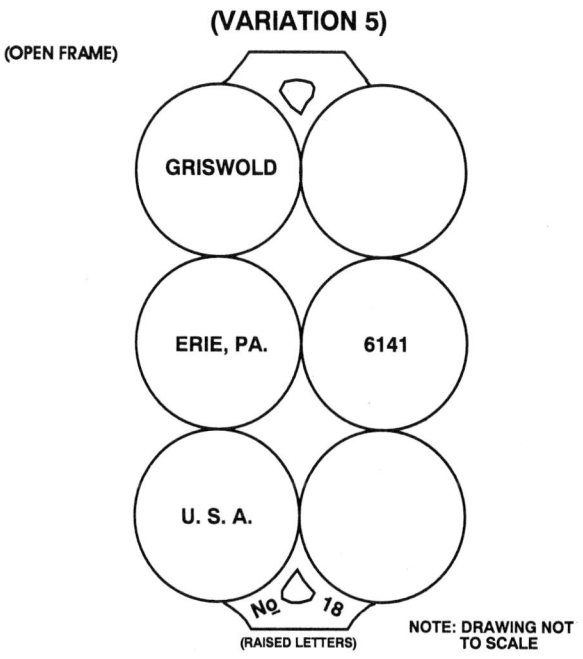

GRISWOLD

ERIE, PA.   6141

U. S. A.

No 18

(RAISED LETTERS)

NOTE: DRAWING NOT
TO SCALE

VIEW OF UNDERSIDE

NO 18 POPOVER PAN
P/N 6141

VARIATION 6 RARITY: 3

(VARIATION 6)

(OPEN FRAME)

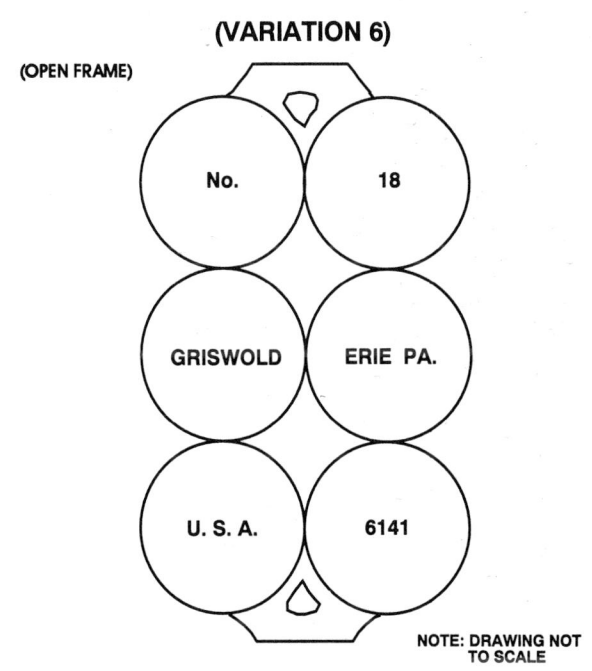

No.   18

GRISWOLD   ERIE PA.

U. S. A.   6141

NOTE: DRAWING NOT
TO SCALE

VIEW OF UNDERSIDE

Top view of Variation 7 of No 18 Popover Pan

NO 18 POPOVER PAN
P/N 6141

VARIATION 7 RARITY: 2

(VARIATION 7)

(OPEN FRAME)

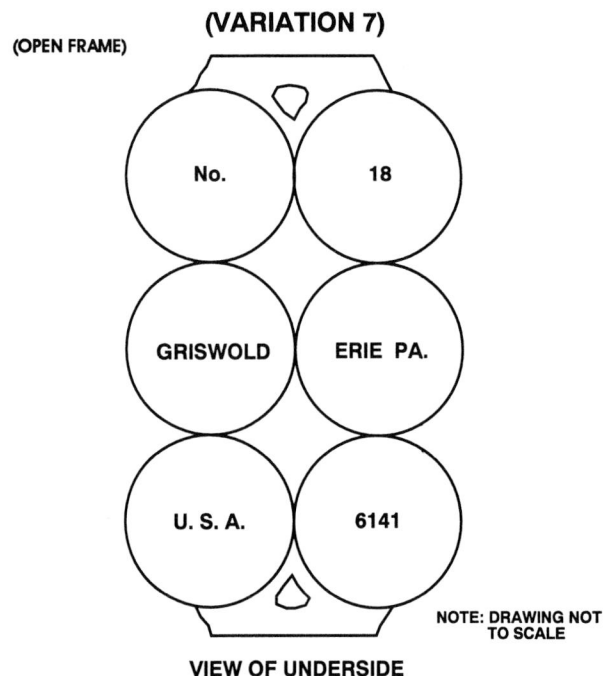

No.   18

GRISWOLD   ERIE PA.

U. S. A.   6141

NOTE: DRAWING NOT TO SCALE

VIEW OF UNDERSIDE

NOTE: THE ONLY DIFFERENCE FROM VARIATION 6 IS THE SIGNIFICANTLY WIDER HANDLE.

Underside of Variation 7 of No 18 Popover Pan

No 19 Golfball Pan

P/N 966
No. of cups: 6
Dimensions: 7 3/4" x 4 5/8"
Production Date: 1910s to 1940s
Variation 1: Rarity 10; Value Unknown
Variation 2: Rarity 8; Value $500 to $600
Variation 3: Rarity 8; Value $500 to $600

The No 19 Golfball Pan is the half pan version of the No 9 Golfball Pan. Variation 1 is not presently known in the collecting community. It was illustrated in Griswold catalogs 47 and 49. Catalog 49 showed them packed 25 dozen in a barrel and priced at $5.50 per dozen. These were sold for at least two years and there just have to be some of them in attics or cupboards. The other variations of the No 19 Golfball Pan are uncommon.

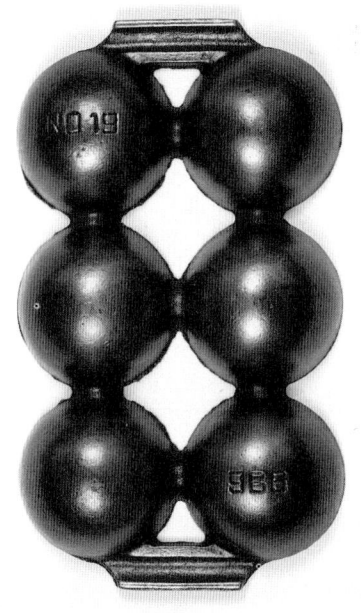

Illustration of Variation 1 of No 19 Golfball Pan from Bulletin E-5 of Catalog No 47

Underside of Variation 2 of No 19 Golfball Pan

NO 19 GOLFBALL PAN
P/N 966

VARIATION 1 RARITY: 10

(VARIATION 1)

(OPEN FRAME)

NOTE: DRAWING NOT
TO SCALE

VIEW OF UNDERSIDE

NOTE: THE MARKINGS ON THIS PAN ARE UNKNOWN AS THERE ARE NO
EXAMPLES OF IT IN THE COLLECTOR COMMUNITY AT THIS TIME.
ITS EXISTENCE IS BASED ON ILLUSTRATIONS IN GRISWOLD
CATALOGS 47 AND 49.

NO 19 GOLFBALL PAN
P/N 966

VARIATION 2 RARITY: 8

(VARIATION 2)

(OPEN FRAME)

NO 19

966

NOTE: DRAWING NOT
TO SCALE

GRISWOLD IMPRINTED
ON TOP OF HANDLE

VIEW OF UNDERSIDE

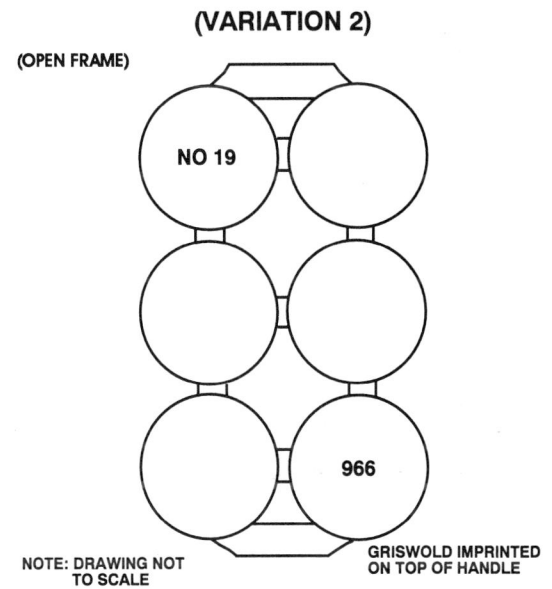

79

Top view of Variation 3 of No 19 Golfball Pan

NO 19 GOLFBALL PAN
P/N 966

VARIATION 3 RARITY: 8

(VARIATION 3)

(OPEN FRAME)

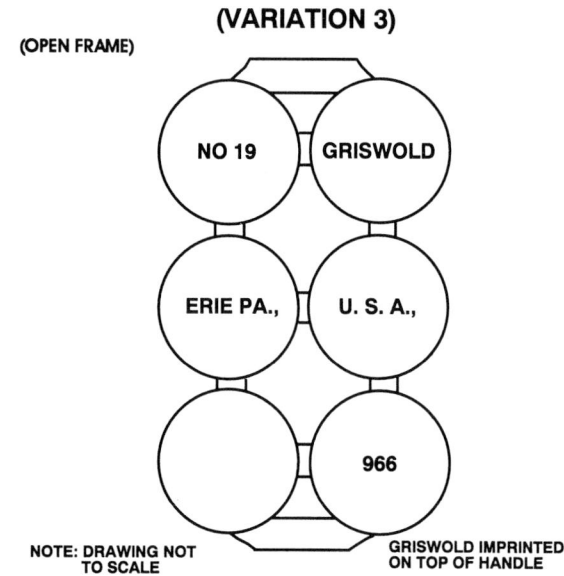

NO 19   GRISWOLD

ERIE PA.,   U. S. A.,

966

NOTE: DRAWING NOT
TO SCALE

GRISWOLD IMPRINTED
ON TOP OF HANDLE

VIEW OF UNDERSIDE

Underside of Variation 3 of No 19 Golfball Pan

No 20 Turk Head Pan

P/N 953
No. of cups: 11
Dimensions: 10 7/16" x 7 3/16"; Late 10 3/8" x 7"
Production Date: 1880s to 1920s
Variation 1: Rarity 7; Value $250 to $300
Variation 2: Rarity 7; Value $200 to $250
Variation 3: Rarity 8; Value $300 to $350
Variation 4: Rarity 8; Value $300 to $350
Variation 5: Rarity 8; Value $300 to $350
Variation 6: Rarity 8; Value $550 to $650
Variation 7: Rarity 8; Value $650 to $700
Variation 8: Rarity 8; Value $700 to $800

    The No 20 Turk Head Pan has a swirled design in the cups. The No 20 Turk Head Pan is small, dainty, and fragile. It makes an excellent wall display. Variation 8 is the most fully marked pan and is most desired by collectors.

NO 20 TURK HEAD PAN
P/N 953

VARIATION 1 RARITY: 7

(OPEN FRAME)

(VARIATION 1)

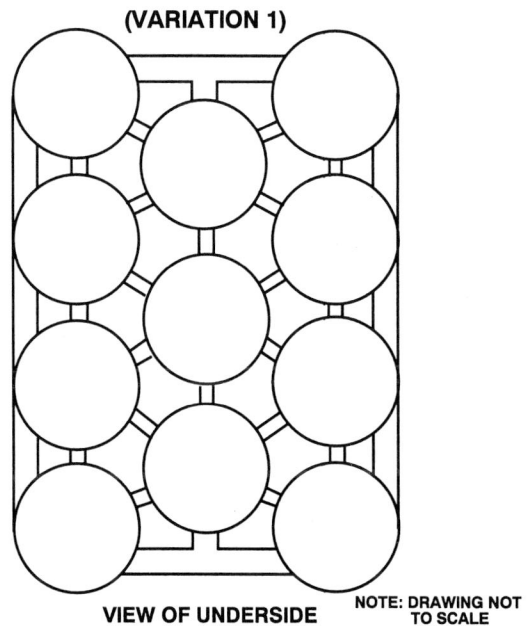

VIEW OF UNDERSIDE

NOTE: DRAWING NOT TO SCALE

NOTE: THE CORNERS ARE ROUND FROM THE HANDLES TO THE SIDE RAIL
NOTE: THERE ARE NO MARKINGS ON THIS PAN. THE WORKMANSHIP AND QUALITY ARE IDENTICAL TO THE EARLY MARKED PANS.

NO 20 TURK HEAD PAN
P/N 953

VARIATION 2 RARITY: 7

(OPEN FRAME)

(VARIATION 2)

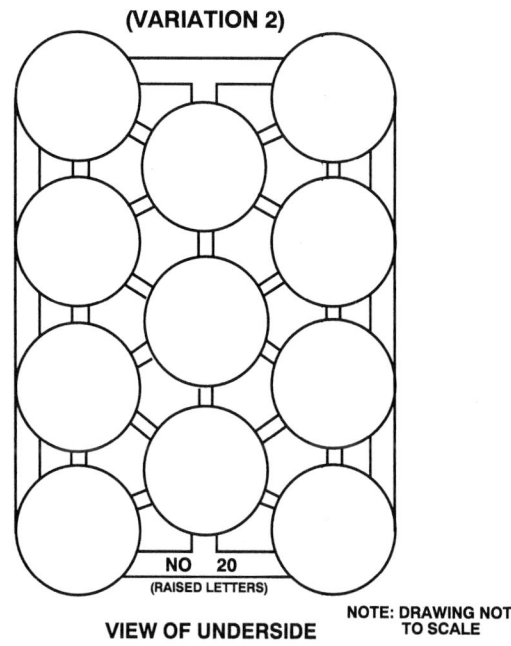

NO   20
(RAISED LETTERS)

VIEW OF UNDERSIDE

NOTE: DRAWING NOT TO SCALE

NOTE: THE CORNERS ARE ROUND FROM THE HANDLES TO THE SIDE RAIL

Top view of Variation 3 of No 20 Turk Head Pan

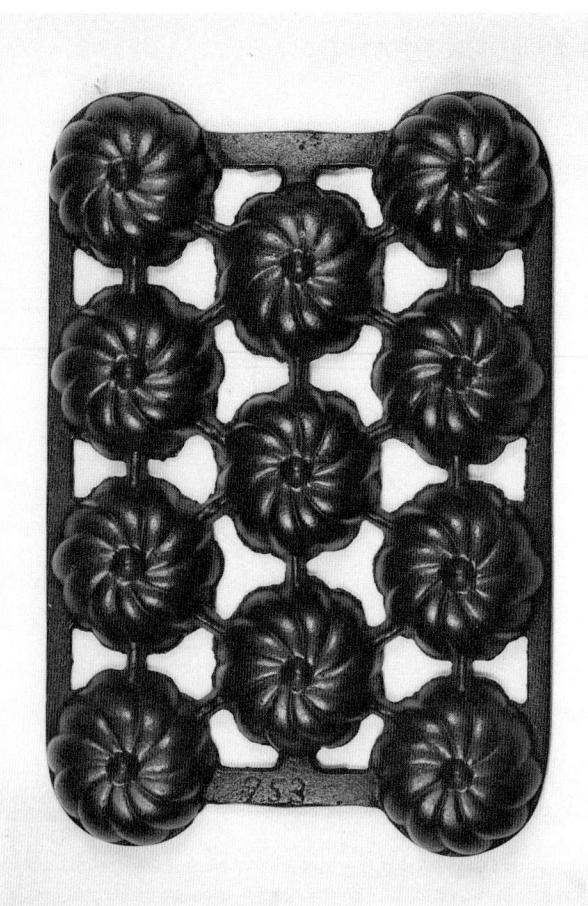

Underside of Variation 3 of No 20 Turk Head Pan

NO 20 TURK HEAD PAN
P/N 953

VARIATION 4 RARITY: 8

(OPEN FRAME)

(VARIATION 4)

(RAISED LETTERS)

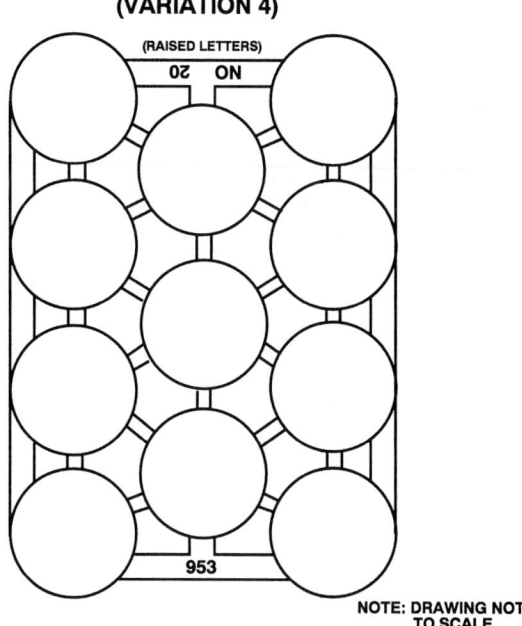

NO 20

953

NOTE: DRAWING NOT TO SCALE

VIEW OF UNDERSIDE

NOTE: THE CORNERS ARE ROUND FROM THE HANDLES TO THE SIDE RAIL

NO 20 TURK HEAD PAN
P/N 953

VARIATION 3 RARITY: 8

(OPEN FRAME)

(VARIATION 3)

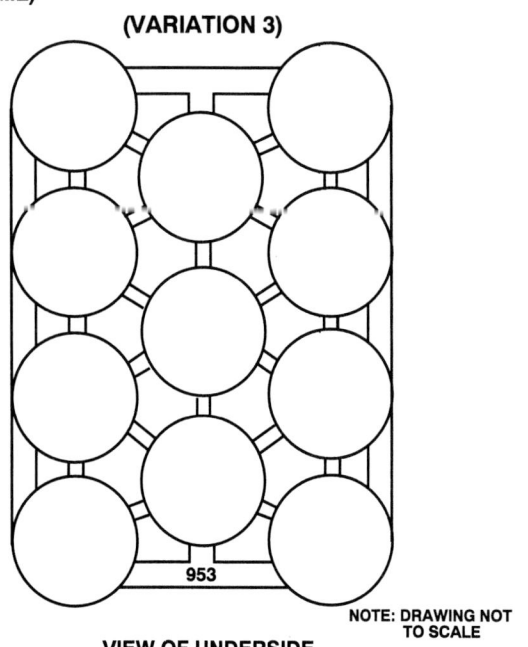

953

NOTE: DRAWING NOT TO SCALE

VIEW OF UNDERSIDE

NOTE: THE CORNERS ARE ROUND FROM THE HANDLES TO THE SIDE RAIL

Top view of Variation 5 of No 20 Turk Head Pan

Underside of Variation 5 of No 20 Turk Head Pan

NO 20 TURK HEAD PAN
P/N 953

VARIATION 6 RARITY: 8

(OPEN FRAME)

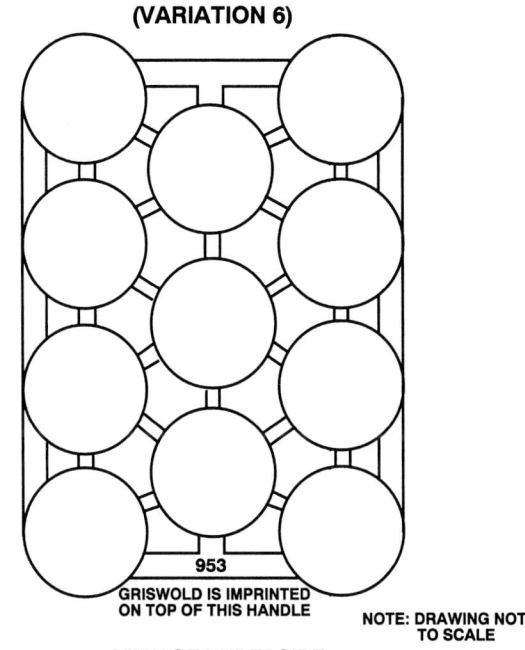

(VARIATION 6)

953

GRISWOLD IS IMPRINTED
ON TOP OF THIS HANDLE

NOTE: DRAWING NOT
TO SCALE

VIEW OF UNDERSIDE

NOTE: THE CORNERS ARE SCALLOPED FROM THE HANDLES TO THE SIDE RAIL

NO 20 TURK HEAD PAN
P/N 953

VARIATION 5 RARITY: 8

(OPEN FRAME)

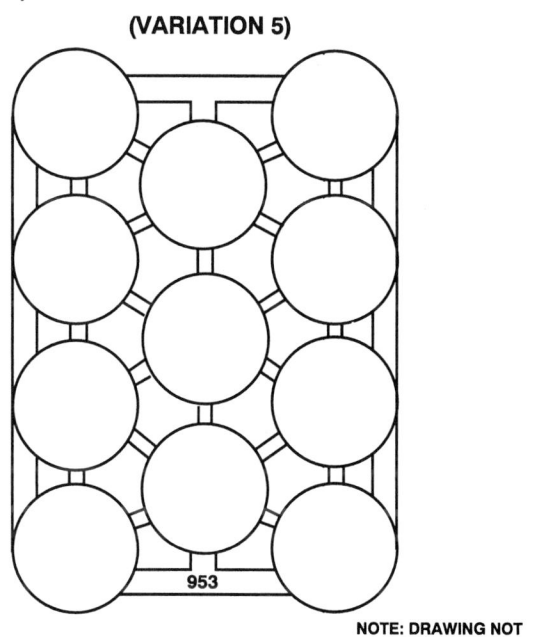

(VARIATION 5)

953

NOTE: DRAWING NOT
TO SCALE

VIEW OF UNDERSIDE

NOTE: THE CORNERS ARE SCALLOPED FROM THE HANDLES TO THE SIDE RAIL

NO 20 TURK HEAD PAN
P/N 953

VARIATION 7 RARITY: 8

(OPEN FRAME)

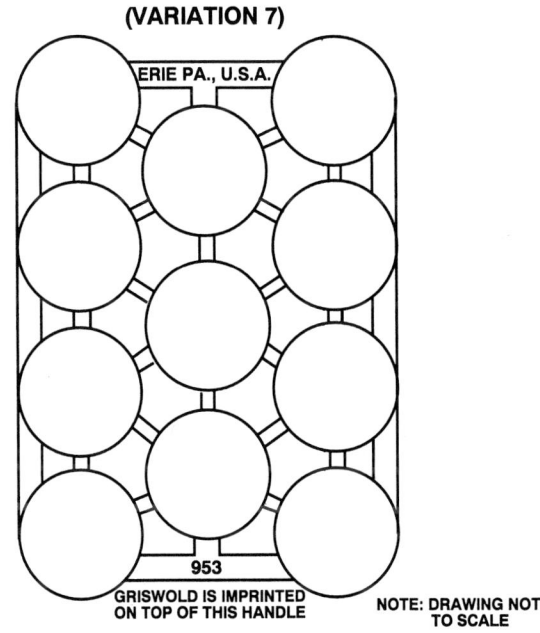

(VARIATION 7)

ERIE PA., U.S.A.

953

GRISWOLD IS IMPRINTED
ON TOP OF THIS HANDLE

NOTE: DRAWING NOT
TO SCALE

VIEW OF UNDERSIDE

NOTE: THE CORNERS ARE SCALLOPED FROM THE HANDLES TO THE SIDE RAIL

Top view of Variation 8 of No 20 Turk Head Pan

NO 20 TURK HEAD PAN
P/N 953

VARIATION 8 RARITY: 8

(OPEN FRAME)   **(VARIATION 8)**

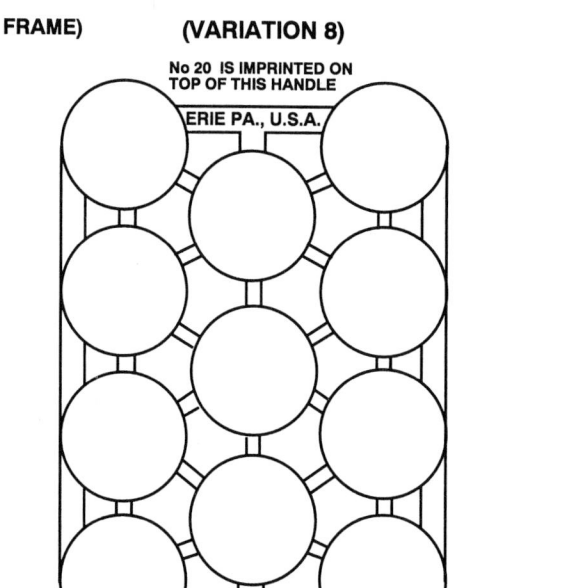

No 20 IS IMPRINTED ON
TOP OF THIS HANDLE

ERIE PA., U.S.A.

953

GRISWOLD IS IMPRINTED
ON TOP OF THIS HANDLE   NOTE: DRAWING NOT
TO SCALE

VIEW OF UNDERSIDE

NOTE: THE CORNERS ARE SCALLOPED FROM THE HANDLES TO THE SIDE RAIL

Underside of Variation 8 of No 20 Turk Head Pan

No 21 Bread Stick Pan

P/N 961
No. of cups: 7
Dimensions: 9 1/2" x 7 1/2"
Production Date: 1920s to 1940s
Rarity: 5
Value: $150 to $200
 The No 21 Bread Stick Pan is a 7 cup pan. It was made in only one variation.

Underside of No 21 Bread Stick Pan

Top view of No 21 Bread Stick Pan

NO 21 BREAD STICK PAN
P/N 961

NO 21 (961) RARITY: 5

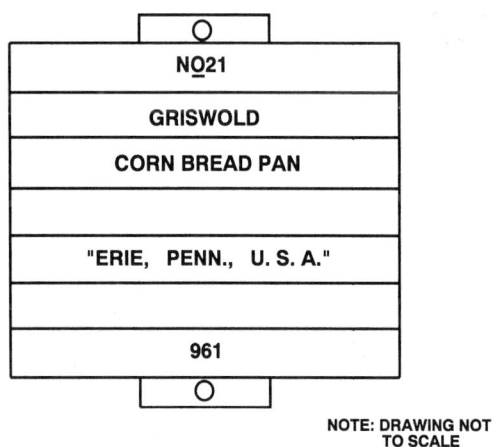

| NO21 |
| GRISWOLD |
| CORN BREAD PAN |
| "ERIE, PENN., U. S. A." |
| 961 |

NOTE: DRAWING NOT TO SCALE

VIEW OF UNDERSIDE

No 22 Bread Stick Pan

P/N 954
No. of cups: 11
Dimensions: 14 3/8" x 7 3/8"
Production Date: 1880s to 1950s
Variation 1: Rarity 3; Value $70 to $90
Variation 2: Rarity 3; Value $75 to $100
Variation 3: Rarity 2; Value $60 to $80
Variation 4: Rarity 1; Value $50 to $70
Variation 5: Rarity 1; Value $25 to $40
Variation 6: Rarity 1; Value $50 to $70
Variation 7: Rarity 1; Value $50 to $70
Variation 8: Rarity 2; Value $60 to $80
Variation 9: Rarity 1; Value $50 to $70
Variation 10: Rarity 2; Value $60 to $80
Variation 11: Rarity 1; Value $25 to $40
Variation 12: Rarity 1; Value $25 to $40
Variation 13: Rarity 1; Value $30 to $50
Variation 14: Rarity 1; Value $25 to $40
Variation 15: Rarity 1; Value $25 to $40

The No 22 Bread Stick Pan was produced throughout Griswold's history and is one of the most common pans. Variation 2 is one of the two Griswold pans known with a gate mark and a pattern number on the same pan. The early No 22 Bread Stick Pans did not have hang holes while the later ones did. The No 22 Bread Stick Pan is rather mundane and does not generate great interest with the collecting community.

Top view of Variation 2 of No 22 Bread Stick Pan

NO 22   BREAD STICK PAN
P/N 954

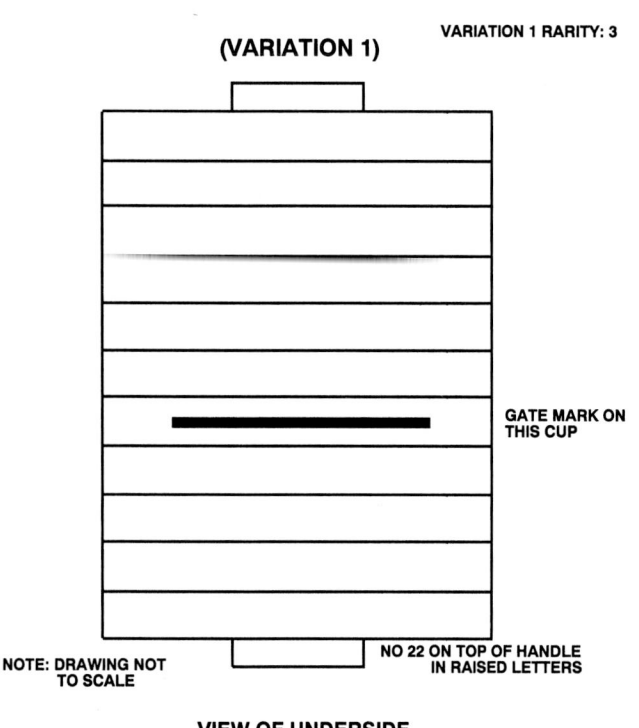

(VARIATION 1)

VARIATION 1 RARITY: 3

GATE MARK ON THIS CUP

NOTE: DRAWING NOT TO SCALE

NO 22 ON TOP OF HANDLE IN RAISED LETTERS

VIEW OF UNDERSIDE

NO 22   BREAD STICK PAN
P/N 954

VARIATION 2 RARITY: 3

(VARIATION 2)

GATE MARK ON THIS CUP

954

NOTE: DRAWING NOT TO SCALE

NO 22 ON TOP OF HANDLE IN RAISED LETTERS

VIEW OF UNDERSIDE

NO 22   BREAD STICK PAN
P/N 954

VARIATION 4 RARITY: 1

(VARIATION 4)

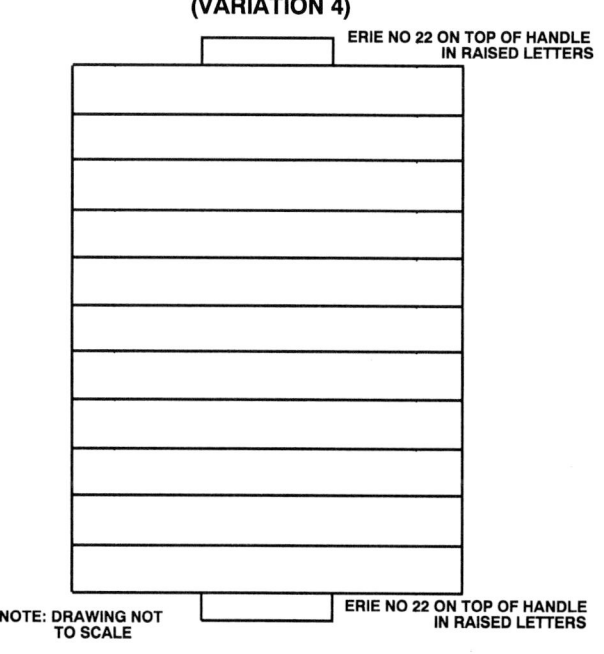

ERIE NO 22 ON TOP OF HANDLE
IN RAISED LETTERS

NOTE: DRAWING NOT
TO SCALE

ERIE NO 22 ON TOP OF HANDLE
IN RAISED LETTERS

VIEW OF UNDERSIDE

Underside of Variation 2 of No 22 Bread Stick Pan

NO 22   BREAD STICK PAN
P/N 954

VARIATION 3 RARITY: 2

(VARIATION 3)

954

NOTE: DRAWING NOT
TO SCALE

VIEW OF UNDERSIDE

NO 22   BREAD STICK PAN
P/N 954

VARIATION 5 RARITY: 1

(VARIATION 5)

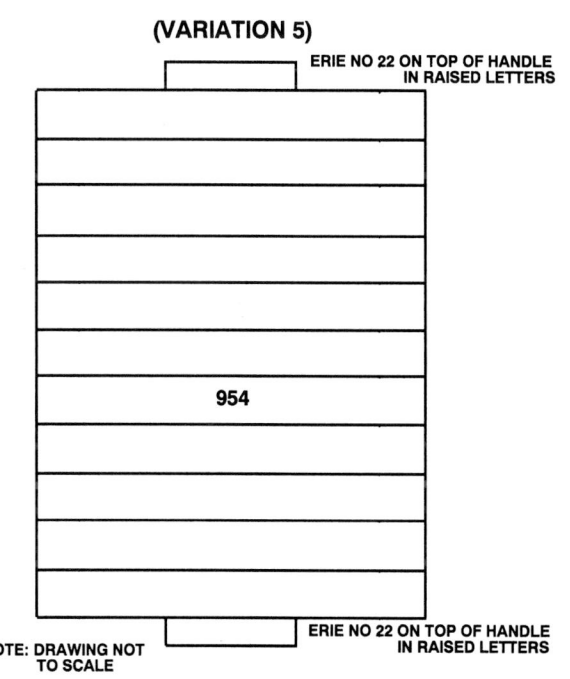

ERIE NO 22 ON TOP OF HANDLE
IN RAISED LETTERS

954

NOTE: DRAWING NOT
TO SCALE

ERIE NO 22 ON TOP OF HANDLE
IN RAISED LETTERS

VIEW OF UNDERSIDE

Underside of Variation 6 of No 22 Bread Stick Pan

NO 22   BREAD STICK PAN
P/N 954

VARIATION 7 RARITY: 1

(VARIATION 7)

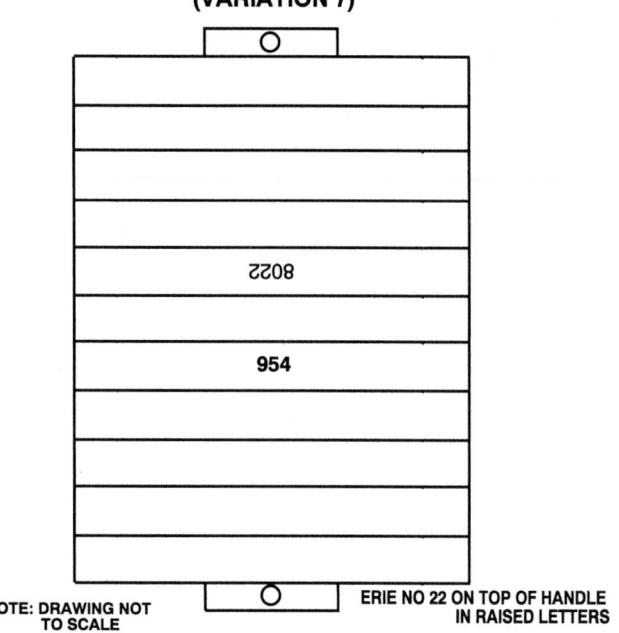

NOTE: DRAWING NOT
TO SCALE

ERIE NO 22 ON TOP OF HANDLE
IN RAISED LETTERS

VIEW OF UNDERSIDE

NOTE: THE 8022, WHICH IS THE PATTERN NUMBER OF THE ALUMINUM BREAD
STICK PAN, IS FAINTER THAN THE 954 ALTHOUGH VERY LEGIBLE.

NO 22   BREAD STICK PAN
P/N 954

VARIATION 6 RARITY: 1

(VARIATION 6)

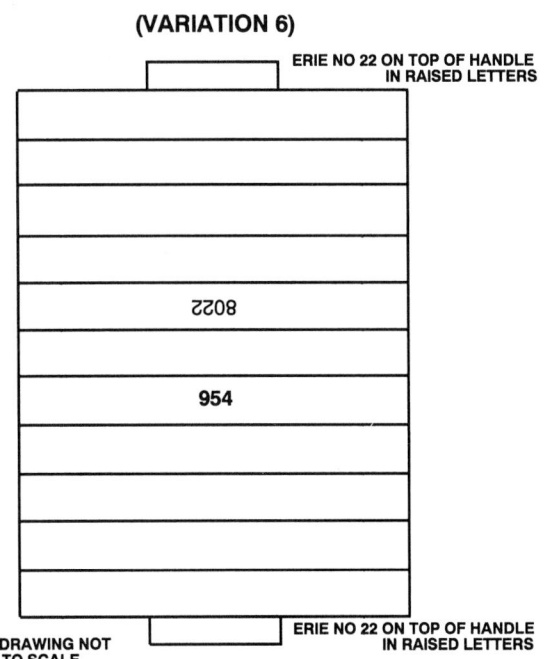

ERIE NO 22 ON TOP OF HANDLE
IN RAISED LETTERS

NOTE: DRAWING NOT
TO SCALE

ERIE NO 22 ON TOP OF HANDLE
IN RAISED LETTERS

VIEW OF UNDERSIDE

NOTE: THE 8022, WHICH IS THE PATTERN NUMBER OF THE ALUMINUM BREAD
STICK PAN, IS FAINTER THAN THE 954 ALTHOUGH VERY LEGIBLE.

NO 22   BREAD STICK PAN
P/N 954

VARIATION 8 RARITY: 2

(VARIATION 8)

ERIE NO 22 ON TOP OF HANDLE
IN RAISED LETTERS

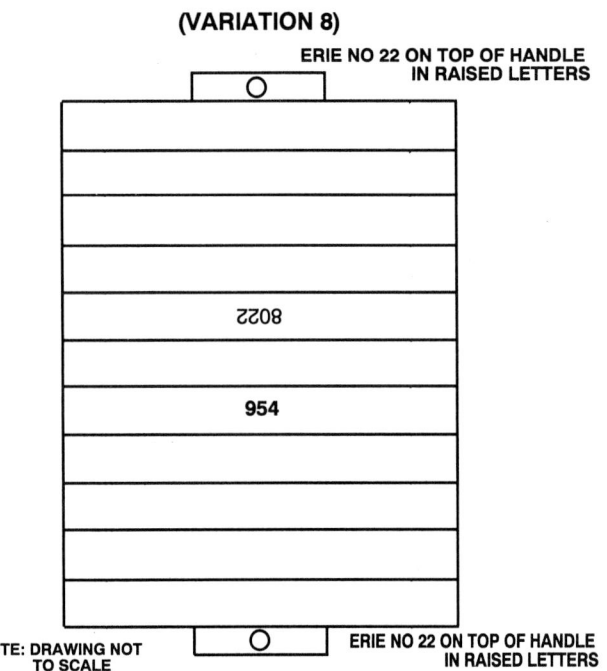

NOTE: DRAWING NOT
TO SCALE

ERIE NO 22 ON TOP OF HANDLE
IN RAISED LETTERS

VIEW OF UNDERSIDE

NOTE: THE 8022, WHICH IS THE PATTERN NUMBER OF THE ALUMINUM BREAD
STICK PAN, IS FAINTER THAN THE 954 ALTHOUGH VERY LEGIBLE.

Top view of Variation 9 of No 22 Bread Stick Pan

NO 22   BREAD STICK PAN
P/N 954

(VARIATION 9)

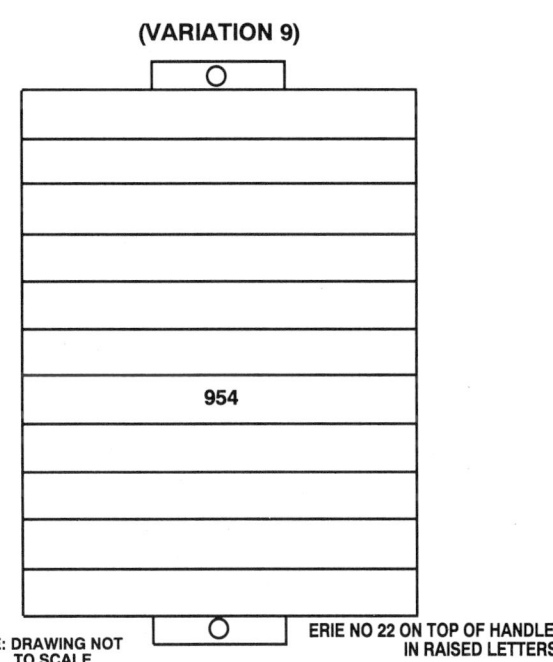

954

NOTE: DRAWING NOT
TO SCALE

ERIE NO 22 ON TOP OF HANDLE
IN RAISED LETTERS

VIEW OF UNDERSIDE

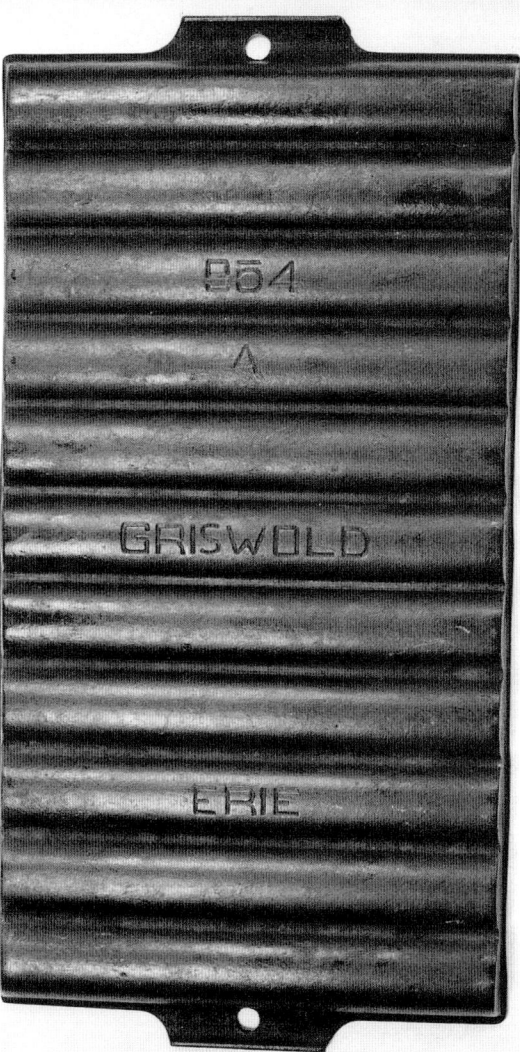

Underside of Variation 10 of No 22 Bread Stick Pan

NO 22   BREAD STICK PAN
P/N 954

(VARIATION 10)

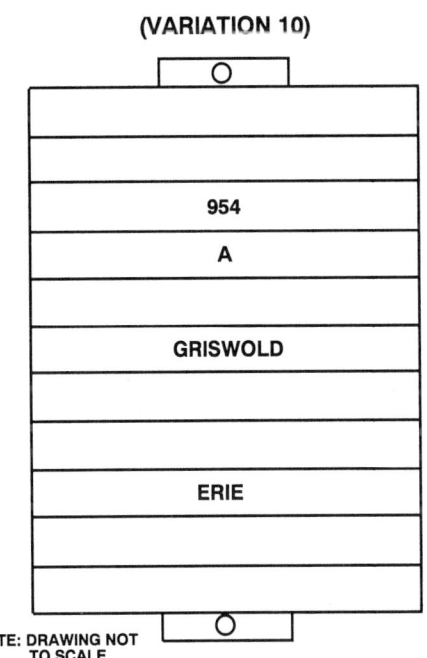

954

A

GRISWOLD

ERIE

NOTE: DRAWING NOT
TO SCALE

VIEW OF UNDERSIDE

NO 22 BREAD STICK PAN
P/N 954

(VARIATION 11)

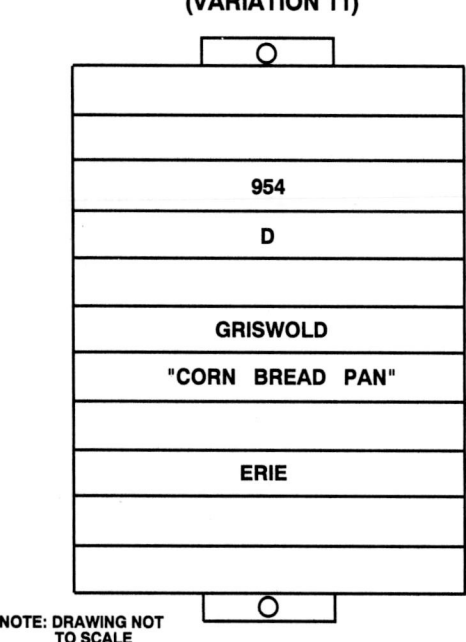

NOTE: DRAWING NOT
TO SCALE

VIEW OF UNDERSIDE

NO 22 BREAD STICK PAN
P/N 954

(VARIATION 13)

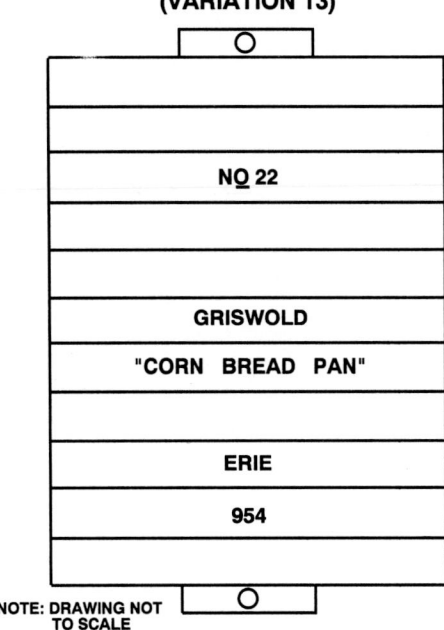

NOTE: DRAWING NOT
TO SCALE

VIEW OF UNDERSIDE

NO 22 BREAD STICK PAN
P/N 954

(VARIATION 12)

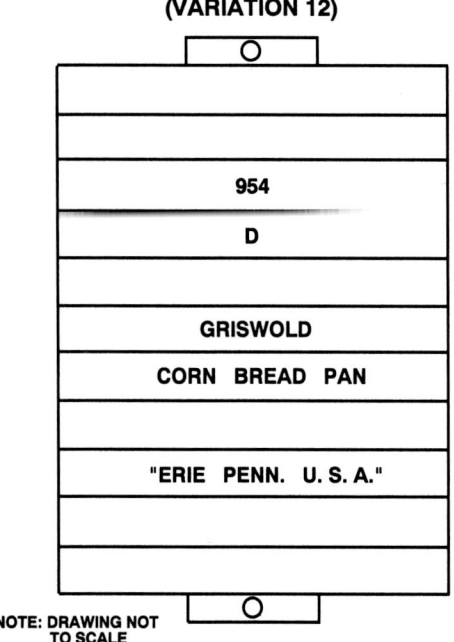

NOTE: DRAWING NOT
TO SCALE

VIEW OF UNDERSIDE

NO 22 BREAD STICK PAN
P/N 954

(VARIATION 14)

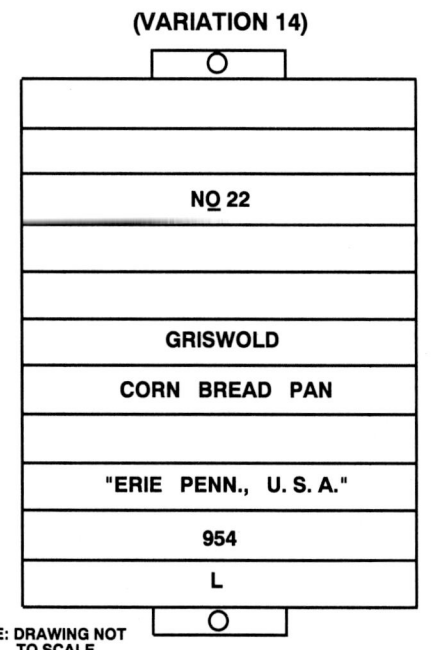

NOTE: DRAWING NOT
TO SCALE

VIEW OF UNDERSIDE

No 23 Bread Stick Pan

P/n 955
No. of cups: 22
Dimensions: 14 1/2" x 7 1/2"
Production Date: 1920s to 1950s
Variation 1: Rarity 3; Value $80 to $100
Variation 2: Rarity 3; Value $80 to $100
    The No 23 Bread Stick Pan is basically the same as the No 22 Bread Stick Pan with a divider down the center to make 22 short bread sticks. The No 23 Bread Stick Pan is a common pan.

Underside of Variation 15 of No 22 Bread Stick Pan

Top view of Variation 1 of No 23 Bread Stick Pan

NO 22 BREAD STICK PAN
P/N 954

VARIATION 15 RARITY: 1

NO 23 BREAD STICK PAN
P/N 955

VARIATION 1 RARITY: 3

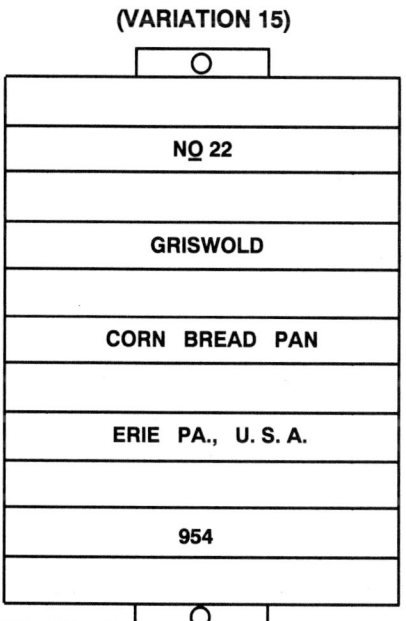

(VARIATION 15)

NO 22

GRISWOLD

CORN BREAD PAN

ERIE PA., U. S. A.

954

NOTE: DRAWING NOT TO SCALE

VIEW OF UNDERSIDE

(VARIATION 1)

NO 23

BREAD STICK PAN

GRISWOLD

ERIE. PA., U. S. A.

955

NOTE: DRAWING NOT TO SCALE

VIEW OF UNDERSIDE

Underside of Variation 1 of No 23 Bread Stick Pan

NO 23   BREAD STICK PAN
P/N 955

VARIATION 2 RARITY: 3

(VARIATION 2)

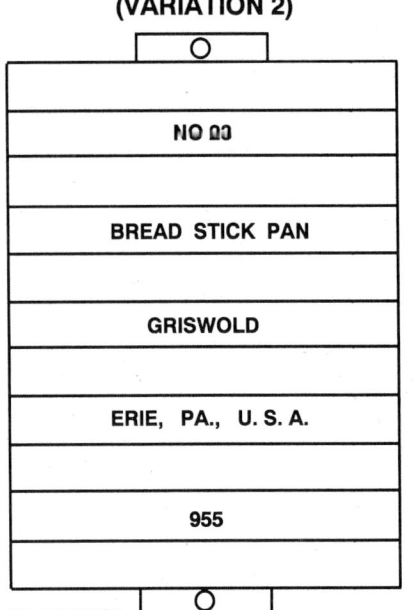

| NO 23 |
| BREAD STICK PAN |
| GRISWOLD |
| ERIE, PA., U. S. A. |
| 955 |

**NOTE: DRAWING NOT
TO SCALE**

VIEW OF UNDERSIDE

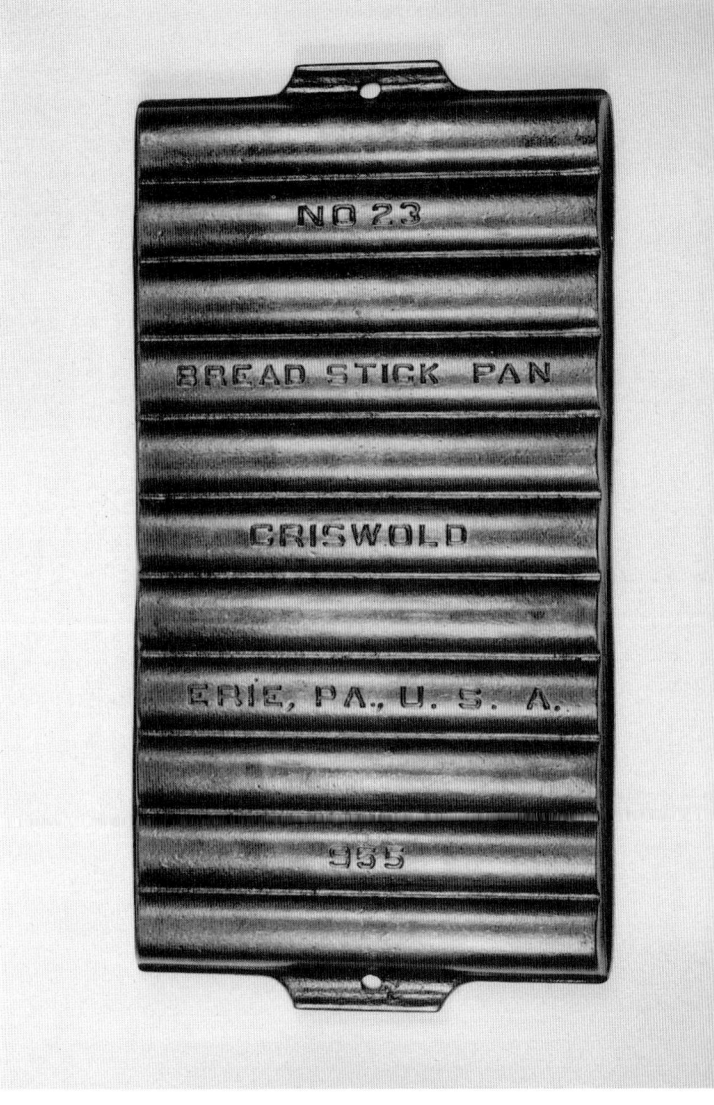

Underside of Variation 2 of No 23 Bread Stick Pan

No 24 Bread Pan

P/N 959
No. of cups: 6
Dimensions: 13 7/8" x 7 5/8"
Production Date: 1900s to 1910s
Variation 1: Rarity 9; Value $1000 to $1200
Variation 2: Rarity 9; Value $1200 to $1400

The No 24 Pan is an early 6 cup bread pan. It is a rare pan and is difficult to obtain. The No 24 Bread Pan, with what appear to be very thin walls, is one of the most fragile pans made by Griswold. The No 24 Bread Pan is part of the Erie Bread Pan series and Variation 2 has "ERIE No 24" on top of one handle.

Top view of Variation 1 of No 24 Bread Pan

NO 24   BREAD PAN
P/N 959

VARIATION 1 RARITY: 9

(VARIATION 1)

959

NOTE: DRAWING NOT
TO SCALE

VIEW OF UNDERSIDE

Top view of Variation 2 of No 24 Bread Pan

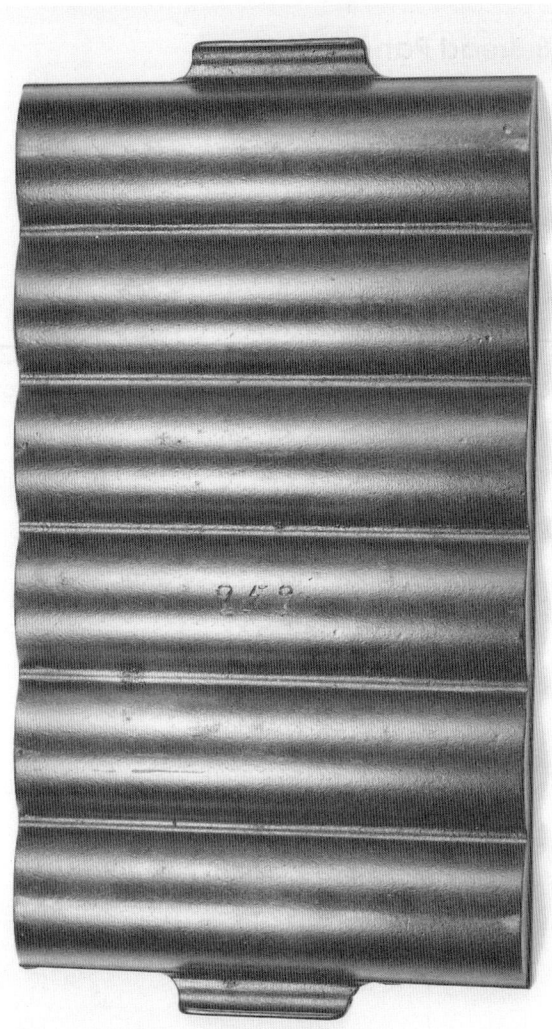

Underside of Variation 2 of No 24 Bread Pan

NO 24   BREAD PAN
P/N 959

VARIATION 2 RARITY: 9

(VARIATION 2)

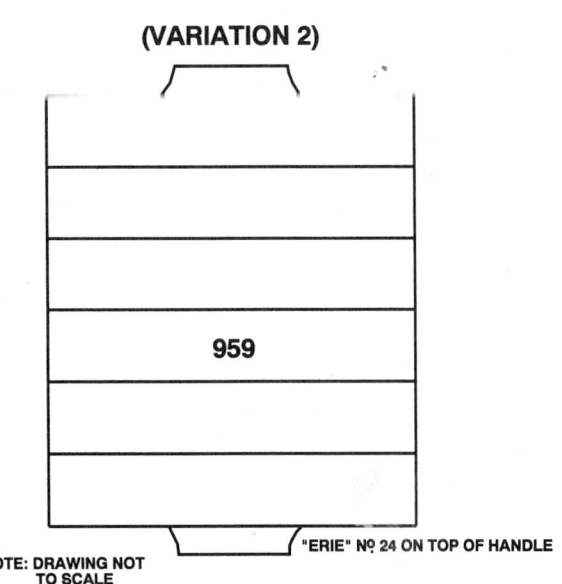

959

NOTE: DRAWING NOT
TO SCALE

"ERIE" N⁰ 24 ON TOP OF HANDLE

VIEW OF UNDERSIDE

No 24 Bread Stick Pan

P/N 957
No. of cups: 7
Dimensions: 9 1/2" x 7 1/2"
Production Date: Unknown (Probably 1920s or 1930s)
Rarity: 9
Value: $800 to $1000

The No 24 Bread Stick Pan is a mysterious pan. It is a duplication of the No 21 Bread Stick Pan and was probably made in the same era. The No 24 Bread Stick Pan has limited markings and it is unclear why it was made or who it was made for. The No 24 Bread Stick Pan is a rare pan but it is not highly coveted by collectors.

Top view of No 24 Bread Stick Pan

Underside of No 24 Bread Stick Pan

NO 24   BREAD STICK PAN
P/N 957

NO 24 (957) RARITY: 9

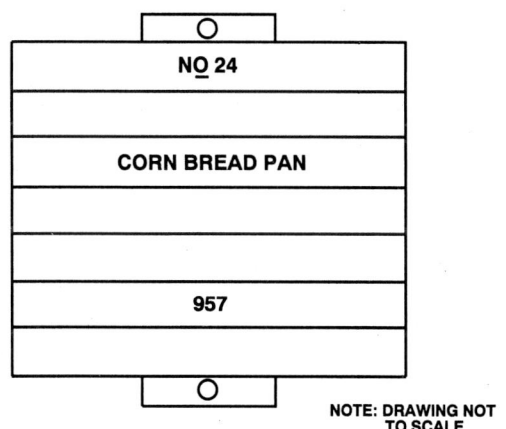

NOTE: DRAWING NOT TO SCALE

VIEW OF UNDERSIDE

No 26 Bread Pan

P/N 960
No. of cups: 2
Dimensions: 13 5/8" x 6 5/16"
Production Date: 1900s to 1910s
Variation 1: Rarity 10; Value $2500 to $3000
Variation 2: Rarity 10; Value $2500 to $3000

   The No 26 Bread Pan is one of the rarest of the Griswold pans and is very difficult to obtain. Variation 2 is marked with P/N 960 and "ERIE No 26" on top of one handle.

NO 26 BREAD PAN
P/N 960

VARIATION 1 RARITY: 10

(VARIATION 1)

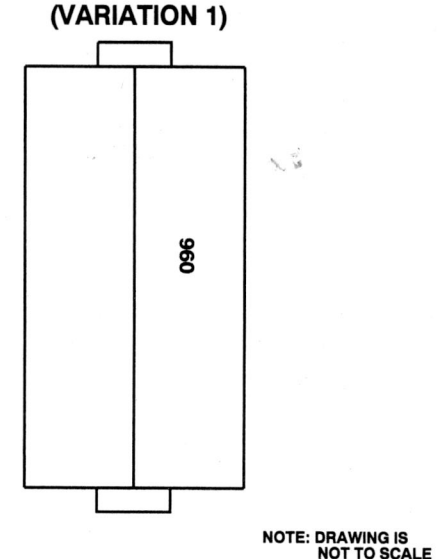

NOTE: DRAWING IS NOT TO SCALE

VIEW OF UNDERSIDE

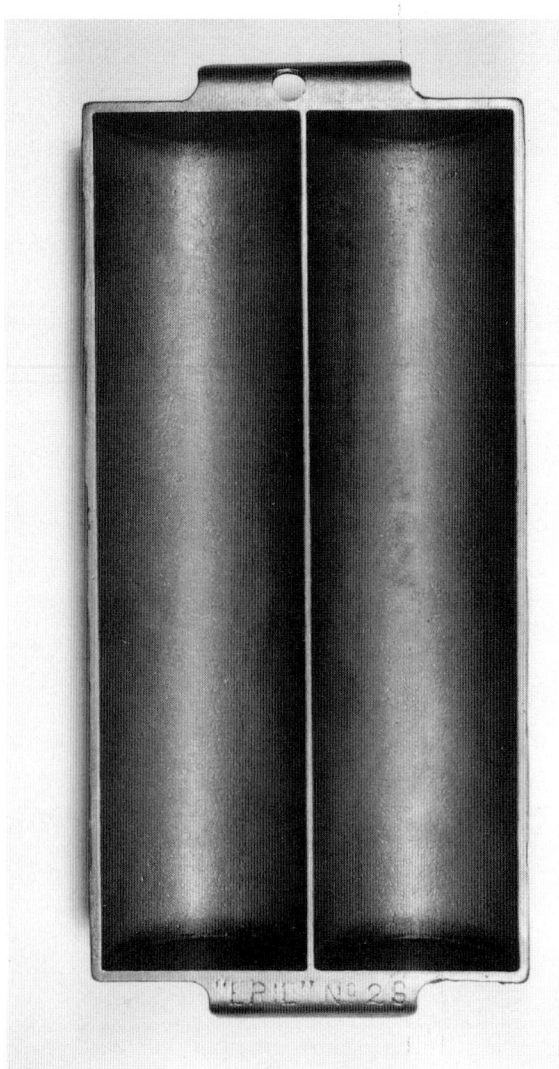

VARIATION 2 RARITY: 10

(VARIATION 2)

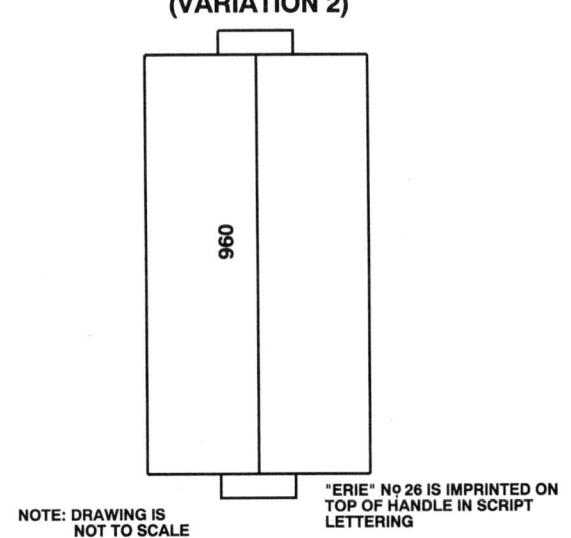

960

NOTE: DRAWING IS
NOT TO SCALE

"ERIE" No 26 IS IMPRINTED ON
TOP OF HANDLE IN SCRIPT
LETTERING

VIEW OF UNDERSIDE

Top view of Variation 2 of No 26 Bread Pan. The hang hole was drilled by someone other than Griswold.

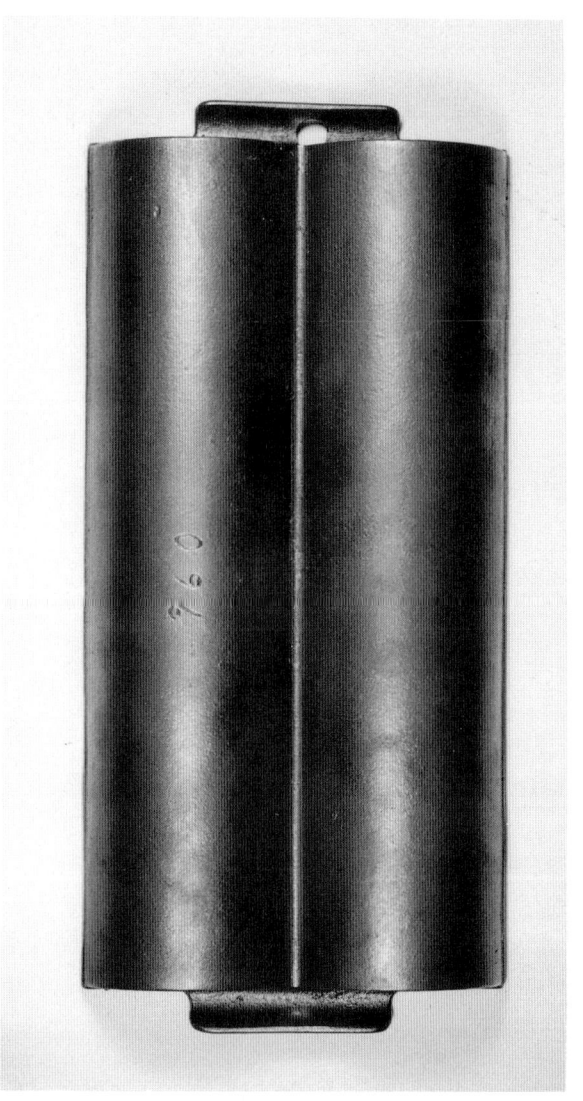

Underside of Variation 2 of No 26 Bread Pan. The hang hole was drilled by someone other than Griswold.

NO 26 BREAD PAN
P/N 960

No 26 Vienna Roll Pan

P/N 958
No. of cups: 6
Dimensions: 12 3/8" x 6 1/4"
Production Date: 1920s to 1940s
Variation 1: Rarity 4; Value $175 to $225
Variation 2: Rarity 4; Value $175 to $225

The No 26 Vienna Roll Pan is the same as the No 6 Vienna Roll Pan. It appears that the No 6 was changed to No 26 to avoid confusion with the No 6 Gem Pan that was being produced at the same time. The No 26 Vienna Roll Pan is a common pan and is readily obtainable.

Underside of Variation 1 of No 26 Vienna Roll Pan

Top view of Variation 1 of No 26 Vienna Roll Pan

NO 26 VIENNA ROLL PAN
P/N 958

VARIATION 1 RARITY: 4

(VARIATION 1)

(OPEN FRAME)

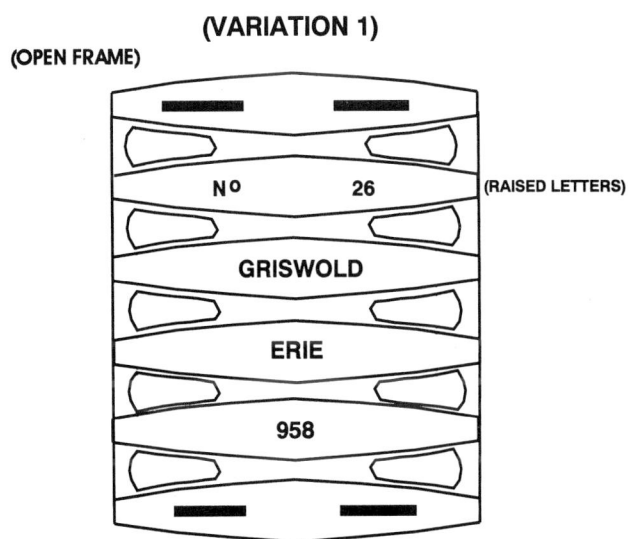

(RAISED LETTERS)

N° 26

GRISWOLD

ERIE

958

NOTE: DRAWING IS
NOT TO SCALE

VIEW OF UNDERSIDE

Underside of Variation 2 of No 26 Vienna Roll Pan

NO 26 VIENNA ROLL PAN
P/N 958

VARIATION 2 RARITY: 4

(VARIATION 2)

(OPEN FRAME)

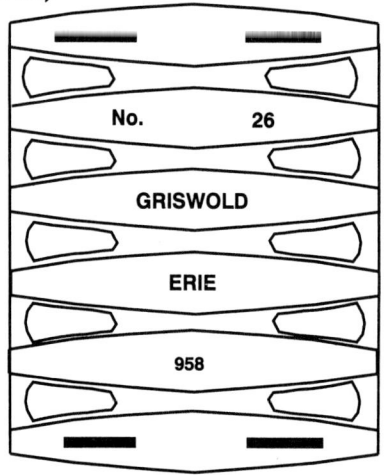

No.   26

GRISWOLD

ERIE

958

NOTE: DRAWING IS
NOT TO SCALE

VIEW OF UNDERSIDE

No 27 Wheat Stick Pan

P/N 638
No. of cups: 6
Dimensions: 10 7/8" x 5 7/8"
Production Date: 1920s
Variation 1: Rarity 6; Value $275 to $300
Variation 2: Rarity 7; Value $275 to $300
Variation 3: Rarity 9; Value $600 to $800
Variation 4: Rarity 7; Value $300 to $325

    The No 27 Wheat Stick Pan is one of the prettiest pans made by Griswold. Griswold obtained a patent (73,326) on this design and the patent number is on Variation 4. Variation 3, marked PAT. APPL'D. FOR., is the rarest variation.

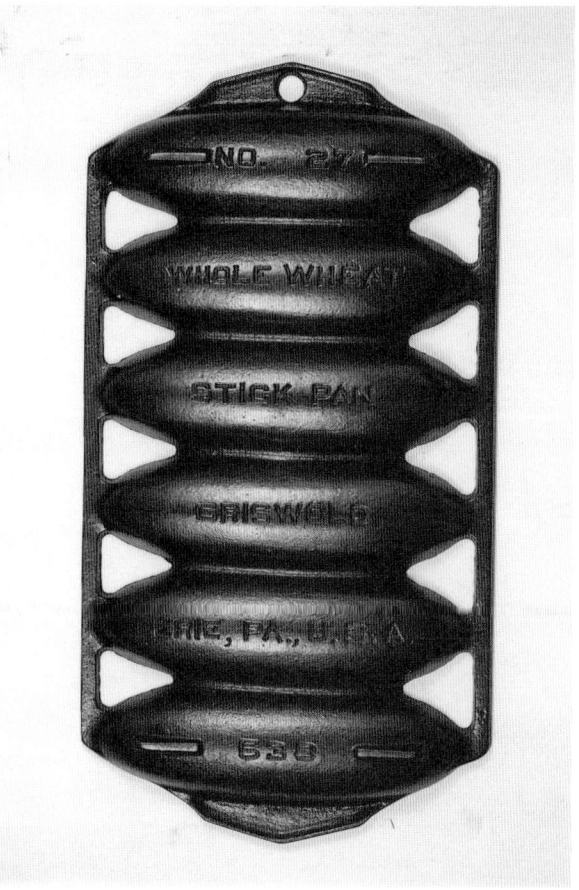

Underside of Variation 1 of No 27 Wheat Stick Pan

NO 27 WHEAT STICK PAN
P/N 638

VARIATION 1 RARITY: 6

(VARIATION 1)

(OPEN FRAME)

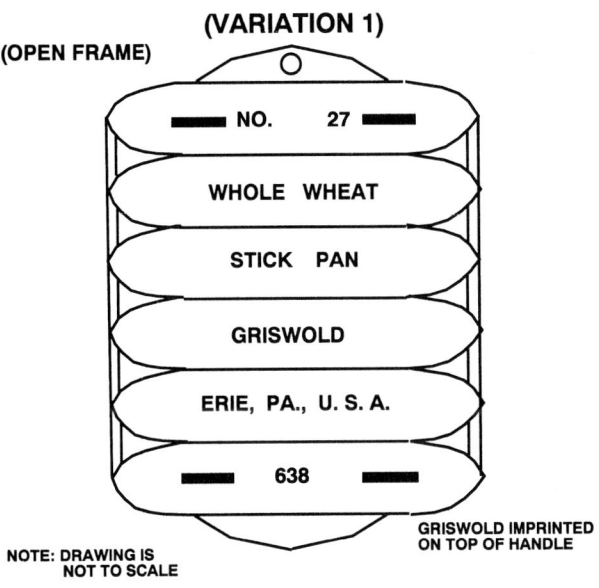

━━ NO. 27 ━━

WHOLE   WHEAT

STICK   PAN

GRISWOLD

ERIE, PA., U. S. A.

━━ 638 ━━

GRISWOLD IMPRINTED
ON TOP OF HANDLE

NOTE: DRAWING IS
NOT TO SCALE

VIEW OF UNDERSIDE

NO 27 WHEAT STICK PAN
P/N 638

VARIATION 2 RARITY: 7

(VARIATION 2)

(OPEN FRAME)

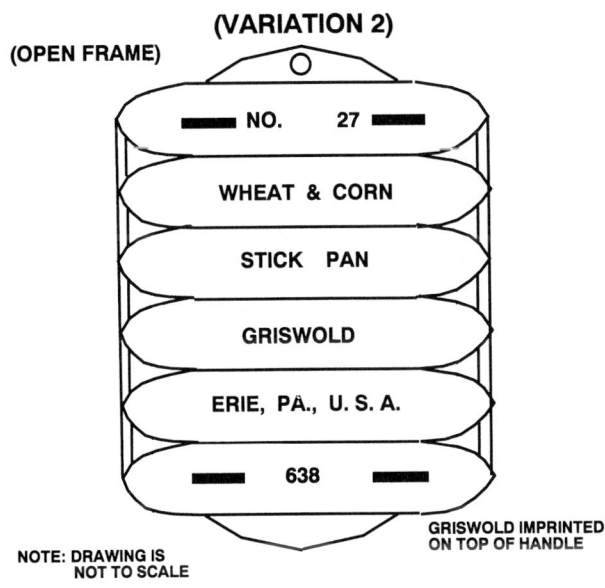

━━ NO. 27 ━━

WHEAT & CORN

STICK   PAN

GRISWOLD

ERIE, PA., U. S. A.

━━ 638 ━━

GRISWOLD IMPRINTED
ON TOP OF HANDLE

NOTE: DRAWING IS
NOT TO SCALE

VIEW OF UNDERSIDE

Top view of Variation 3 of No 27 Wheat Stick Pan

99

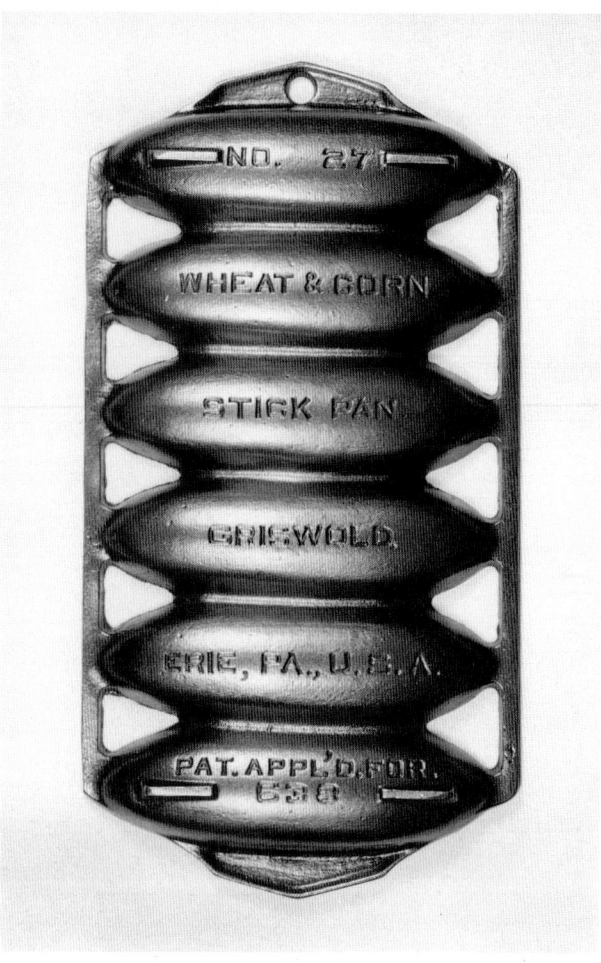

Underside of Variation 3 of No 27 Wheat Stick Pan

NO 27 WHEAT STICK PAN
P/N 638

VARIATION 3 RARITY: 8

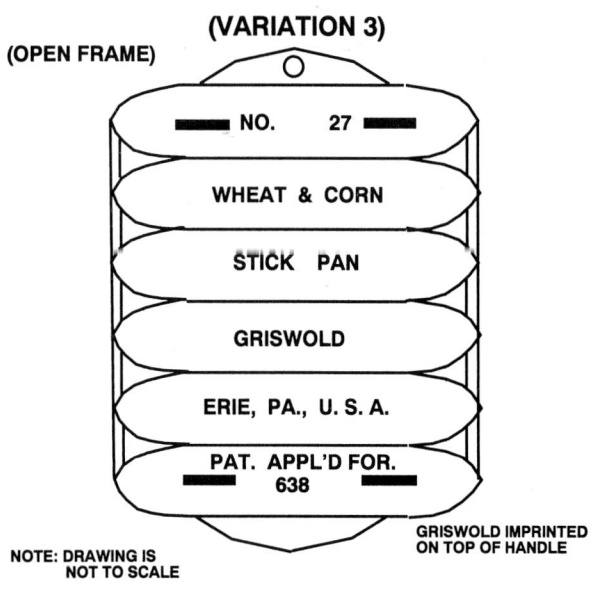

(VARIATION 3)

(OPEN FRAME)

NO. 27

WHEAT & CORN

STICK PAN

GRISWOLD

ERIE, PA., U. S. A.

PAT. APPL'D FOR.
638

GRISWOLD IMPRINTED
ON TOP OF HANDLE

NOTE: DRAWING IS
NOT TO SCALE

VIEW OF UNDERSIDE

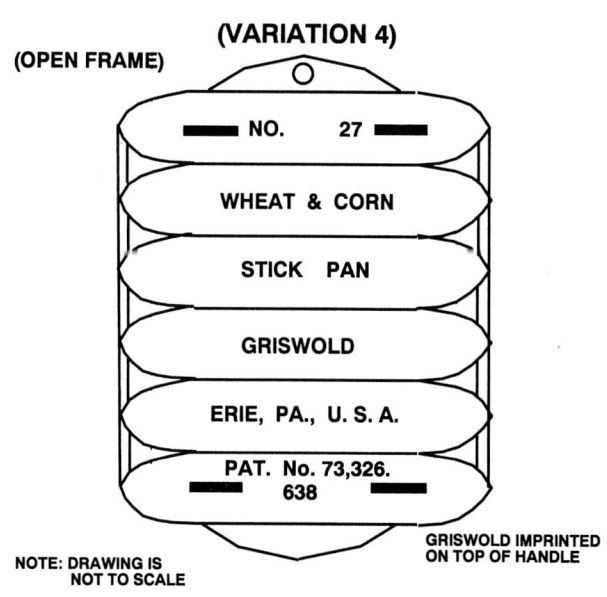

Underside of Variation 4 of No 27 Wheat Stick Pan

NO 27 WHEAT STICK PAN
P/N 638

VARIATION 4 RARITY: 7

(VARIATION 4)

(OPEN FRAME)

NO. 27

WHEAT & CORN

STICK PAN

GRISWOLD

ERIE, PA., U. S. A.

PAT. No. 73,326.
638

GRISWOLD IMPRINTED
ON TOP OF HANDLE

NOTE: DRAWING IS
NOT TO SCALE

VIEW OF UNDERSIDE

No 28 Bread Pan

P/N 961?
No. of cups: 1
Dimensions: 12" x 4" (from an early catalog)
Production Date: 1900s
Rarity: 10
Value: Unknown

The No. 28 Bread Pan is only known because of an illustration of it in an early (circa 1905) catalog. There are no known examples of this pan in the collecting community. Since it is illustrated in a catalog, it was probably manufactured. It would be an outstanding find and would probably have P/N 961 on it.

Illustration of No 28 Bread Pan from Catalog No 40

NO 28 BREAD PAN
P/N 961?

NO 28 (961?) RARITY: 10

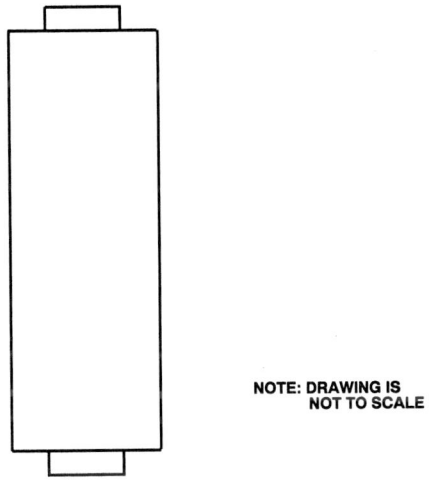

NOTE: DRAWING IS
NOT TO SCALE

VIEW OF UNDERSIDE

NOTE: THERE ARE PRESENTLY NO EXAMPLES OF THIS PAN KNOWN TO THE COLLECTOR COMMUNITY. ITS EXISTENCE IS BASED ON A DRAWING IN AN EARLY (CIRCA 1905) GRISWOLD CATALOG. CONSIDERING THE OTHER PANS IN THIS SERIES (NO. 24 AND NO. 26 BREAD PANS) ONE WOULD EXPECT THERE WOULD BE A PATTERN NUMBER (PROBABLY 961) ON THE UNDERSIDE.

No 28 Wheat Stick Pan

P/N 639
No. of cups: 6
Dimensions: 12 5/8" x 7"
Production Date: 1920s
Variation 1: Rarity 6; Value $275 to $300
Variation 2: Rarity 6; Value $275 to $300
Variation 3: Rarity 8; Value $600 to $800
Variation 4: Rarity 6; Value $300 to $325

The No 28 Wheat Stick Pan is a large version of the No 27 Wheat Stick Pan. The variations of the No 28 Wheat Stick Pan parallel the variations of the No 27 Wheat Stick Pan and are of approximately the same value.

Underside of Variation 1 of No 28 Wheat Stick Pan

NO 28 WHEAT STICK PAN
P/N 639

VARIATION 1 RARITY: 6

(VARIATION 1)

(OPEN FRAME)

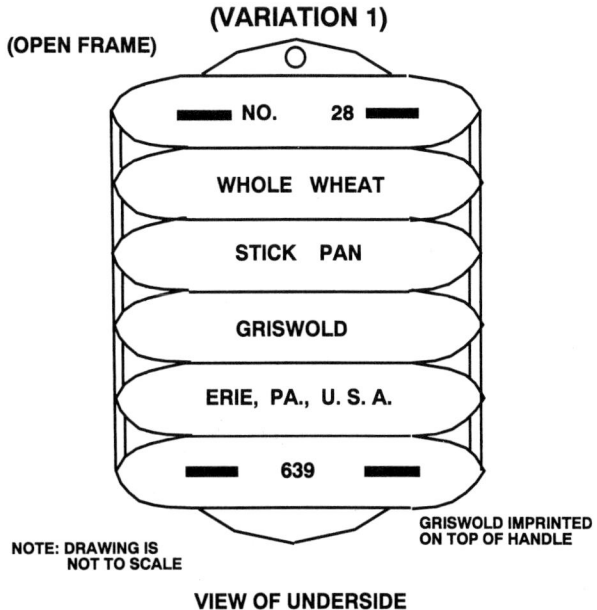

NO.   28

WHOLE   WHEAT

STICK   PAN

GRISWOLD

ERIE, PA., U. S. A.

639

NOTE: DRAWING IS
NOT TO SCALE

GRISWOLD IMPRINTED
ON TOP OF HANDLE

VIEW OF UNDERSIDE

Underside of Variation 2 of No 28 Wheat Stick Pan

NO 28 WHEAT STICK PAN
P/N 639

VARIATION 2 RARITY: 6

(VARIATION 2)

(OPEN FRAME)

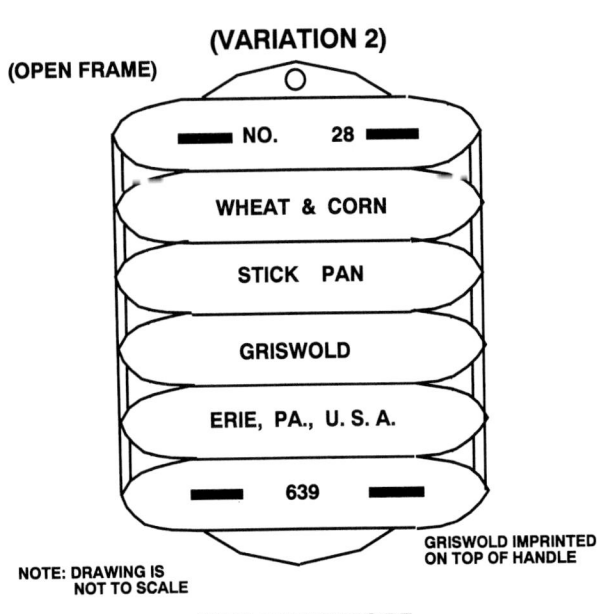

NO.   28

WHEAT & CORN

STICK   PAN

GRISWOLD

ERIE, PA., U. S. A.

639

NOTE: DRAWING IS
NOT TO SCALE

GRISWOLD IMPRINTED
ON TOP OF HANDLE

VIEW OF UNDERSIDE

NO 28 WHEAT STICK PAN
P/N 639

VARIATION 3 RARITY: 8

(VARIATION 3)

(OPEN FRAME)

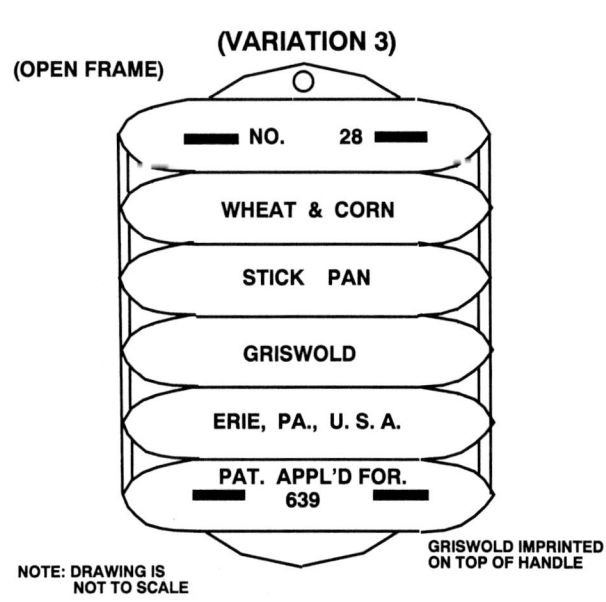

NO.   28

WHEAT & CORN

STICK   PAN

GRISWOLD

ERIE, PA., U. S. A.

PAT. APPL'D FOR.
639

NOTE: DRAWING IS
NOT TO SCALE

GRISWOLD IMPRINTED
ON TOP OF HANDLE

VIEW OF UNDERSIDE

NOTE: THERE ARE NO EXAMPLES OF THIS PAN IN THE COLLECTOR COMMUNITY
AT THE PRESENT TIME. ITS EXISTENCE IS BASED ON SIMILARITY OF THE
VARIATIONS WITH THE VARIATIONS OF THE NO 27 WHEAT STICK PAN.

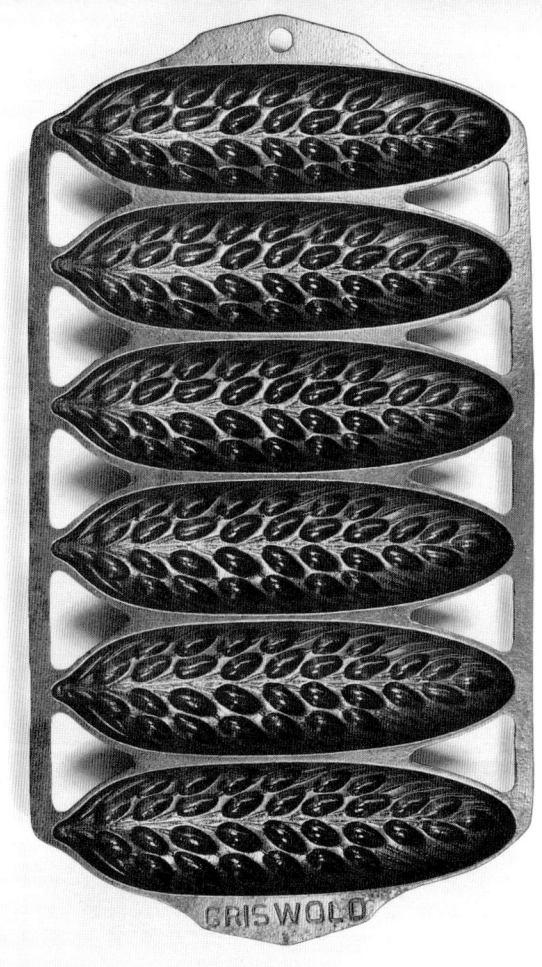

Top view of Variation 4 of No 28 Wheat Stick Pan

NO 28 WHEAT STICK PAN
P/N 639

VARIATION 4 RARITY: 6

(VARIATION 4)

(OPEN FRAME)

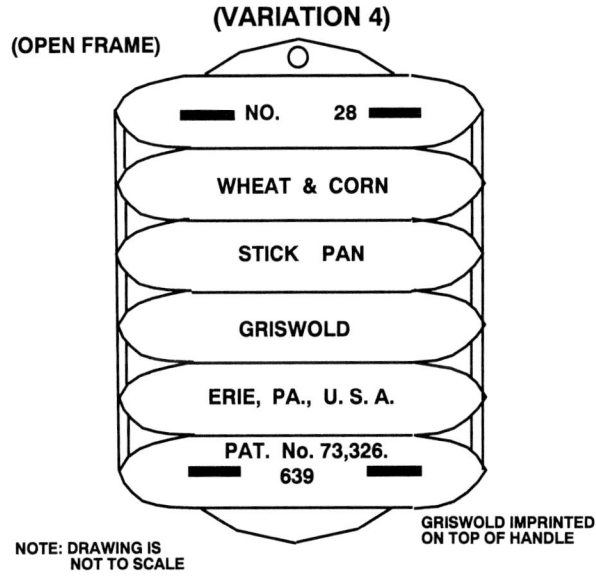

NO. 28

WHEAT & CORN

STICK PAN

GRISWOLD

ERIE, PA., U. S. A.

PAT. No. 73,326.
639

GRISWOLD IMPRINTED
ON TOP OF HANDLE

NOTE: DRAWING IS
NOT TO SCALE

VIEW OF UNDERSIDE

Underside of Variation 4 of No 28 Wheat Stick Pan

No 31 Danish Cake Pan

P/N 963
No. of cups: 7
Dimensions: 9" (diameter)
Production Date: 1900s to 1940s
Variation 1: Rarity 5; Value $175 to $200
Variation 2: Rarity 5; Value $175 to $200
Variation 3: Rarity 5; Value $175 to $200
Variation 4: Rarity 5; Value $200 to $225

    The No 31 Danish Cake Pan is similar to the No 32 Danish Cake Pan with the exception that it does not have the top rim. The No 31 Danish Cake Pan is uncommon but obtainable.

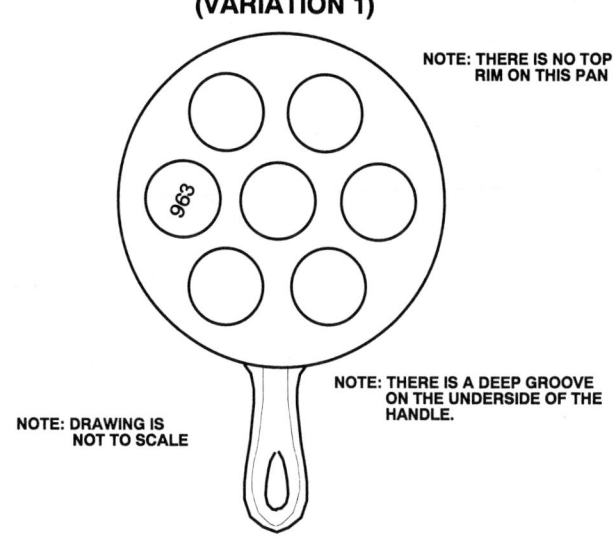

NO 31 DANISH CAKE PAN
P/N 963

VARIATION 1 RARITY: 5

(VARIATION 1)

NOTE: THERE IS NO TOP RIM ON THIS PAN

NOTE: THERE IS A DEEP GROOVE ON THE UNDERSIDE OF THE HANDLE.

NOTE: DRAWING IS NOT TO SCALE

VIEW OF UNDERSIDE

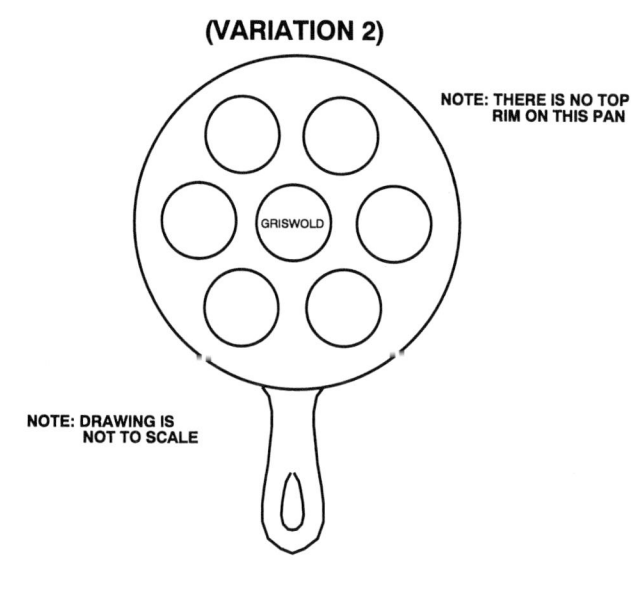

NO 31 DANISH CAKE PAN
P/N 963

VARIATION 2 RARITY: 5

(VARIATION 2)

NOTE: THERE IS NO TOP RIM ON THIS PAN

GRISWOLD

NOTE: DRAWING IS NOT TO SCALE

VIEW OF UNDERSIDE

Underside of Variation 1 of No 31 Danish Cake Pan

Underside of Variation 3 of No 31 Danish Cake Pan

NO 31 DANISH CAKE PAN
P/N 963

VARIATION 3 RARITY: 5

(VARIATION 3)

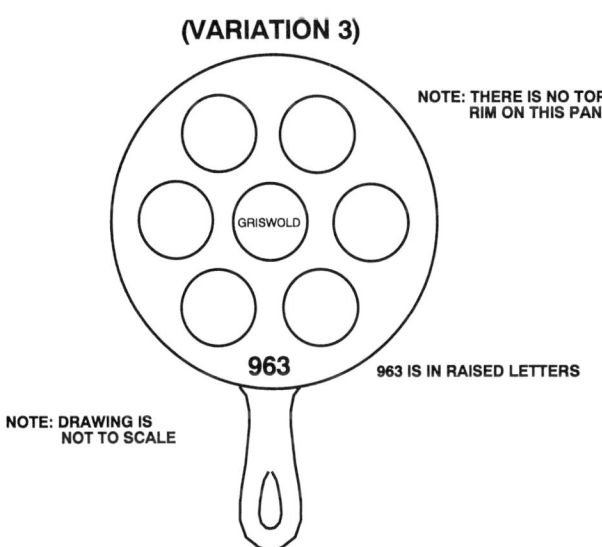

NOTE: THERE IS NO TOP
RIM ON THIS PAN

GRISWOLD

963

963 IS IN RAISED LETTERS

NOTE: DRAWING IS
NOT TO SCALE

VIEW OF UNDERSIDE

Top view of Variation 4 of No 31 Danish Cake Pan

Underside of Variation 4 of No 31 Danish Cake Pan

NO 31 DANISH CAKE PAN
P/N 963

VARIATION 4 RARITY: 5

(VARIATION 4)

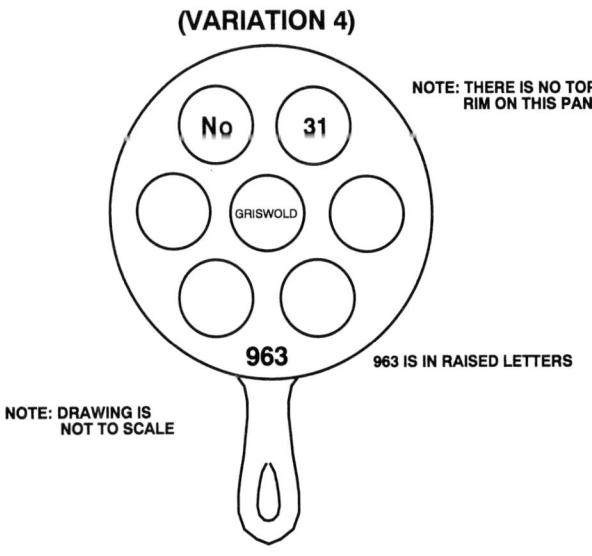

NOTE: THERE IS NO TOP RIM ON THIS PAN

No   31

GRISWOLD

963

963 IS IN RAISED LETTERS

NOTE: DRAWING IS NOT TO SCALE

VIEW OF UNDERSIDE

No 32 Danish Cake Pan

P/N 962
No. of cups: 7
Dimensions: 9" (diameter)
Production Date: 1900s to 1950s
Variation 1: Rarity 4; Value $175 to $225
Variation 2: Rarity 3; Value $140 to $160
Variation 3: Rarity 2; Value $50 to $75
Variation 4: Rarity 2; Value $50 to $75
Variation 5: Rarity 1; Value $30 to $50
Variation 6: Rarity 1; Value $25 to $35
Variation 7: Rarity 1; Value $20 to $30

The No 32 Danish Cake Pan is one of the most common pans. Variation 1 is the only Griswold muffin pan with the diamond ERIE logo. Variation 2 is the only Griswold muffin pan marked with G M Co. Variations 6 and 7 were made after Griswold was sold and production was moved from Erie, Pennsylvania.

Underside of Variation 1 of No 32 Danish Cake Pan

NO 32 DANISH CAKE PAN
P/N 962

VARIATION 1 RARITY: 4

(VARIATION 1)

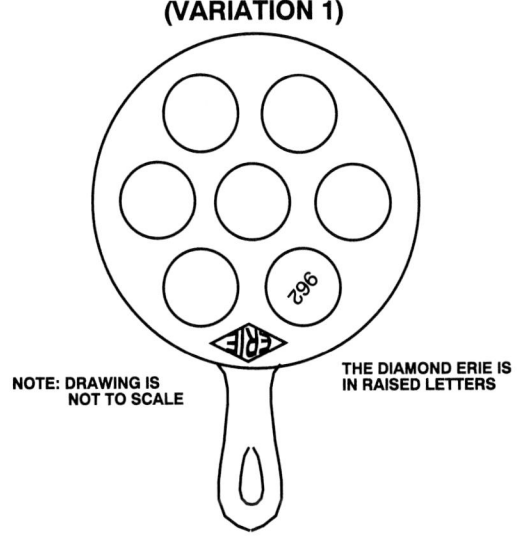

NOTE: DRAWING IS
NOT TO SCALE

THE DIAMOND ERIE IS
IN RAISED LETTERS

VIEW OF UNDERSIDE

Underside of Variation 2 of No 32 Danish Cake Pan

NO 32 DANISH CAKE PAN
P/N 962

VARIATION 2 RARITY: 3

(VARIATION 2)

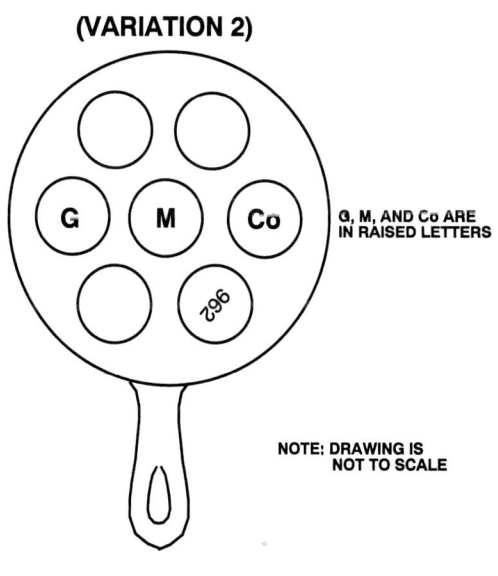

G, M, AND Co ARE
IN RAISED LETTERS

NOTE: DRAWING IS
NOT TO SCALE

VIEW OF UNDERSIDE

Top view of Variation 2 of No 32 Danish Cake Pan

Underside of Variation 3 of No 32 Danish Cake Pan

NO 32 DANISH CAKE PAN
P/N 962

VARIATION 3 RARITY: 2

(VARIATION 3)

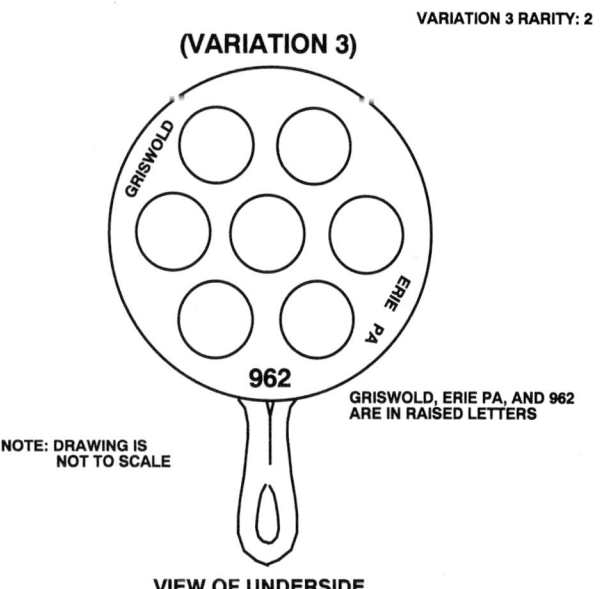

GRISWOLD, ERIE PA, AND 962
ARE IN RAISED LETTERS

NOTE: DRAWING IS
NOT TO SCALE

VIEW OF UNDERSIDE

NO 32 DANISH CAKE PAN
P/N 962

VARIATION 4 RARITY: 2

(VARIATION 4)

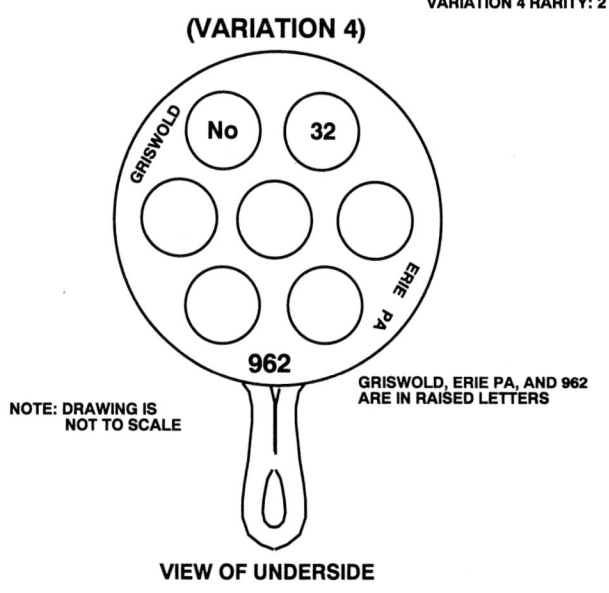

NOTE: DRAWING IS
NOT TO SCALE

GRISWOLD, ERIE PA, AND 962
ARE IN RAISED LETTERS

VIEW OF UNDERSIDE

NO 32 DANISH CAKE PAN
P/N 962

VARIATION 5 RARITY: 1

(VARIATION 5)

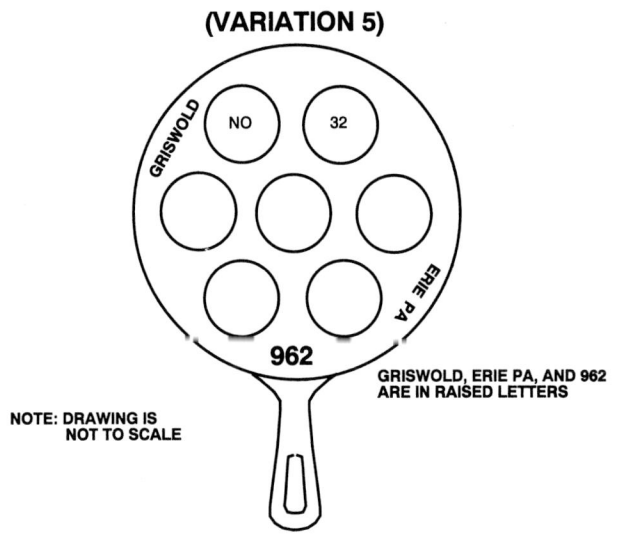

NOTE: DRAWING IS
NOT TO SCALE

GRISWOLD, ERIE PA, AND 962
ARE IN RAISED LETTERS

VIEW OF UNDERSIDE

NO 32 DANISH CAKE PAN
P/N 962

VARIATION 6 RARITY: 1

(VARIATION 6)

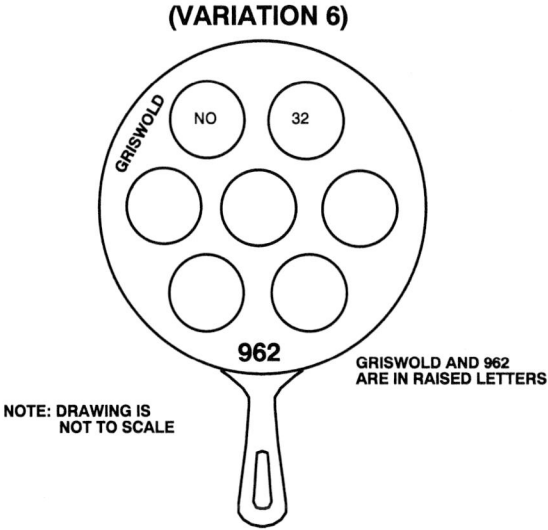

NOTE: DRAWING IS
NOT TO SCALE

GRISWOLD AND 962
ARE IN RAISED LETTERS

VIEW OF UNDERSIDE

NOTE: THIS VARIATION WAS MADE AFTER 1957 WHEN GRISWOLD WAS SOLD
AND MOVED FROM ERIE, PA.

NO 32 DANISH CAKE PAN
P/N 962

VARIATION 7 RARITY: 1

(VARIATION 7)

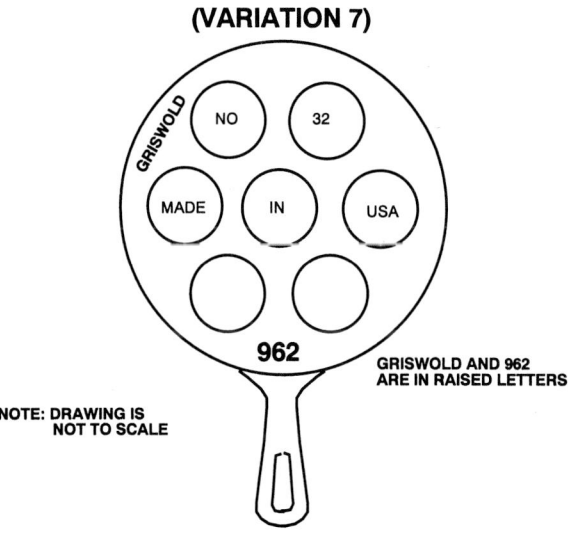

NOTE: DRAWING IS
NOT TO SCALE

GRISWOLD AND 962
ARE IN RAISED LETTERS

VIEW OF UNDERSIDE

NOTE: THIS VARIATION WAS MADE AFTER 1957 WHEN GRISWOLD WAS SOLD
AND MOVED FROM ERIE, PA.

No 33 Munk Pan

P/N 2992
No. of cups: 7
Dimensions: 9" (diameter)
Production Date: 1920s to 1940s
Variation 1: Rarity 6; Value $275 to $325
Variation 2: Rarity 6; Value $275 to $325

The No 33 Munk Pan is similar to the No 32 Danish Cake Pan, except for the fact that it does not have the skirt down the sides. It is not known why 2992 is the pattern number for this pan. The No 33 Munk Pan is of moderate rarity.

Underside of Variation 1 of No 33 Munk Pan

NO 33 MUNK PAN
P/N 2992

VARIATION 1 RARITY: 6

(VARIATION 1)

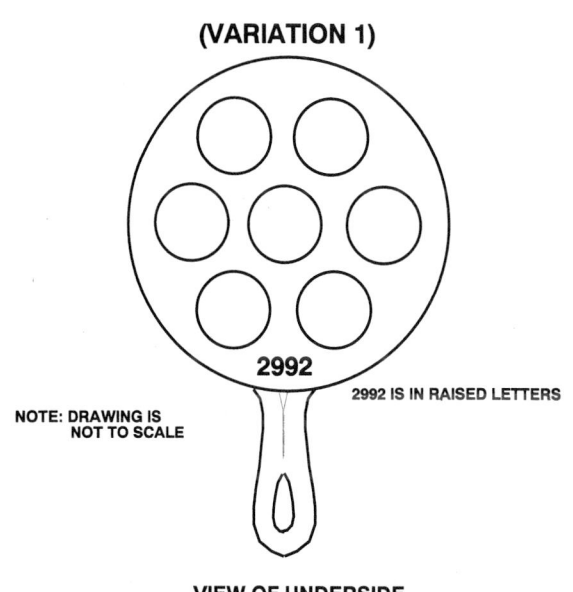

NOTE: DRAWING IS
NOT TO SCALE

2992 IS IN RAISED LETTERS

VIEW OF UNDERSIDE

Top view of Variation 2 of No 33 Munk Pan

NO 33 MUNK PAN
P/N 2992

(VARIATION 2)

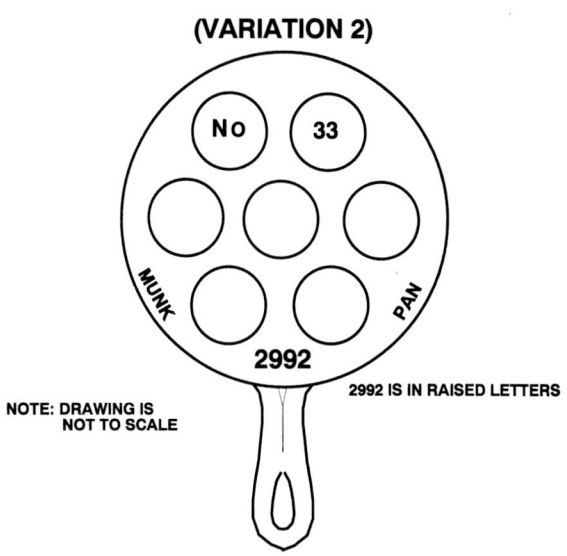

NOTE: DRAWING IS
NOT TO SCALE

2992 IS IN RAISED LETTERS

VIEW OF UNDERSIDE

Underside of Variation 2 of No 33 Munk Pan

No 34 Plett Pan

P/N 2980
No. of cups: 7
Dimensions: 9 1/2" (diameter)
Production Date: 1910s to 1950s
Variation 1: Rarity 2; Value $60 to $80
Variation 2: Rarity 3; Value $75 to $100
Variation 3: Rarity 2; Value $50 to $70
Variation 4: Rarity 1; Value $20 to $25
Variation 5: Rarity 1; Value $15 to $20

   The No 34 Plett Pan is a very common pan. The plett pan is of Scandinavian origin. Variations 4 and 5 were made after Griswold was sold and production was moved from Erie, Pennsylvania.

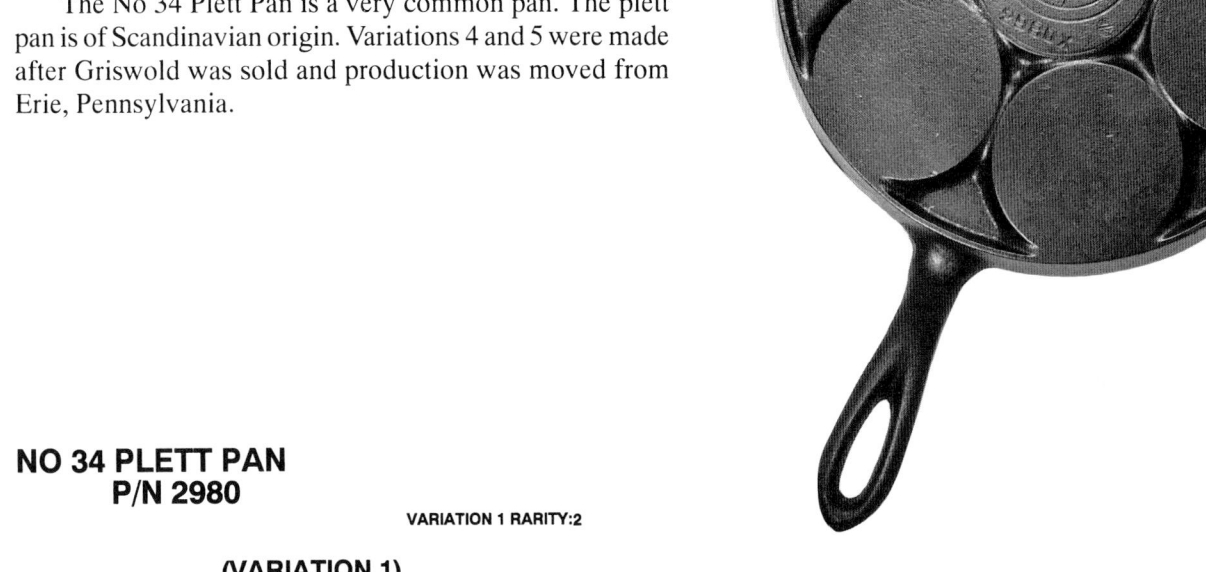

Underside of Variation 2 of No 34 Plett Pan

NO 34 PLETT PAN
P/N 2980

VARIATION 1 RARITY:2

(VARIATION 1)

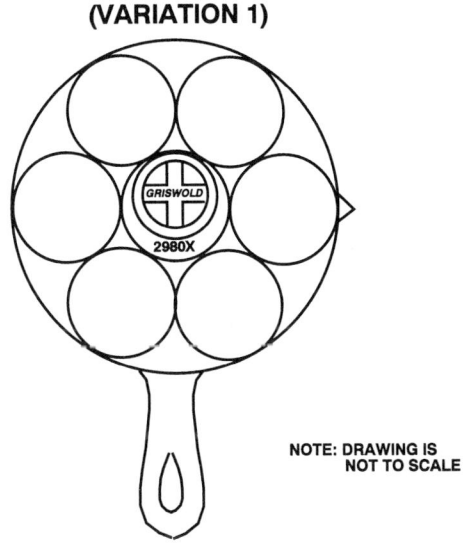

NOTE: DRAWING IS
NOT TO SCALE

VIEW OF UNDERSIDE

NO 34 PLETT PAN
P/N 2980

VARIATION 2 RARITY:3

(VARIATION 2)

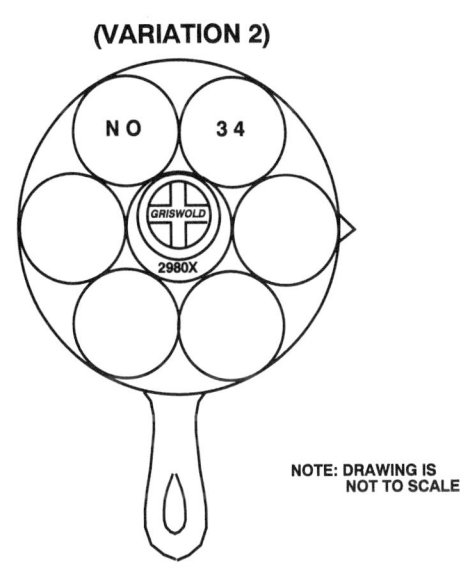

NOTE: DRAWING IS
NOT TO SCALE

VIEW OF UNDERSIDE

NO 34 PLETT PAN
P/N 2980

(VARIATION 3)

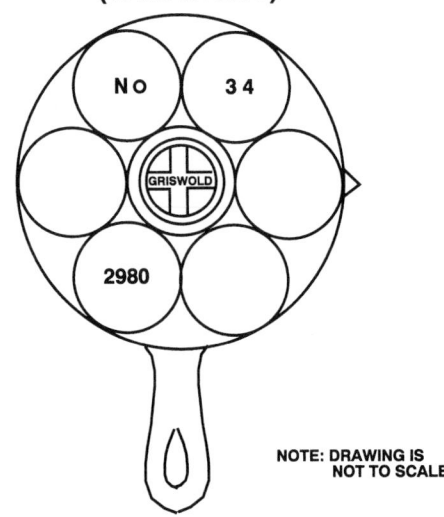

NO   34

GRISWOLD

2980

NOTE: DRAWING IS
NOT TO SCALE

VIEW OF UNDERSIDE

Top view of Variation 3 of No 34 Plett Pan

Underside of Variation 3 of No 34 Plett Pan

Underside of Variation 4 of No 34 Plett Pan

112

NO 34 PLETT PAN
P/N 2980

VARIATION 4 RARITY: 1

(VARIATION 4)

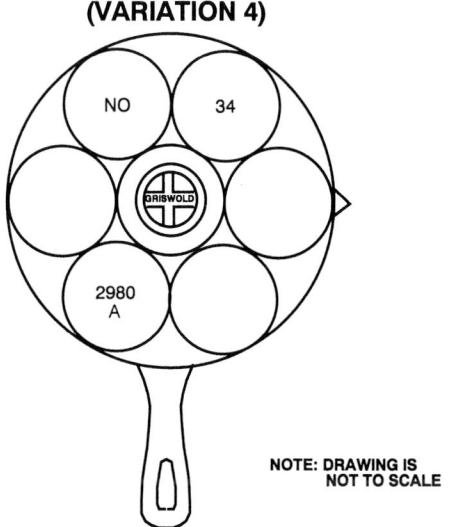

VIEW OF UNDERSIDE

NO 34 PLETT PAN
P/N 2980

VARIATION 5 RARITY: 1

(VARIATION 5)

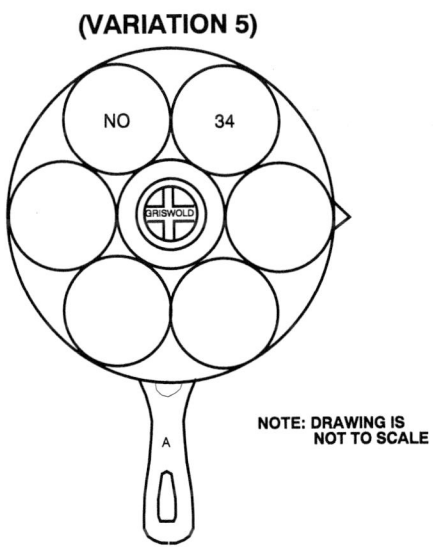

VIEW OF UNDERSIDE

NOTE: THIS VARIATION WAS MADE AFTER 1957 WHEN GRISWOLD WAS SOLD
AND MOVED FROM ERIE, PA.

No 34 Plett Pan (Milled Bottom)

P/N 969
No. of cups: 7
Dimensions: 9 1/2" (diameter)
Production Date: 1940s
Rarity 7
Value: $225 to $275

The No 34 Plett Pan (Milled Bottom) is part of a set of cookware that was specially made to be used on electric stoves. This was an example of Griswold trying to keep up with society and produce cookware for all situations for all people. The No 34 Plett Pan (Milled Bottom) is of moderate rarity.

Top view of No 34 Plett Pan (Milled Bottom)

113

Underside of No 34 Plett Pan (Milled Bottom)

NO 34 PLETT PAN (MILLED BOTTOM)
P/N 969

NO 34 (969) RARITY: 7

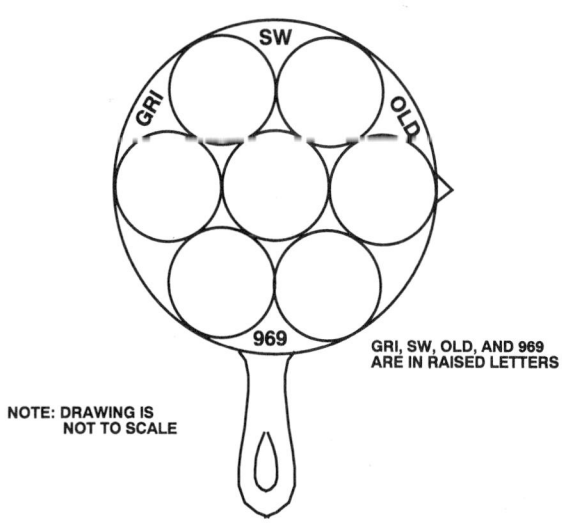

SW

GRI

OLD

969

GRI, SW, OLD, AND 969
ARE IN RAISED LETTERS

NOTE: DRAWING IS
NOT TO SCALE

VIEW OF UNDERSIDE

NOTE: THE BOTTOM OF THIS PAN WAS MILLED AND IT WAS PART OF A SET OF
SPECIAL MACHINED BOTTOM UTENSILS FOR USE ON ELECTRIC STOVES.

No 50 Hearts/Star Pan

P/N 959
No. of cups: 6 hearts & 1 star
Dimensions: 6 1/2" x 6 1/2"
Production Date: 1920s
Rarity: 10
Value: $2100 to $2400

The No 50 Hearts/Star Pan is the smallest pan that Griswold made. Griswold was awarded a patent on the heart and star design on May 18, 1920. This date appears on both the No 50 and No 100 Hearts/Star Pan. The No 50 Hearts/Star pan is a rare pan that is desirable to heart collectors as well as to cast iron collectors. The No 50 Hearts/Star Pan has 6 hearts surrounding a 6 pointed star.

Top view of No 50 Hearts/Star Pan

NO 50 HEARTS/STAR PAN
P/N 959

NO 50 (959) RARITY: 10

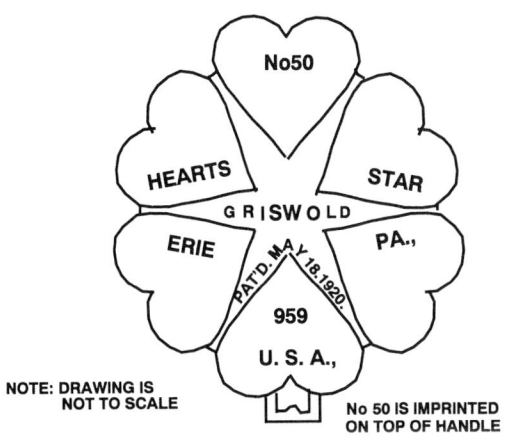

NOTE: DRAWING IS NOT TO SCALE

No 50 IS IMPRINTED ON TOP OF HANDLE

VIEW OF UNDERSIDE

Underside of No 50 Hearts/Star Pan

No 100 Hearts/Star Pan

P/N 960
No. of cups: 5 hearts & 1 star
Dimensions: 7 3/4" x 7 3/4"
Production Date: 1920s
Rarity: 9
Value: $900 to $1100

The No 100 Hearts/Star Pan is larger than the No 50 Hearts/Star Pan. The No 100 Hearts/Star Pan has 5 hearts surrounding a 5 pointed star. The No 50 and No 100 Hearts/Star Pans are very pretty and make an excellent display. The No 100 Hearts/Star Pan is rare but not as rare as the No 50 Hearts/Star Pan.

Top view of No 100 Hearts/Star Pan

115

Underside of No 100 Hearts/Star Pan

NO 100 HEARTS/STAR PAN
P/N 960

NO 100 (960) RARITY: 9

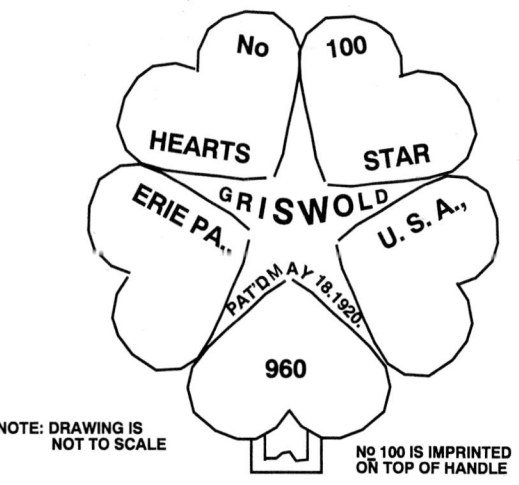

NOTE: DRAWING IS
NOT TO SCALE

NO 100 IS IMPRINTED
ON TOP OF HANDLE

VIEW OF UNDERSIDE

No 130 Turk Head Pan

P/N 634
No. of cups: 6
Dimensions: 10" x 5 9/16"
Production Date: 1930s to 1940s
Rarity: 9
Value: $800 to $900

The No 130 Turk Head Pan is a 6 cup version of the No 140 Turk Head Pan. The 130 Turk Head Pan is quite rare and desirable.

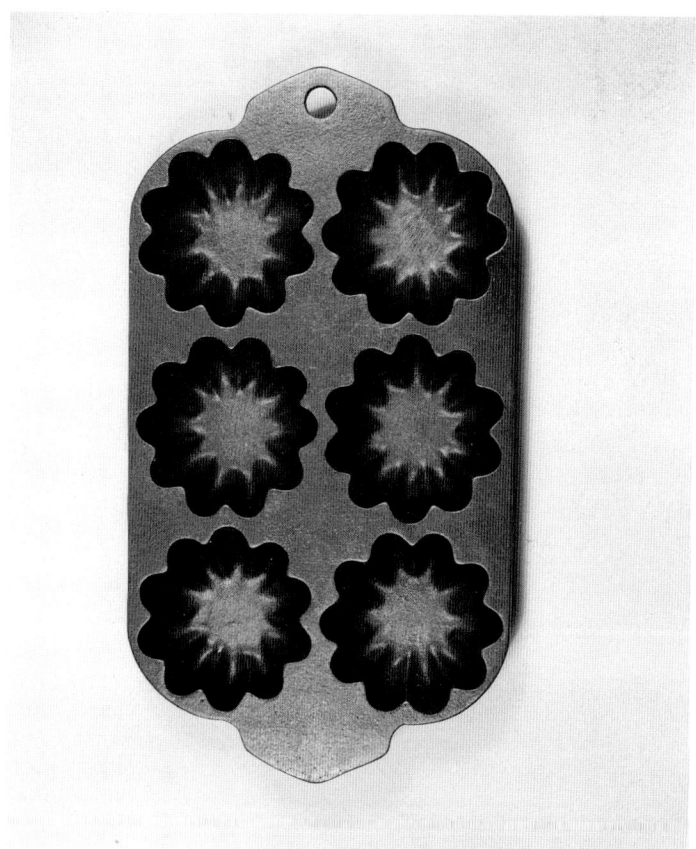

Top view of No 130 Turk Head Pan

Underside of No 130 Turk Head Pan

NO 130 TURK HEAD PAN
P/N 634

NO 130 (634) RARITY: 9

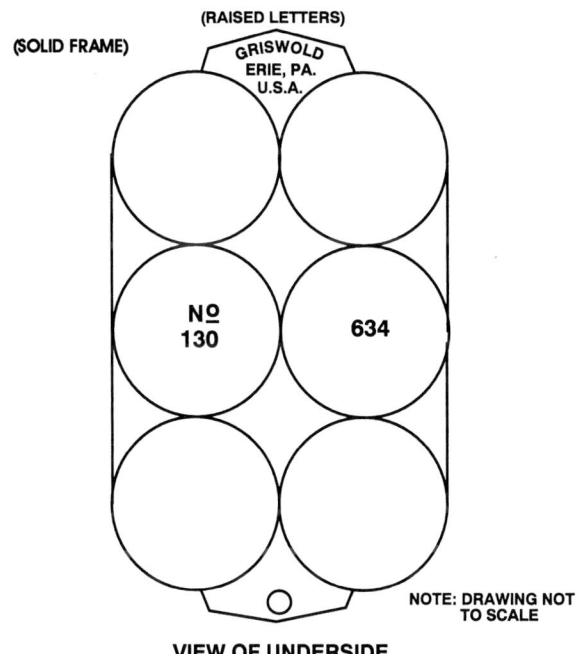

(SOLID FRAME) (RAISED LETTERS)

GRISWOLD
ERIE, PA.
U.S.A.

N⁰ 130   634

NOTE: DRAWING NOT TO SCALE

VIEW OF UNDERSIDE

No 140 Turk Head Pan

P/N 635
No. of cups: 12
Dimensions: 12 5/8" x 8 1/4"
Production Date: 1930s to 1950s
Rarity: 5
Value: $175 to $200

   This is a twelve cup version of the No 130 Turk Head Pan. The No 140 Turk Head Pan is the most common of the Griswold Turk Head Pans.

Top view of No 140 Turk Head Pan

Underside of No 140 Turk Head Pan

NO 140 TURK HEAD PAN
P/N 635

NO 140 (635) RARITY: 5

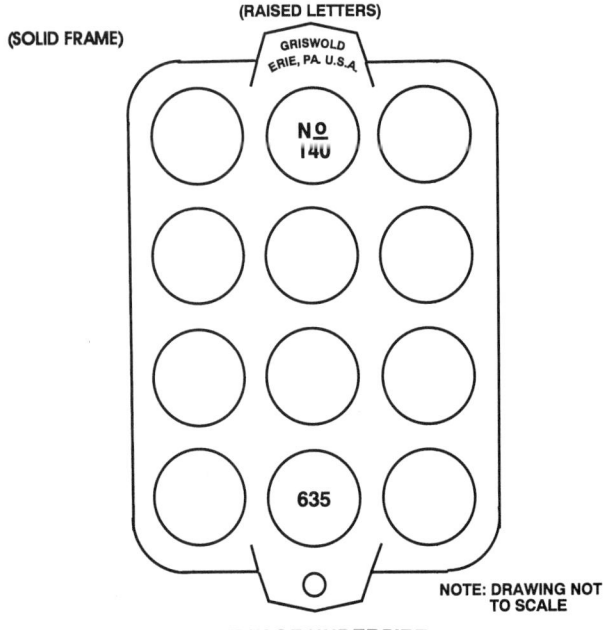

(SOLID FRAME)

(RAISED LETTERS)

GRISWOLD
ERIE, PA. U.S.A.

NO
140

635

NOTE: DRAWING NOT
TO SCALE

VIEW OF UNDERSIDE

No 240 Turk Head Pan

P/N 631
No. of cups: 12
Dimensions: 14 5/8" x 10"
Production Date: 1930s to 1940s
Rarity 8
Value: $450 to $500

This is a 12 cup Turk head pan that was made in the 1930s and 1940s. It is larger than the No 140 Turk Head Pan and has a rim around the outside edge. It is fairly uncommon but is obtainable.

Top view of No 240 Turk Head Pan

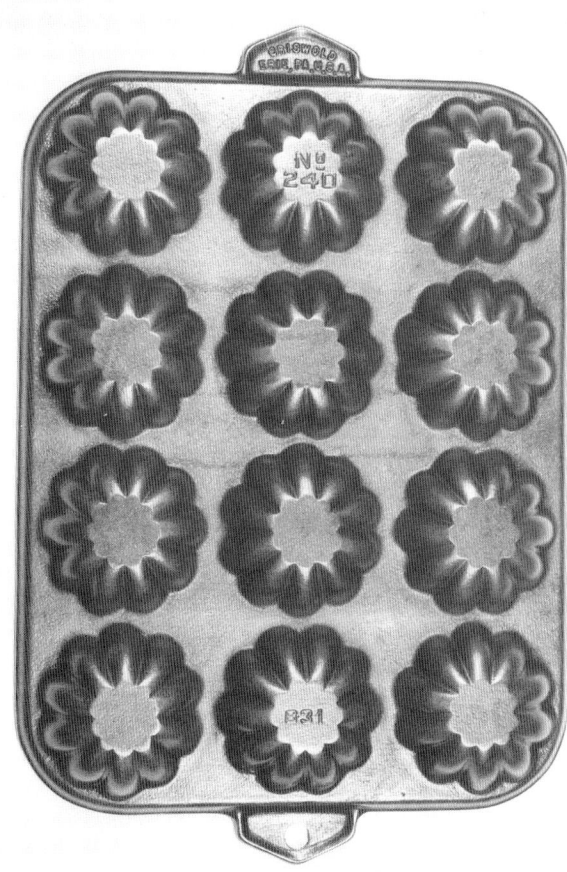

Underside of No 240 Turk Head Pan

NO 240 TURK HEAD PAN
P/N 631

NO 240 (631) RARITY: 8

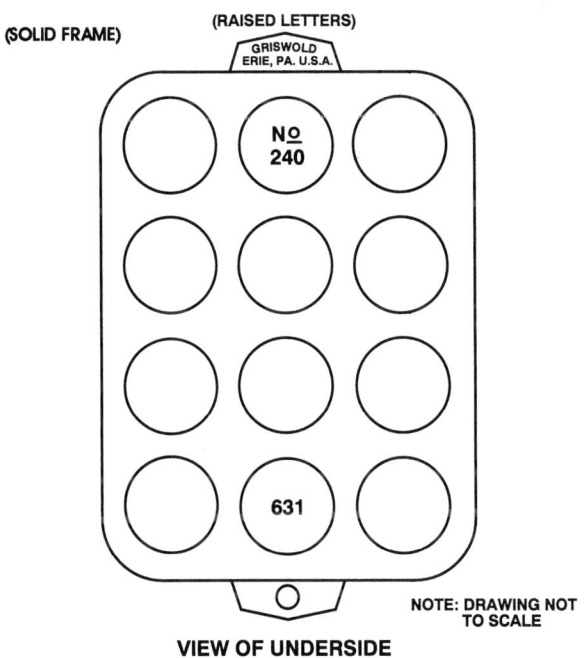

VIEW OF UNDERSIDE

No 262 Corn Stick Pan

P/N 625
No. of cups: 7
Dimensions: 8 1/2" x 4 1/8"
Production Date: 1930s to 1950s
Variation 1: Rarity 2; Value $75 to $100
Variation 2: Rarity 2; Value $60 to $80

This pan is the tea size corn stick pan. This is a common pan that is readily available. Variation 2 does not have ERIE PA., U. S. A. on it as it was made after Griswold was sold and moved from Erie.

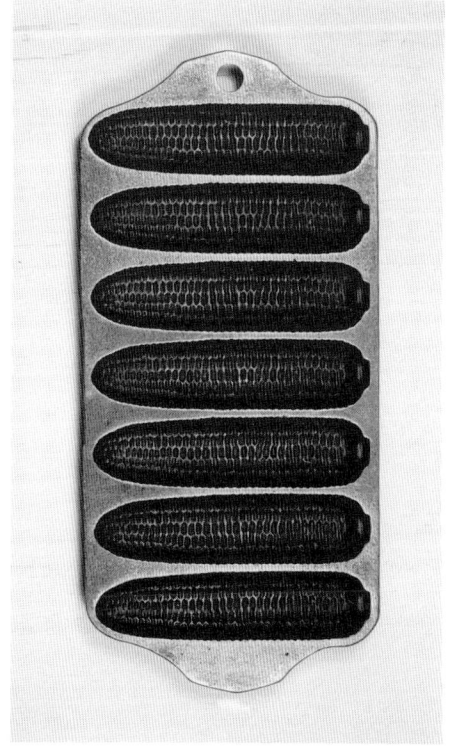

Top view of Variation 1 of No 262 Corn Stick Pan

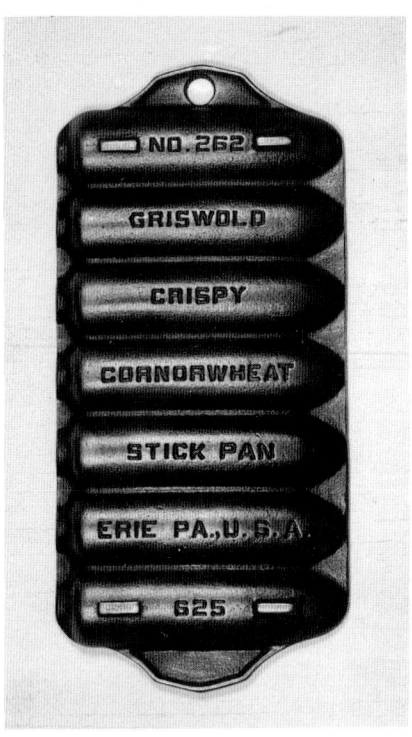

Underside of Variation 1 of No 262 Corn Stick Pan

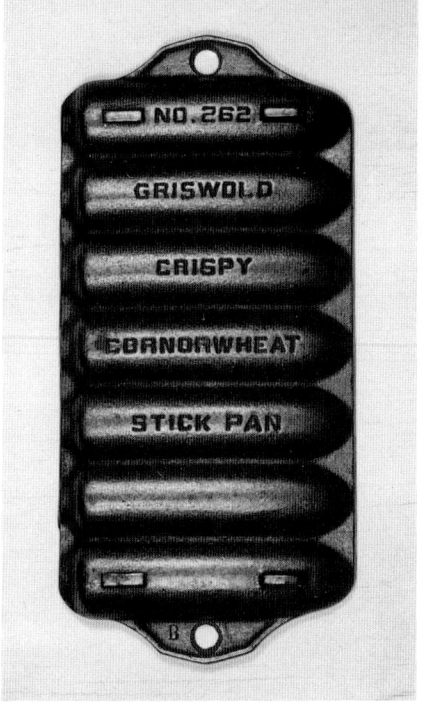

Underside of Variation 2 of No 262 Corn Stick Pan

NO 262 CORN STICK PAN
P/N 625

VARIATION 1 RARITY: 2

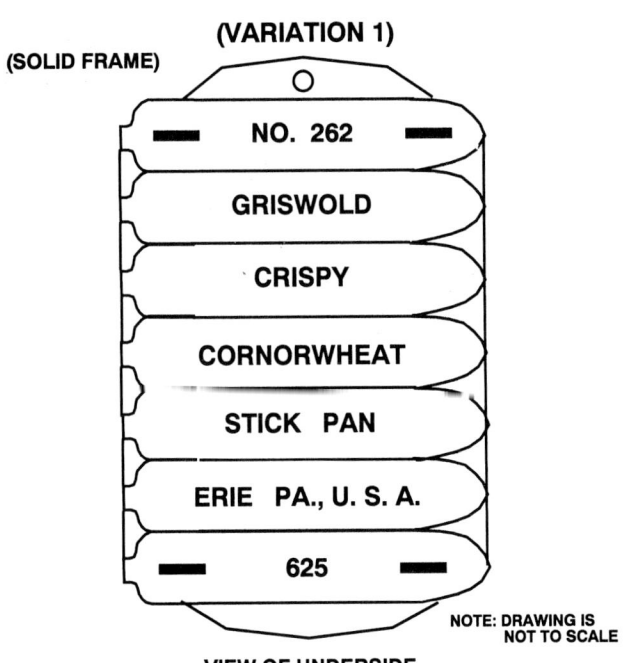

NO 262 CORN STICK PAN
P/N 625

VARIATION 2 RARITY: 2

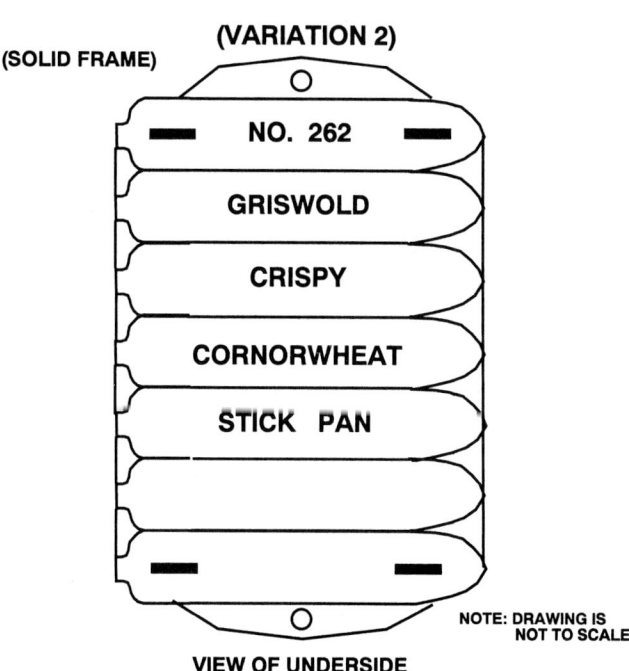

NOTE: THIS VARIATION WAS MADE AFTER 1957 WHEN GRISWOLD WAS SOLD AND MOVED FROM ERIE, PA.

No 270 Corn or Wheat Stick Pan

P/N 636
No. of cups: 7
Dimensions: 13 1/4" x 5 3/4"
Production Date: 1920s
Rarity: 8
Value: $500 to $600

This pan is the small version of the No 280 Corn or Wheat Stick Pan. It is not understood why this pan has patent number 73,326 imprinted on it since that is the design patent for the wheat stick pan.

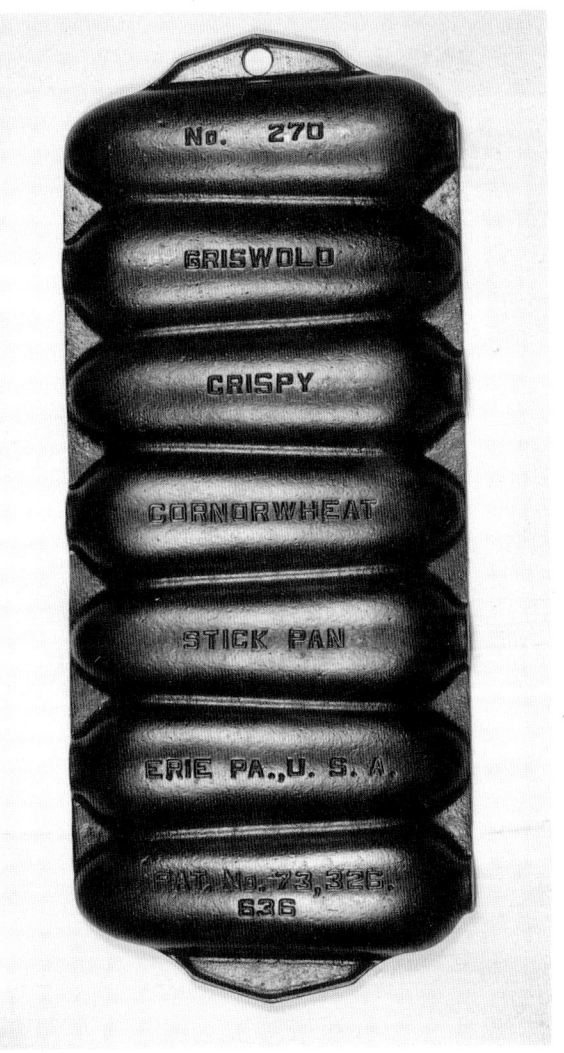

Underside of No 270 Corn or Wheat Stick Pan

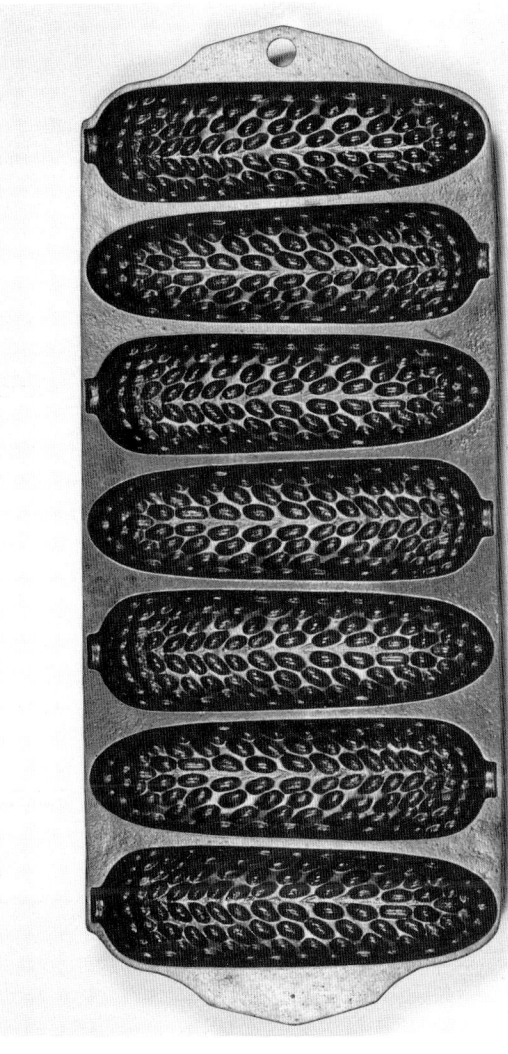

Top view of No 270 Corn or Wheat Stick Pan

NO 270 CORN OR WHEAT STICK PAN
P/N 636

NO 270 (636) RARITY: 8

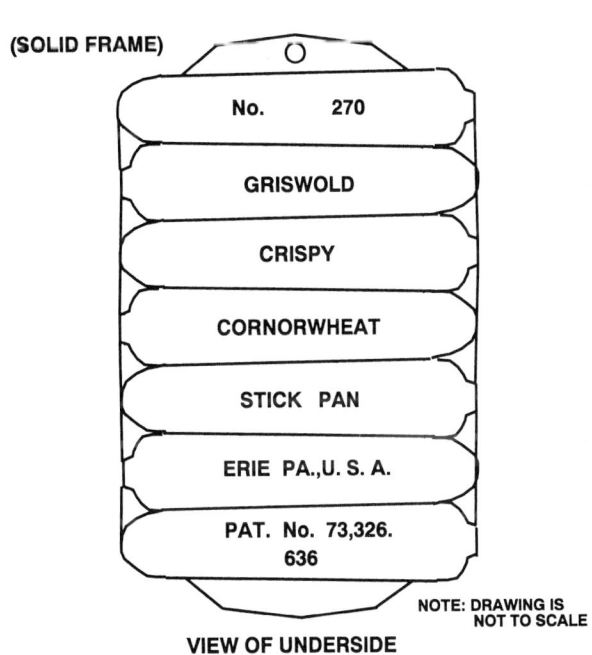

(SOLID FRAME)

No. 270

GRISWOLD

CRISPY

CORNORWHEAT

STICK PAN

ERIE PA.,U. S. A.

PAT. No. 73,326.
636

NOTE: DRAWING IS NOT TO SCALE

VIEW OF UNDERSIDE

No 272 Corn or Wheat Stick Pan

P/N 629
No. of cups: 7
Dimensions: 13 1/4" x 5 3/4"
Production Date: 1930s
Variation 1: Rarity 5; Value $175 to $200
Variation 2: Rarity 5; Value $200 to $225

    This pan is the small version of the No 282 Corn or Wheat Stick Pan. It is fairly common and obtainable.

Underside of Variation 1 of No 272 Corn or Wheat Stick Pan

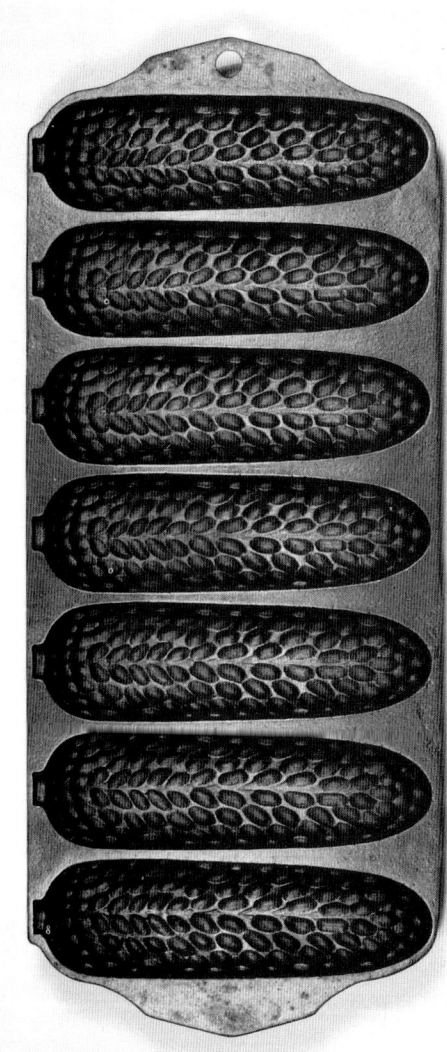

Top view of Variation 1 of No 272 Corn or Wheat Stick Pan

NO 272 CORN OR WHEAT STICK PAN
P/N 629

VARIATION 1 RARITY: 5

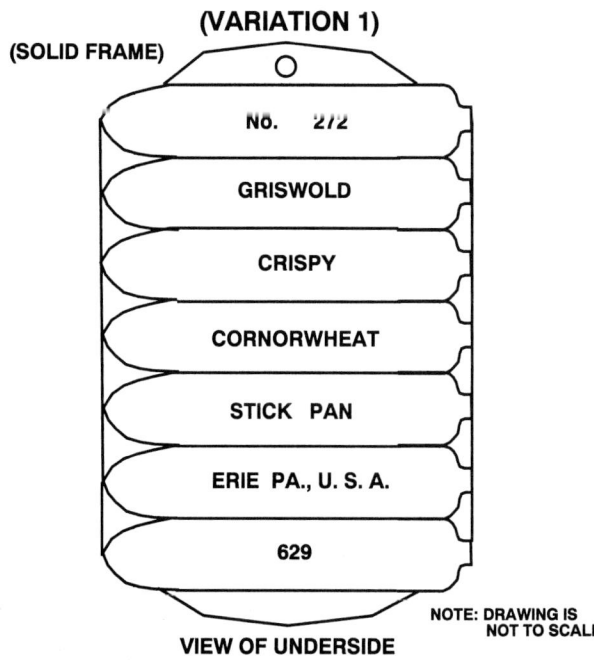

(VARIATION 1)

(SOLID FRAME)

NO. 272

GRISWOLD

CRISPY

CORNORWHEAT

STICK PAN

ERIE PA., U. S. A.

629

VIEW OF UNDERSIDE

NOTE: DRAWING IS NOT TO SCALE

Underside of Variation 2 of No 272 Corn or Wheat Stick Pan

NO 272 CORN OR WHEAT STICK PAN
P/N 629

VARIATION 2 RARITY: 5

(VARIATION 2)

(SOLID FRAME)

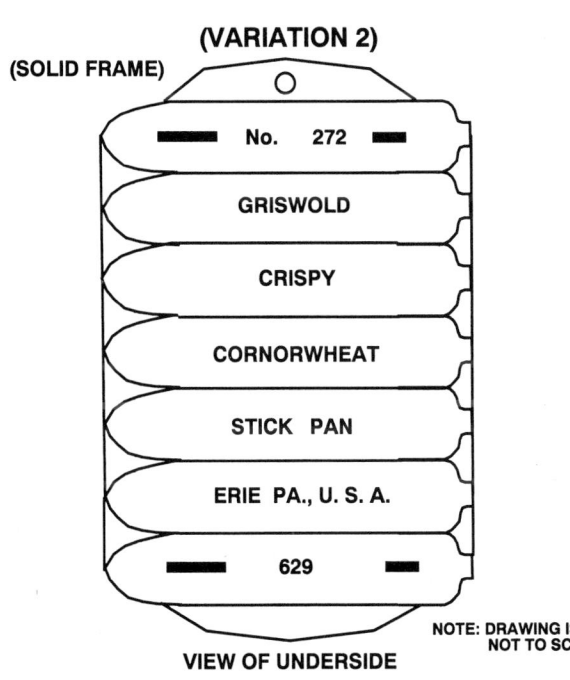

No. 272

GRISWOLD

CRISPY

CORNORWHEAT

STICK PAN

ERIE PA., U. S. A.

629

NOTE: DRAWING IS
NOT TO SCALE

VIEW OF UNDERSIDE

No 273 Corn Stick Pan

P/N 930
No. of cups: 7
Dimensions: 13 1/4" x 5 3/4"
Production Date: 1930s to 1950s
Rarity: 1
Value: $20 to $30

The No 273 Corn Stick Pan is the most common Griswold pan. These are excellent pans to use to make corn sticks. Many times you see these pans for ridiculously high prices. They are easily obtainable in the $20 to $30 price range.

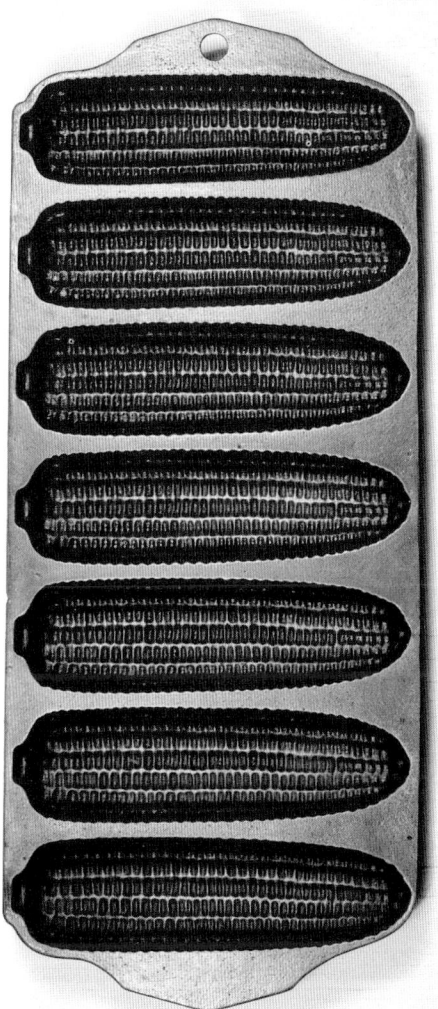

Top view of No 273 Corn Stick Pan

123

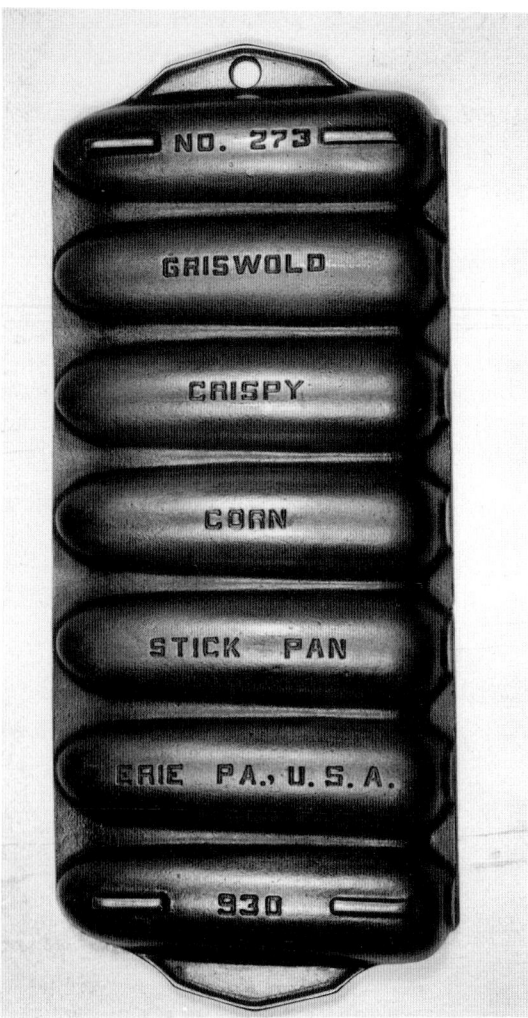

Underside of No 273 Corn Stick Pan

NO 273 CORN STICK PAN
P/N 930

NO 273 (930) RARITY: 1

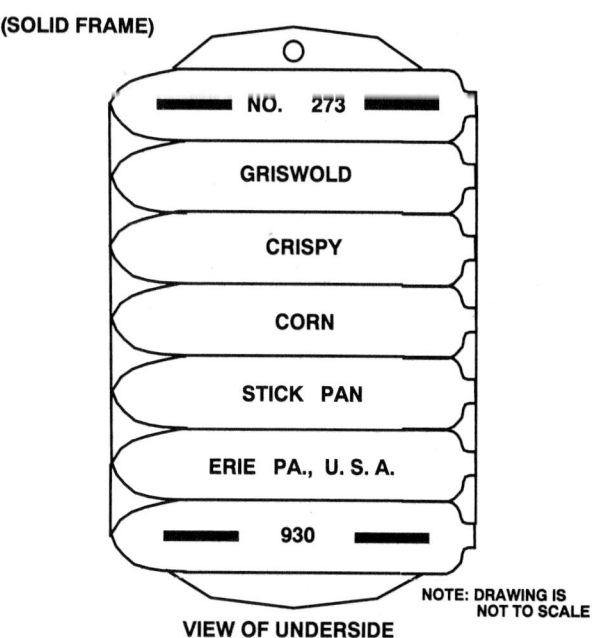

(SOLID FRAME)

NO. 273

GRISWOLD

CRISPY

CORN

STICK PAN

ERIE PA., U. S. A.

930

NOTE: DRAWING IS
NOT TO SCALE

VIEW OF UNDERSIDE

No 273 Corn Stick Pan (Hammered)

P/N 2073
No. of cups: 7
Dimensions: 13 1/4" x 5 3/4"
Production Date: 1940s
Rarity: 7
Value: $325 to $375

This pan is the hammered version of the common No 273 Corn Stick Pan. It is part of a set of hammered cookware that was made by Griswold in the 1940s. The hammered effect is cast into the pan and not added after manufacture. These very pretty pans are fairly uncommon.

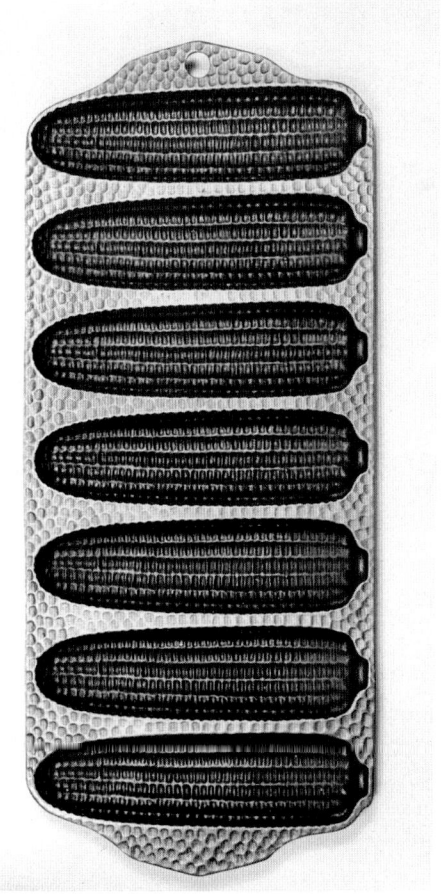

Top view of No 273 Corn Stick Pan (Hammered)

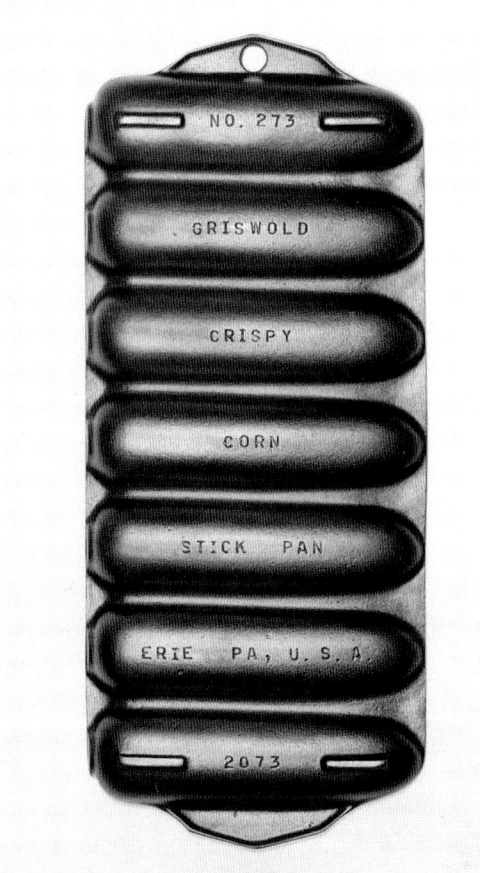

Underside of No 273 Corn Stick Pan (Hammered)

NO 273 CORN STICK PAN (HAMMERED)
P/N 2073

NO 273 (2073) RARITY: 7

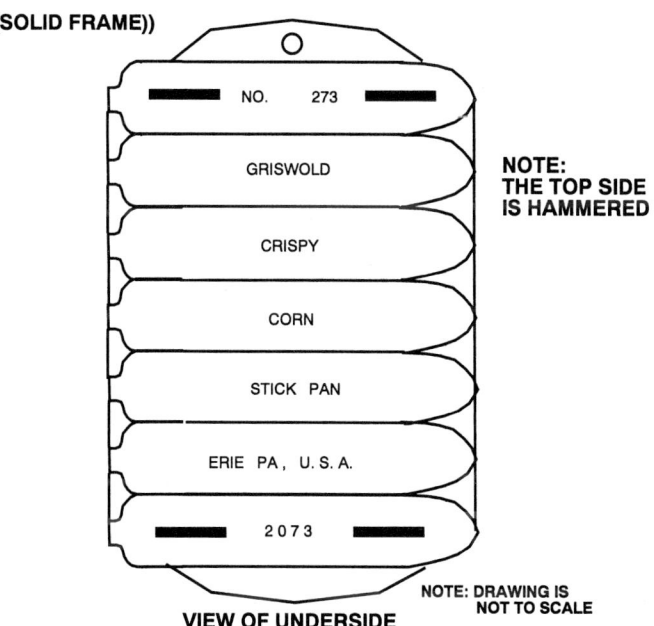

(SOLID FRAME))

NO.   273

GRISWOLD

CRISPY

CORN

STICK   PAN

ERIE PA, U.S.A.

2073

NOTE:
THE TOP SIDE
IS HAMMERED

NOTE: DRAWING IS
NOT TO SCALE

VIEW OF UNDERSIDE

No 280 Corn or Wheat Stick Pan

P/N 637
No. of cups: 7
Dimensions: 14" x 7 5/8"
Production Date: 1920s
Rarity: 10
Value: $1400 to $1600

This pan is a large version of The No 270 Corn or Wheat Stick Pan. This is a rare pan and is very difficult to find. It is not known why the patent number 73,326 is imprinted on this pan. That patent was a design patent for the wheat stick pan. If the patent number belongs on this pan, why isn't it on the No 272 and No 282 pans?

Top view of No 280 Corn or Wheat Stick Pan

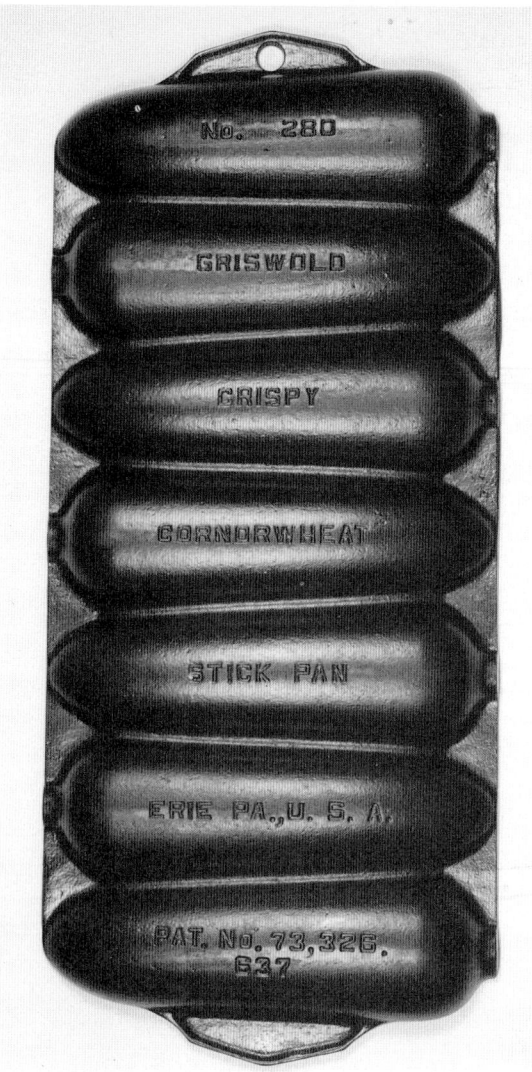

Underside of No 280 Corn or Wheat Stick Pan

NO 280 CORN OR WHEAT STICK PAN
P/N 637

NO 280 (637) RARITY: 10

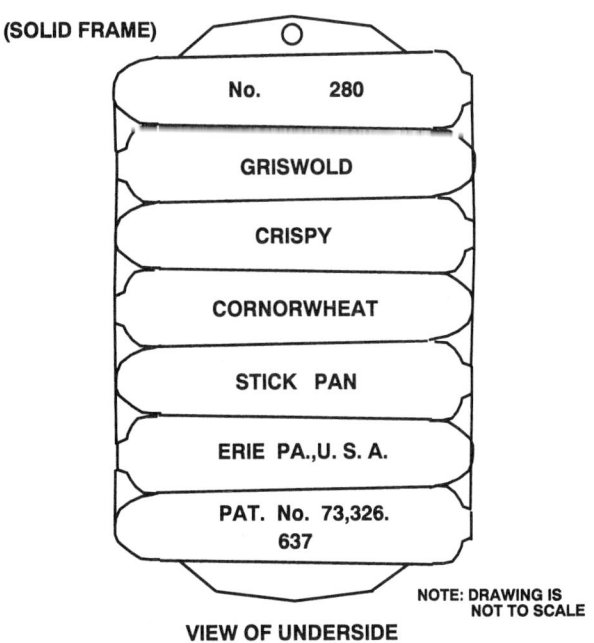

(SOLID FRAME)

| No. 280 |
| GRISWOLD |
| CRISPY |
| CORNORWHEAT |
| STICK PAN |
| ERIE PA.,U. S. A. |
| PAT. No. 73,326. 637 |

NOTE: DRAWING IS
NOT TO SCALE

VIEW OF UNDERSIDE

No 282 Corn or Wheat Stick Pan

P/N 630
No. of cups: 7
Dimensions: 14" x 7 5/8"
Production Date: 1930s
Variation 1: Rarity 8; Value $400 to $500
Variation 2: Rarity 8; Value $450 to $550

This pan is a large version of the No 272 Corn or Wheat Stick Pan. It is relatively uncommon. Variation 2, the variation with feet, is more difficult to find than Variation 1.

Top view of Variation 1 of No 282 Corn or Wheat Stick Pan

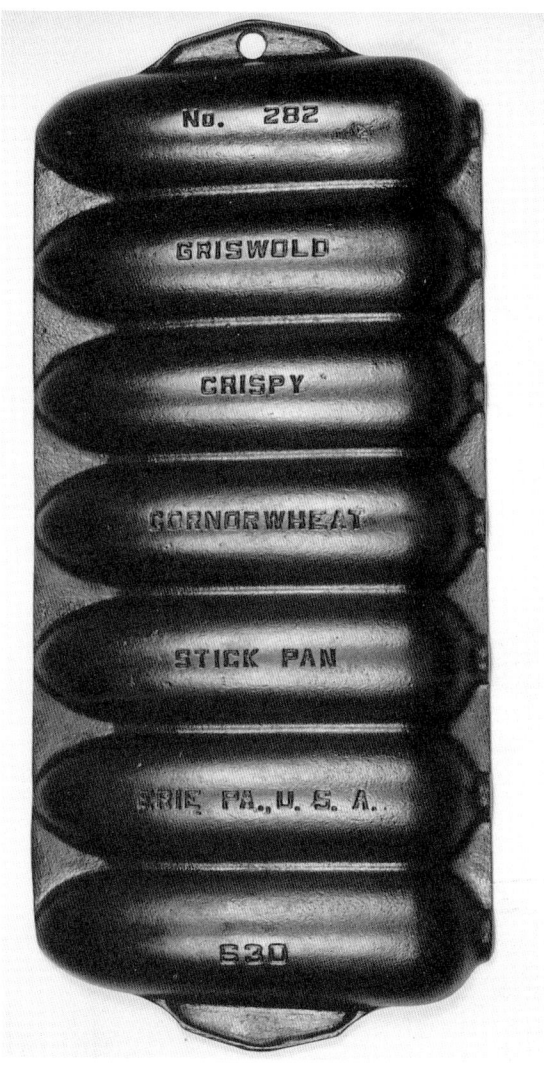

Underside of Variation 1 of No 282 Corn or Wheat Stick Pan

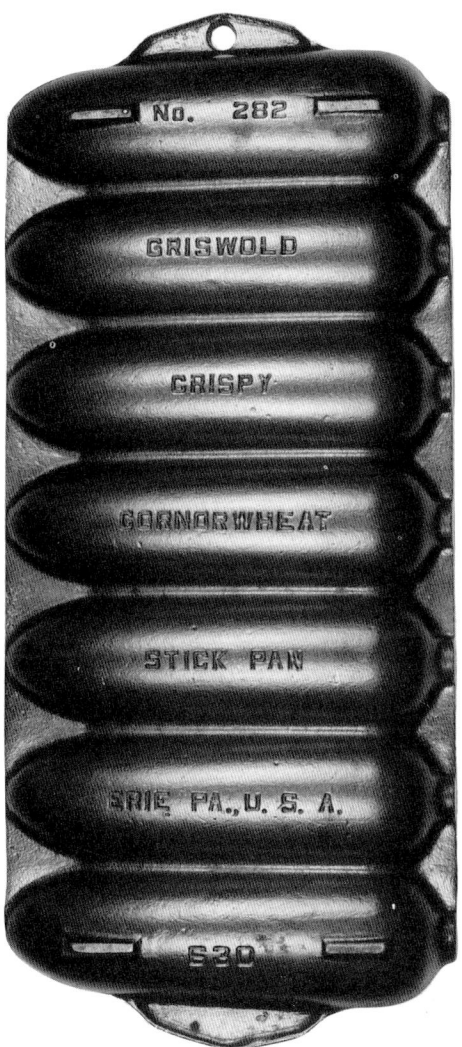

Underside of Variation 2 of No 282 Corn or Wheat Stick Pan

NO 282 CORN OR WHEAT STICK PAN
P/N 630

VARIATION 1 RARITY: 8

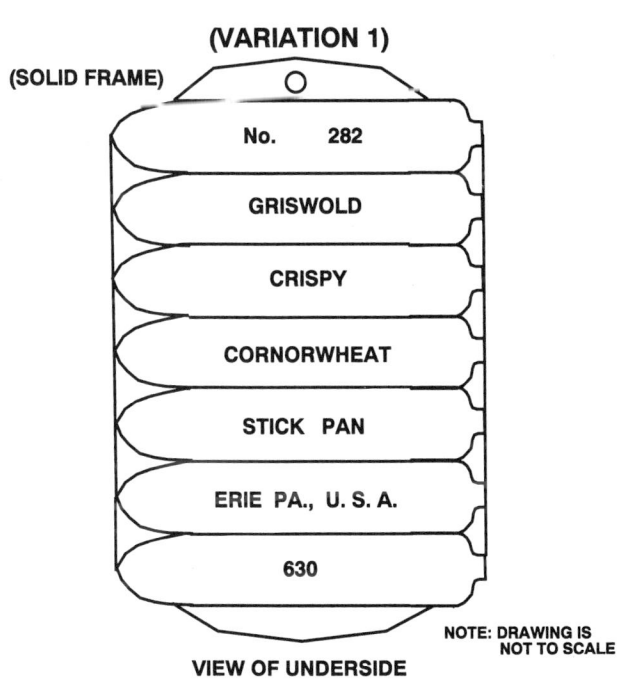

NO 282 CORN OR WHEAT STICK PAN
P/N 630

VARIATION 2 RARITY: 8

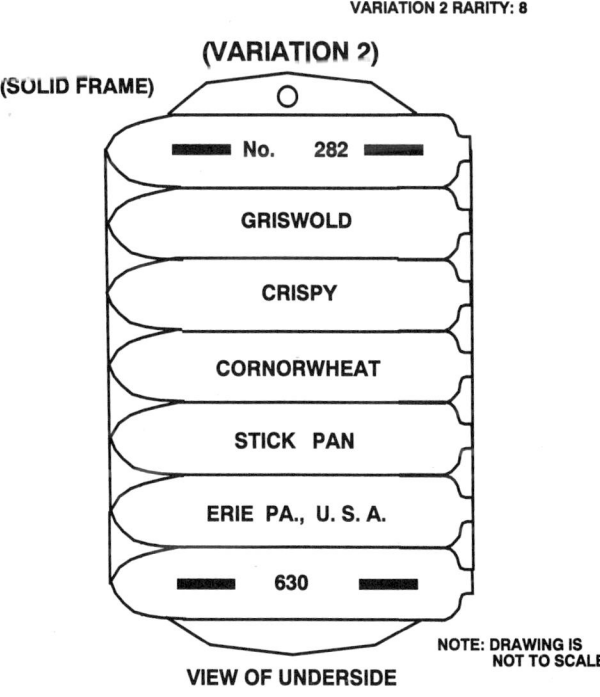

127

No 283 Corn Stick Pan

P/N 931
No. of cups: 7
Dimensions: 14" x 7 5/8"
Production Date: 1930s to 1940s
Rarity: 4
Value: $150 to $200

The No 283 Corn Stick Pan is the large version of the most common Griswold pan, the No 273 Corn Stick Pan. This pan is fairly common.

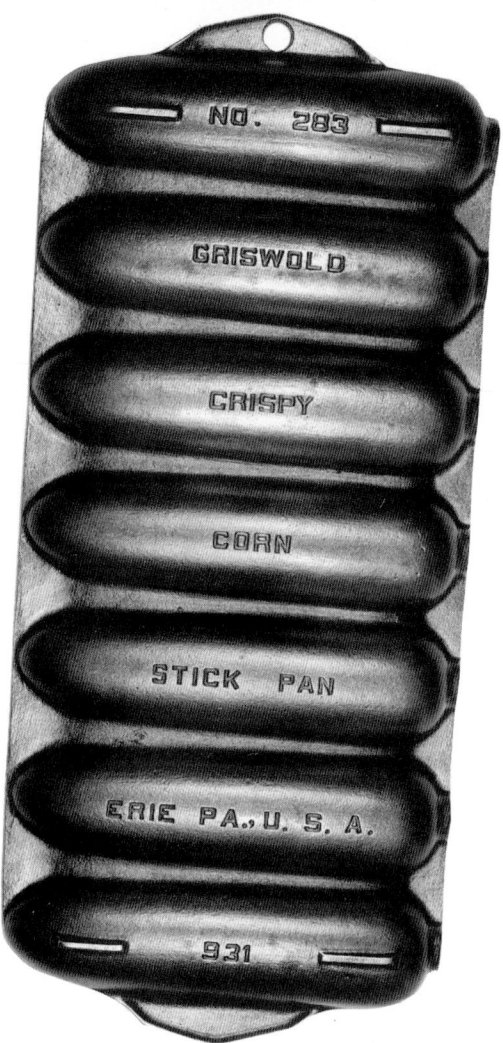

Underside of No 283 Corn Stick Pan

NO 283 CORN STICK PAN
P/N 931

NO 283 (931) RARITY: 4

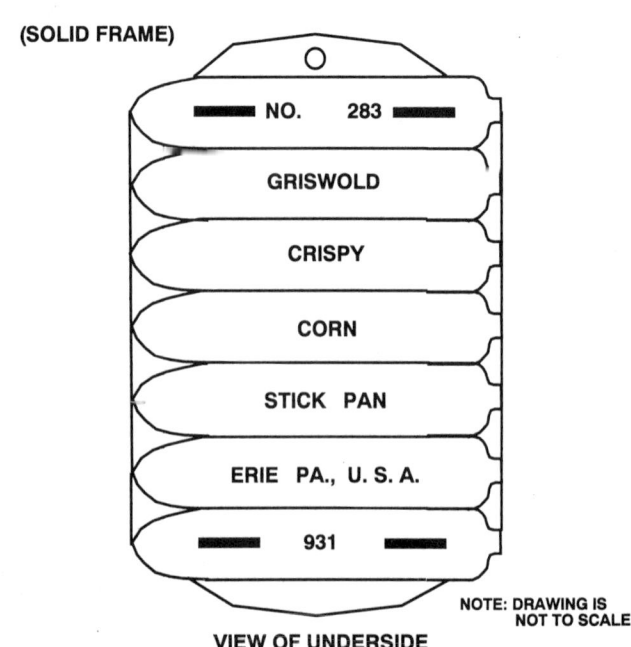

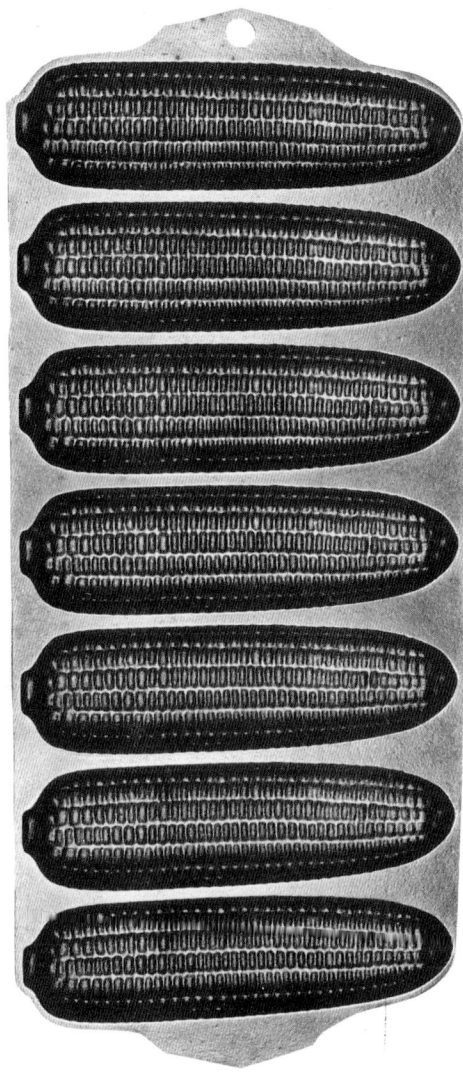

Top view of No 283 Corn Stick Pan

128

No 2700 Wheat Stick Pan

P/N 632
No. of cups: 7
Dimensions: 13 1/8" x 5 3/4"
Production Date: 1920s
Rarity: 8
Value: $500 to $600

This pan is a small version of the No 2800 Wheat Stick Pan. It was made in the late 1920s. The patent number (73,326) is the design patent for the wheat stick pan. The No 2700 Wheat Stick Pan is of moderate rarity, but is obtainable.

Underside of No 2700 Wheat Stick Pan

Top view of No 2700 Wheat Stick Pan

NO 2700 WHEAT STICK PAN
P/N 632

NO 2700 (632) RARITY: 8

(SOLID FRAME)

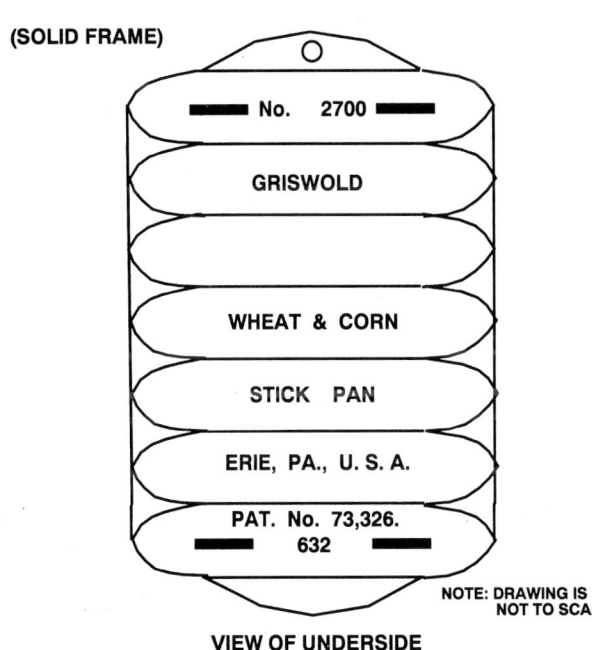

NOTE: DRAWING IS NOT TO SCALE

VIEW OF UNDERSIDE

129

No 2800 Wheat Stick Pan

P/N 633
No. of cups: 7
Dimensions: 15" x 6 3/4"
Production Date: 1920s
Rarity: 10
Value: $2500 to $3000

    This pan is a large version of the No 2700 Wheat Stick Pan. It was made in the late 1920s after patent 73,326 was awarded on August 23, 1927. The No 2800 Wheat Stick Pan is the rarest of the Griswold pans that are fully marked and is quite difficult to find.

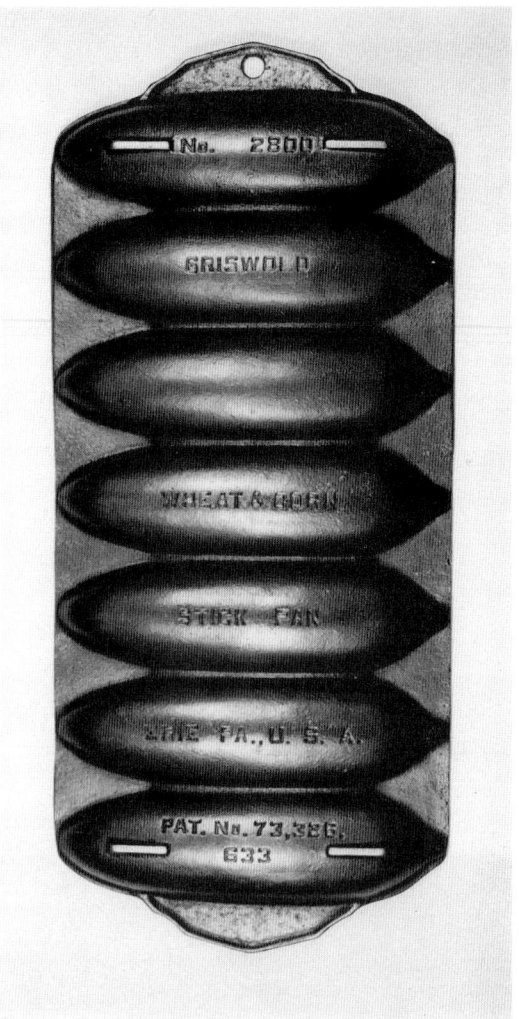

Underside of No 2800 Wheat Stick Pan

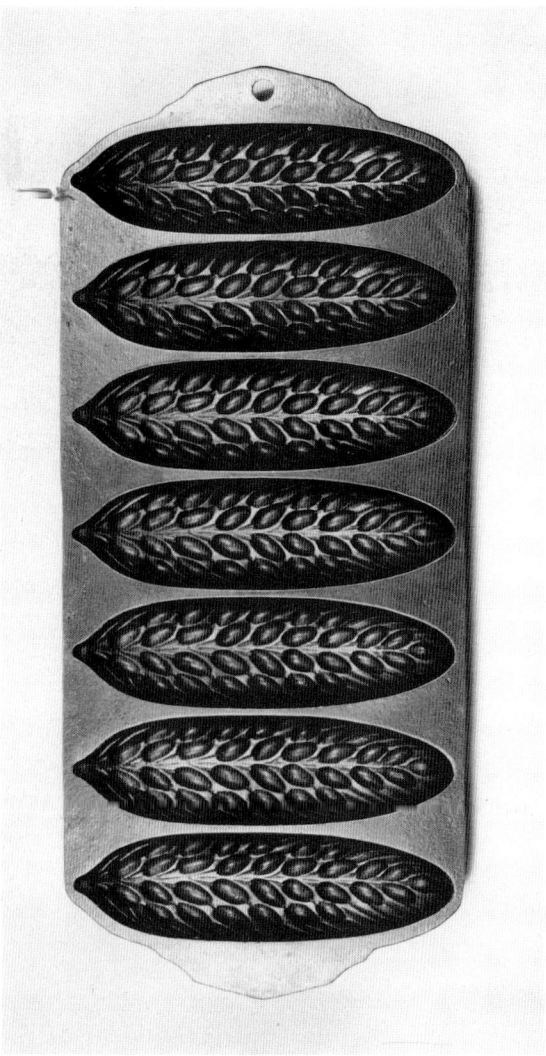

Top view of No 2800 Wheat Stick Pan

NO 2800 WHEAT STICK PAN
P/N 633

NO 2800 (633) RARITY: 10

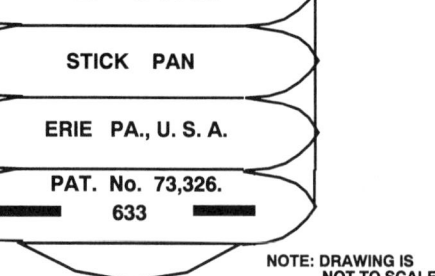

(SOLID FRAME)

No. 2800

GRISWOLD

WHEAT & CORN

STICK PAN

ERIE PA., U. S. A.

PAT. No. 73,326.
633

NOTE: DRAWING IS
NOT TO SCALE

VIEW OF UNDERSIDE

No - Corn or Wheat Stick Pan (P/N 623)

P/N 623
No. of cups: 7
Dimensions: 13 1/4" x 5 3/4"
Production Date: Unknown (Probably 1930s)
Rarity: 10
Value: $1200 to $1500

This pan is a mystery pan. It is identified as a Griswold pan by the P/N and the cups which are identical to the No 272 pan. The handles are different than any other Griswold pan. The hang hole is such that the P/N is upside down when the pan is hanging. Why this pan was made and for what purpose it was made is unknown. This pan is very rare, with only 3 or 4 known in the collecting community.

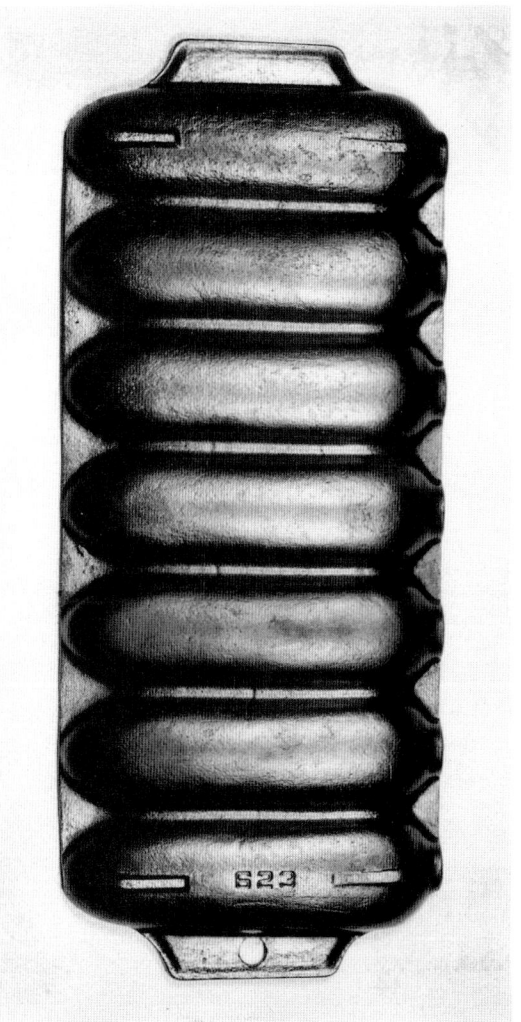

Underside of Corn or Wheat Stick Pan (P/N 623)

NO --- CORN OR WHEAT STICK PAN P/N 623

NO -- (623) RARITY: 10

Top view of Corn or Wheat Stick Pan (P/N 623)

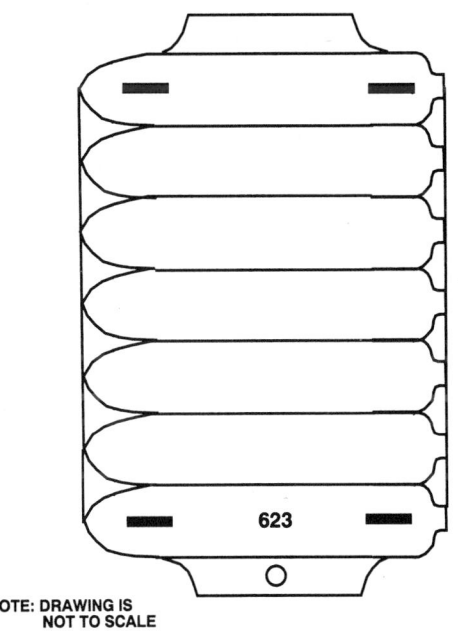

NOTE: DRAWING IS
NOT TO SCALE

VIEW OF UNDERSIDE

Chapter 4.
Variations of Griswold Cast Iron Muffin Pans Made for Others

Summary

This section provides detailed information on the 12 cast iron muffin pans and the 19 variations of them that were made by Griswold for others to market. These are identified as Griswold pans because of the Griswold P/Ns on them or similarity to pans with the P/Ns on them.

Pan No	Description	P/N	No. of Variations
No 10	Popover Pan, Best Made for Sears	1253	2
No 10	Popover Pan, Puritan for Sears	1512	1
No 32	Danish Cake Pan for Favorite Piqua Ware	962	1
No 33	Munk Pan for Alfred Andresen Co.	2992	2
No 33	Munk Pan for Western Importing Co.	2992	1
No 34	Plett Pan for Alfred Andresen Co.	2980	4
No 34	Plett Pan for Western Importing Co.	2980	3
No 34	Plett Pan for Sandvik Saw & Tool Corp.	2980	1
No 34	Plett Pan for Scandinavian Importing Co.	2980	1
No 1270	Wheat Stick Pan, Best Made for Sears	1270	1
No 1270	Wheat Stick Pan, Merit for Sears	1513	1
No 1270	Wheat Stick Pan, Puritan for Sears	1513	1

Top view of Variation 1 of No 10 Popover Pan (Best Made)

Underside of Variation 1 of No 10 Popover Pan (Best Made)

No 10 Popover Pan, Best Made for Sears

P/N 1253
No. of cups: 11
Dimensions: 11 3/16" x 7 5/8"
Production Date: 1920s to 1930s
Variation 1: Rarity 3; Value $60 to $90
Variation 2: Rarity 4; Value $100 to $125

These pans were made by Griswold for Sears to market in its Best Made line of cookware. These pans are identical to the Griswold popover pans of this era. These pans are not as common as the Griswold No 10 Popover Pans. Variation 2 is rather difficult to find.

Underside of Variation 2 of No 10 Popover Pan (Best Made)

NO 10 POPOVER PAN (BEST MADE)
P/N 1253

VARIATION 1 RARITY: 3

(OPEN FRAME) **(VARIATION 1)**

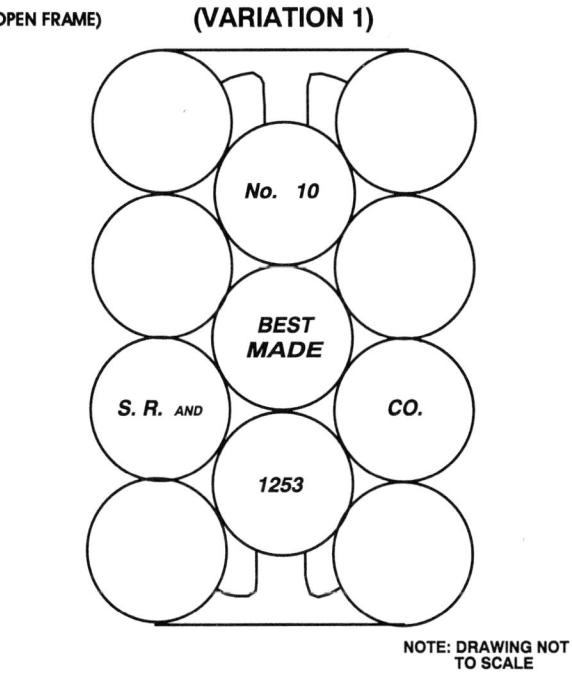

No. 10

BEST MADE

S. R. AND   CO.

1253

NOTE: DRAWING NOT TO SCALE

VIEW OF UNDERSIDE

NO 10 POPOVER PAN (BEST MADE)
P/N 1253

VARIATION 2 RARITY: 4

(SOLID FRAME) **(VARIATION 2)**

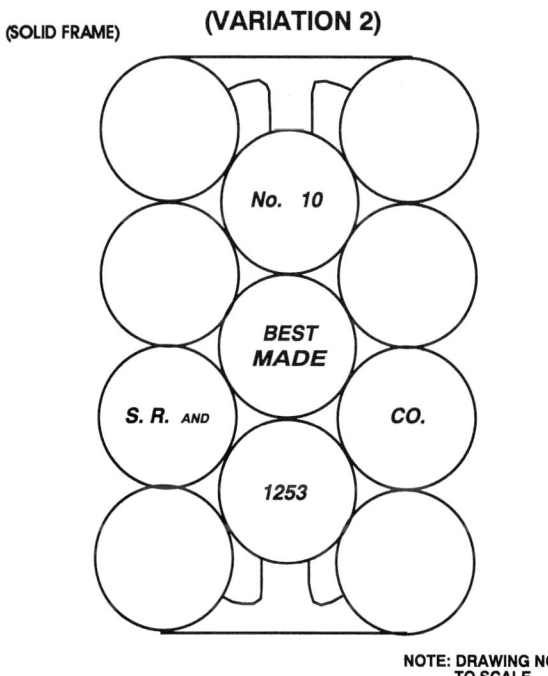

No. 10

BEST MADE

S. R. AND   CO.

1253

NOTE: DRAWING NOT TO SCALE

VIEW OF UNDERSIDE

No 10 Popover Pan, Puritan for Sears

P/N 1512
No. of cups: 11
Dimensions: 11 3/16" x 7 5/8"
Production Date: 1930s
Rarity: 6
Value: $175 to $200

    This pan was made by Griswold for Sears to market under their Puritan cookware line. It is suspected that there may be a variation of this pan with cutouts between the cups; however, no such variation has been identified by the collecting community. The Puritan Popover Pan is somewhat difficult to find.

NO 10 POPOVER PAN (PURITAN)
P/N 1512

NO 10 (1512) RARITY: 6

(SOLID FRAME)

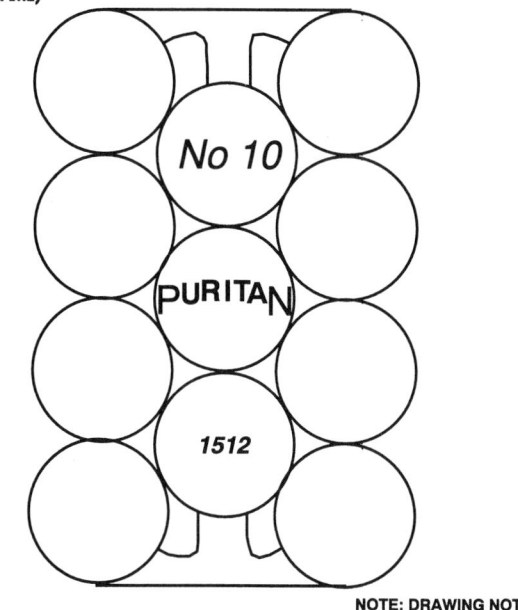

NOTE: DRAWING NOT
TO SCALE

VIEW OF UNDERSIDE

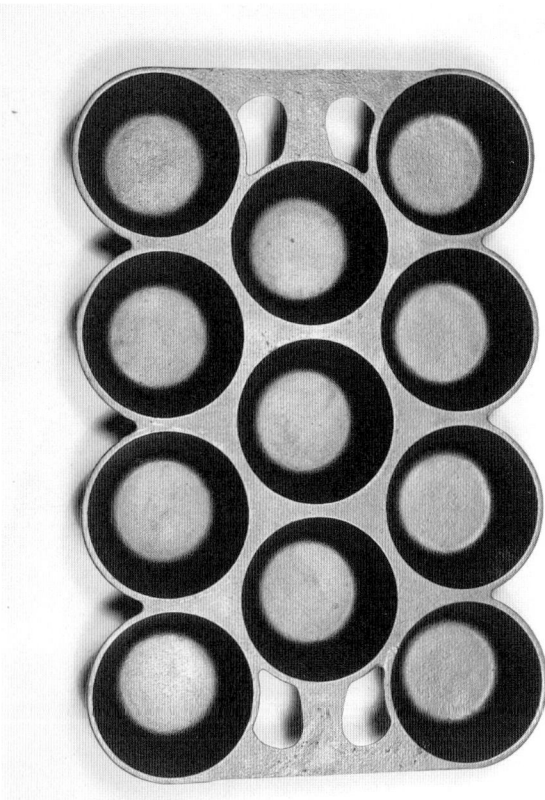

Top view of No 10 Popover Pan (Puritan)

Underside of No 10 Popover Pan (Puritan)

No 32 Danish Cake Pan for Favorite Piqua Ware

P/N 962
No. of cups: 7
Dimensions: 9" (diameter)
Production Date: Unknown (Probably 1900s)
Rarity: 4
Value: $75 to $100

    This pan was made by Griswold for Favorite Piqua Ware. This pan has a handle style similar to the handle on Variation 1 of the Griswold No 31 Danish Cake Pan. Little is known about this piece. It is considered a Griswold made pan because of the Griswold P/N on it.

Underside of No 32 Danish Cake Pan (Favorite Piqua Ware)

NO 32 DANISH CAKE PAN (FAVORITE PIQUA WARE) P/N 962

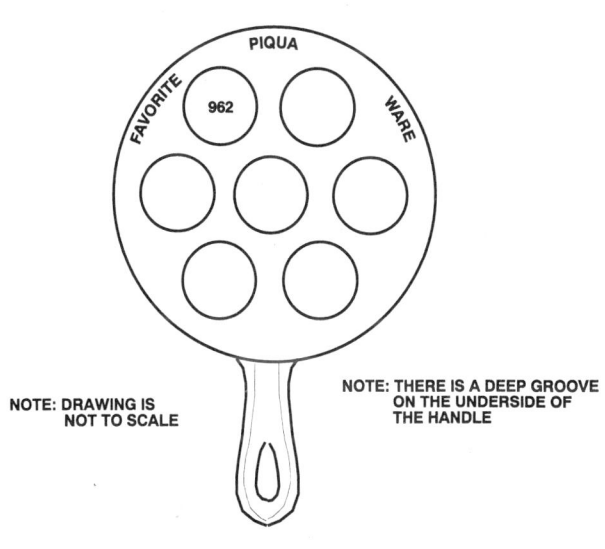

NO 32 (962 - FAVORITE PIQUA WARE) RARITY: 4

NOTE: DRAWING IS NOT TO SCALE

NOTE: THERE IS A DEEP GROOVE ON THE UNDERSIDE OF THE HANDLE

VIEW OF UNDERSIDE

Top view of No 32 Danish Cake Pan (Favorite Piqua Ware)

No 33 Munk Pan for Alfred Andresen Co.

P/N 2992
No. of cups: 7
Dimensions: 9" (diameter)
Production Date: 1900s to 1910s
Variation 1: Rarity 3; Value $75 to $100
Variation 2: Rarity 3; Value $100 to $125

This pan was made by Griswold for the Alfred Andresen Co. The Alfred Andresen Co. was formed by Alfred Andresen to market products made by others. This munk pan has a very different handle that is unique. Variation 2 of this pan is marked ANDRESEN MONK PAN. Monk is an error and should have been munk. Variation 1 of this pan, while just marked with the P/N, is considered an Andresen Pan because of the similar handle style.

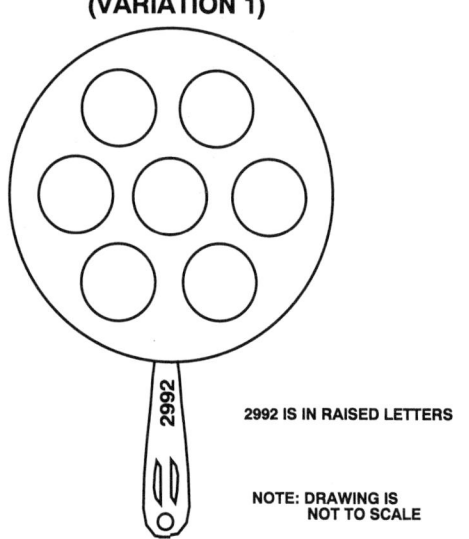

**NO 33 MUNK PAN
        (ALFRED ANDRESEN CO.)
        P/N 2992**

VARIATION 1 RARITY: 3

(VARIATION 1)

2992

2992 IS IN RAISED LETTERS

NOTE: DRAWING IS
NOT TO SCALE

VIEW OF UNDERSIDE

Top view of Variation 2 of No 33 Munk Pan (Alfred Andresen Co.)

Underside of Variation 2 of No 33 Munk Pan (Alfred Andresen Co.)

NO 33 MUNK PAN
(ALFRED ANDRESEN CO.)
P/N 2992

VARIATION 2 RARITY: 3

(VARIATION 2)

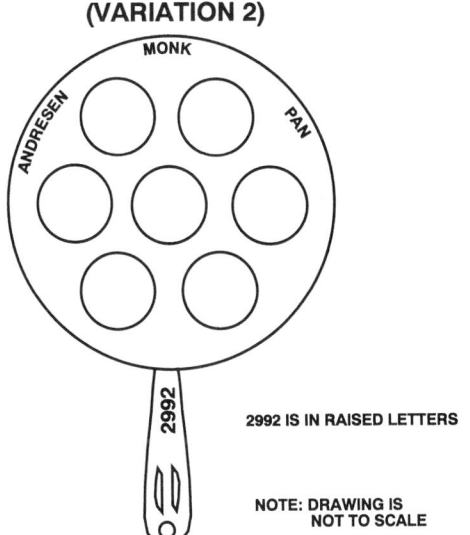

2992 IS IN RAISED LETTERS

NOTE: DRAWING IS
NOT TO SCALE

VIEW OF UNDERSIDE

No 33 Munk Pan for Western Importing Co.

P/N 2992
No. of cups: 7
Dimensions: 9" (diameter)
Production Date: 1910s
Rarity: 3
Value: $90 to $110

This pan was made by Griswold for the Western Importing Co. The Western Importing Co. was the successor company to the Alfred Andresen Co. Except for its markings, this pan is identical to the Griswold Munk Pan.

Underside of No 33 Munk Pan (Western Importing Co.)

NO 33 MUNK PAN
(WESTERN IMPORTING CO.)
P/N 2992

NO 33 (2992 - WESTERN IMPORTING) RARITY: 3

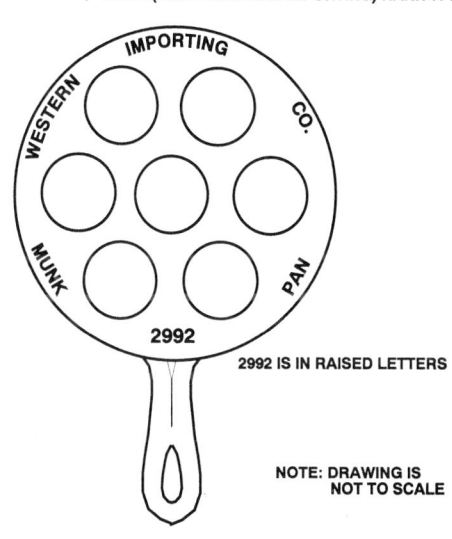

2992 IS IN RAISED LETTERS

NOTE: DRAWING IS
NOT TO SCALE

Top view of No 33 Munk Pan (Western
Importing Co.)

VIEW OF UNDERSIDE

No 34 Plett Pan for Alfred Andresen Co.

P/N 2980
No. of cups: 7
Dimensions: 9 1/2" (diameter)
Production Date: 1900s to 1910s
Variation 1: Rarity 2; Value $70 to $90
Variation 2: Rarity 2; Value $70 to $90
Variation 3: Rarity 2; Value $50 to $75
Variation 4: Rarity 2; Value $50 to $75

    This pan was made by Griswold for the Alfred Andresen Co. The Alfred Andresen Co. was formed by Alfred Andresen to market products that were made by others. Alfred Andresen was a flamboyant entrepreneur. The early Alfred Andresen Plett Pans had long handles while the last variation had a handle similar to the Griswold Plett Pans.

Underside of Variation 1 of No 34 Plett Pan (Alfred Andresen Co.)

NO 34 PLETT PAN (ALFRED ANDRESEN CO.) P/N 2980

VARIATION 1 RARITY: 2

(VARIATION 1)

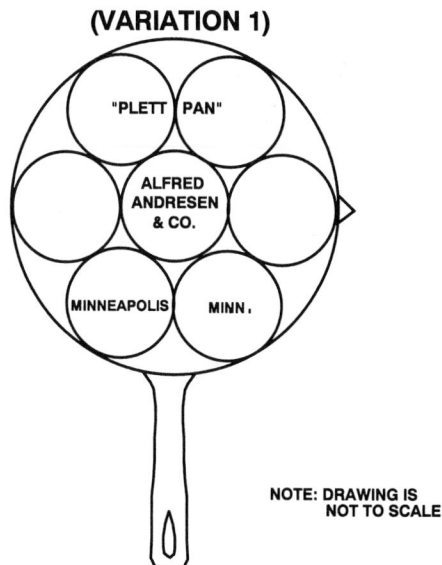

NOTE: DRAWING IS NOT TO SCALE

VIEW OF UNDERSIDE

NO 34 PLETT PAN (ALFRED ANDRESEN CO.) P/N 2980

VARIATION 2 RARITY: 2

(VARIATION 2)

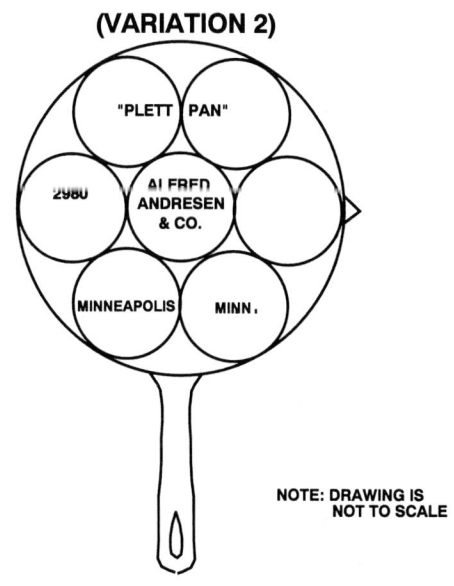

NOTE: DRAWING IS NOT TO SCALE

VIEW OF UNDERSIDE

Top view of Variation 3 of No 34 Plett Pan (Alfred Andresen Co.)

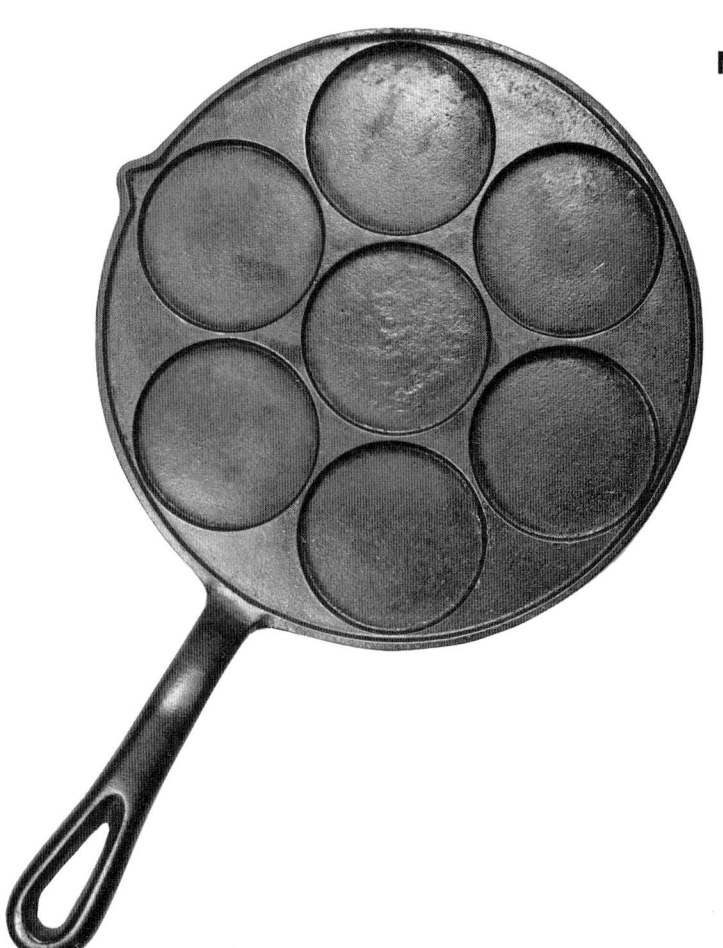

NO 34 PLETT PAN
(ALFRED ANDRESEN CO.)
P/N 2980

VARIATION 3 RARITY: 2

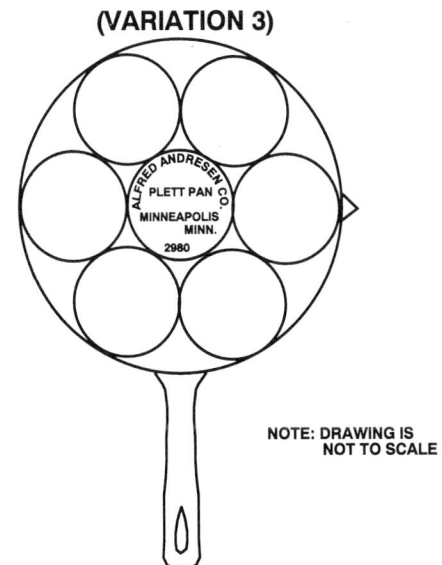

(VARIATION 3)

ALFRED ANDRESEN CO.
PLETT PAN
MINNEAPOLIS
MINN.
2980
NOTE: DRAWING IS NOT TO SCALE

VIEW OF UNDERSIDE

NOTE: THE LETTERING IS ALL RAISED. THE FLAT SURFACE ON THE MIDDLE CUP IS RECESSED SO THAT THE RAISED LETTERS ARE EVEN WITH THE SURFACES OF THE OUTSIDE CUPS

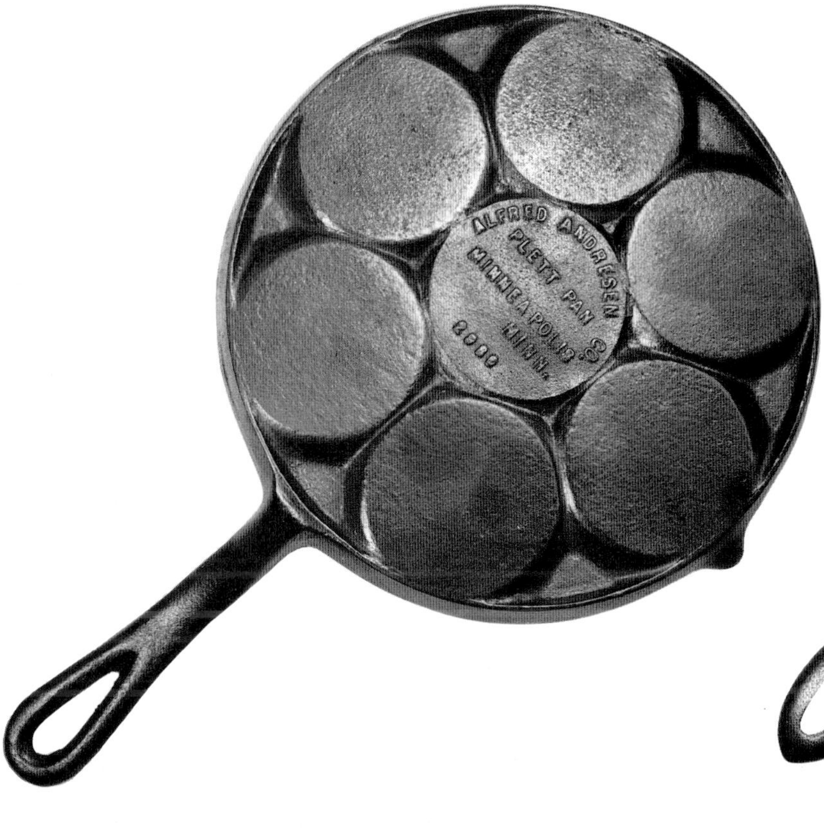

ALFRED ANDRESEN CO.
PLETT PAN
MINNEAPOLIS
MINN.

Underside of Variation 3 of No 34 Plett Pan (Alfred Andresen Co.)

Top view of Variation 4 of No 34 Plett Pan (Alfred Andresen Co.)

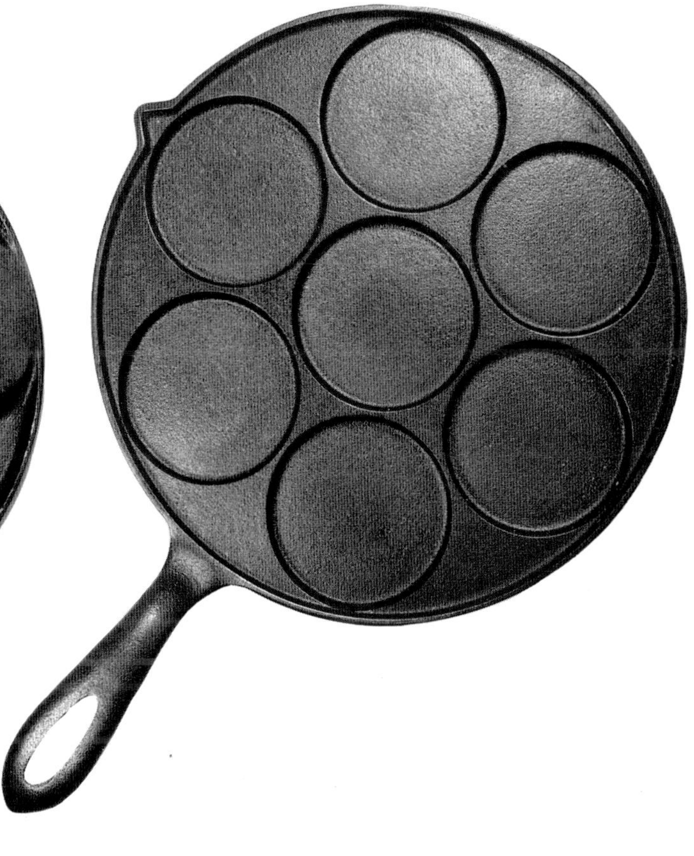

Underside of Variation 4 of No 34 Plett Pan (Alfred Andresen Co.)

NO 34 PLETT PAN
(ALFRED ANDRESEN CO.)
P/N 2980

VARIATION 4 RARITY: 2

(VARIATION 4)

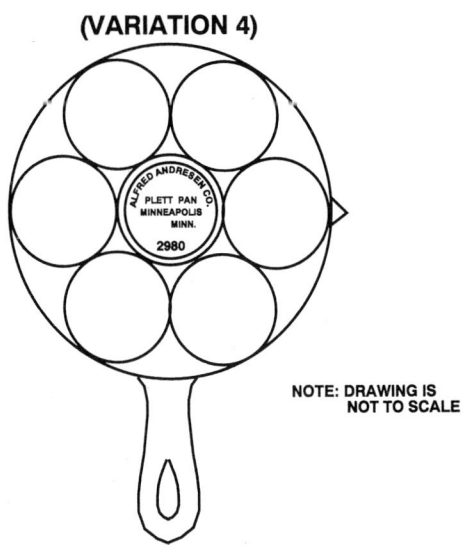

NOTE: DRAWING IS
NOT TO SCALE

VIEW OF UNDERSIDE

NOTE: THE LETTERING IS ALL RAISED. THE FLAT SURFACE ON THE
MIDDLE CUP IS RECESSED SO THAT THE RAISED LETTERS
ARE EVEN WITH THE SURFACES OF THE OUTSIDE CUPS.

No 34 Plett Pan for Western Importing Co.

P/N 2980
No. of cups: 7
Dimensions: 9 1/2" (diameter)
Production Date: 1910s
Variation 1: Rarity 2; Value $40 to $60
Variation 2: Rarity 2; Value $40 to $60
Variation 3: Rarity 2; Value $40 to $60

This plett pan was made by Griswold for the Western Importing Co. The Western Importing Co. was the successor company to the Alfred Andresen Co. and was created after the demise of Alfred Andresen. These plett pans all have the handles similar to the ones on the Griswold Plett Pans.

NO 34 PLETT PAN
(WESTERN IMPORTING CO.)
P/N 2980

VARIATION 1 RARITY: 2

(VARIATION 1)

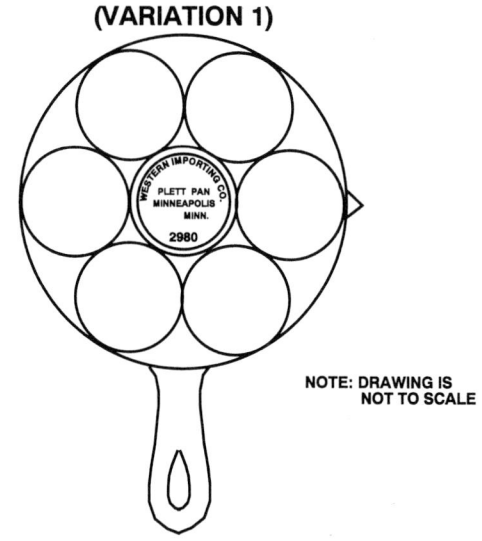

NOTE: DRAWING IS
NOT TO SCALE

VIEW OF UNDERSIDE

NOTE: THE LETTERING IS ALL RAISED. THE FLAT SURFACE ON THE
MIDDLE CUP IS RECESSED SO THAT THE RAISED LETTERS
ARE EVEN WITH THE SURFACES OF THE OUTSIDE CUPS.

Top view of Variation 2 of No 34 Plett Pan (Western Importing Co.)

Underside of Variation 2 of No 34 Plett Pan (Western Importing Co.)

Underside of Variation 3 of No 34 Plett Pan (Western Importing Co.)

NO 34 PLETT PAN (WESTERN IMPORTING CO.) P/N 2980

VARIATION 2 RARITY: 2

(VARIATION 2)

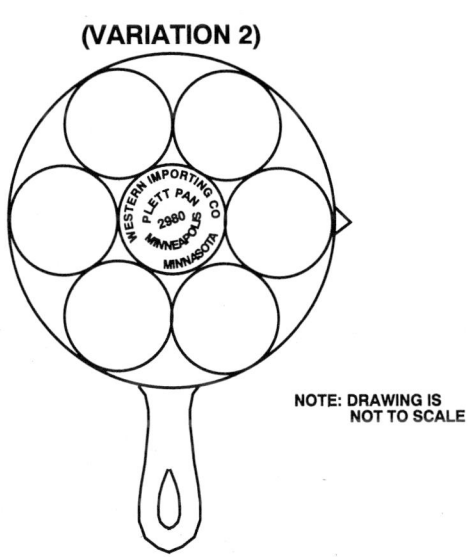

NOTE: DRAWING IS NOT TO SCALE

VIEW OF UNDERSIDE

NOTE: THE LETTERING IS ALL RAISED. THE FLAT SURFACE ON THE MIDDLE CUP IS RECESSED SO THAT THE RAISED LETTERS ARE EVEN WITH THE SURFACES OF THE OUTSIDE CUPS.

NO 34 PLETT PAN (WESTERN IMPORTING CO.) P/N 2980

VARIATION 3 RARITY: 2

(VARIATION 3)

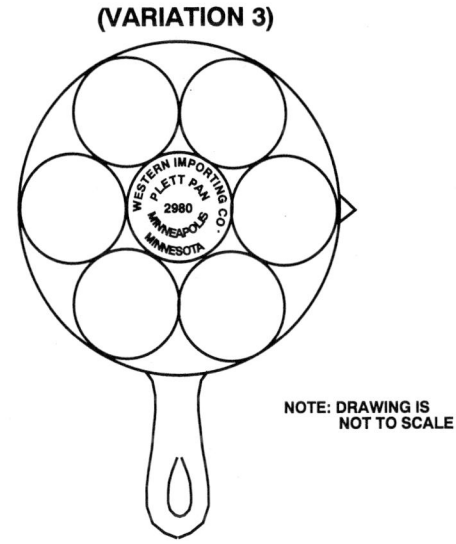

NOTE: DRAWING IS NOT TO SCALE

VIEW OF UNDERSIDE

NOTE: THE LETTERING IS ALL RAISED. THE FLAT SURFACE ON THE MIDDLE CUP IS RECESSED SO THAT THE RAISED LETTERS ARE EVEN WITH THE SURFACES OF THE OUTSIDE CUPS.

No 34 Plett Pan for Sandvik Saw & Tool Corp.

P/N 2980
No. of cups: 7
Dimensions: 9 1/2" (diameter)
Production Date: Unknown
Rarity: 3
Value: $50 to $70

This pan was made by Griswold for the Sandvik Saw & Tool Corp. It is not known if this pan was sold by Sandvik Saw & Tool Corp. or given to customers as a form of advertising. Sandvik Saws & Tools Co. currently exists in Throop, Pa. The small fish-like imprint on the pan may be related to the company logo.

Underside of No 34 Plett Pan (Sandvik Saw & Tool Corp.)

Top view of No 34 Plett Pan (Sandvik Saw & Tool Corp.)

NO 34 PLETT PAN (SANDVIK SAW & TOOL CORP.) P/N 2980

NO 34 (2980 - SANDVIK SAW & TOOL CORP.) RARITY: 3

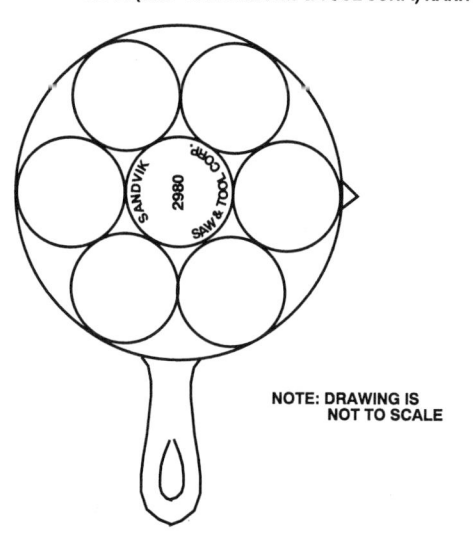

NOTE: DRAWING IS NOT TO SCALE

VIEW OF UNDERSIDE

NOTE: THIS IS AN ADVERTISING PLETT PAN MADE BY GRISWOLD FOR THE SANDVIK SAW & TOOL CORP.

No 34 Plett Pan for Scandinavian Importing Co.

P/N 2980
No. of cups: 7
Dimensions: 9 1/2" (diameter)
Production Date: Unknown (Probably 1910s)
Rarity: 3
Value: $75 to $100

This plett pan was made by Griswold for the Scandinavian Importing Company of Boston, Massachusetts. This plett pan has the long handle similar to the handle on the early Alfred Andresen Plett Pans. Nothing is known about this company. There may be some relationship with this company to Alfred Andresen.

Underside of No 34 Plett Pan (Scandinavian Importing Co.)

NO 34 PLETT PAN (SCANDINAVIAN IMPORTING CO.) P/N 2980

NO 34 (2980 - SCANDINAVIAN IMPORTING CO.) RARITY: 3

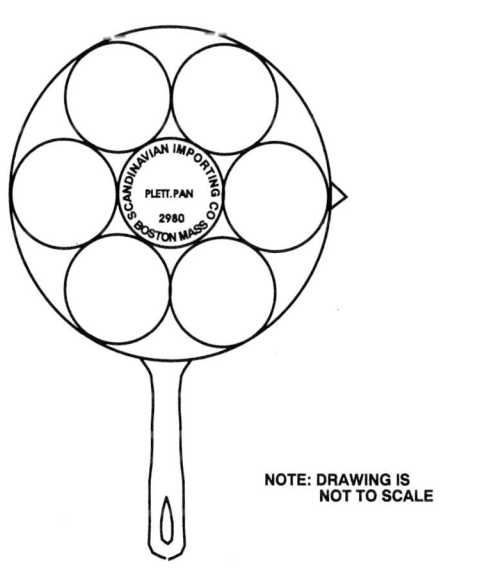

NOTE: DRAWING IS NOT TO SCALE

VIEW OF UNDERSIDE

NOTE: THE LETTERING IS ALL RAISED. THE FLAT SURFACE ON THE MIDDLE CUP IS RECESSED SO THAT THE RAISED LETTERS ARE EVEN WITH THE SURFACES OF THE OUTSIDE CUPS.

Top view of No 34 Plett Pan (Scandinavian Importing Co.)

No 1270 Wheat Stick Pan, Best Made for Sears

P/N 1270
No. of cups: 7
Dimensions: 13 1/8" x 5 3/4"
Production Date: 1920s to 1930s
Rarity: 4
Value $90 to $110

    The Best Made Wheat Stick Pan was made by Griswold for Sears. This was part of the Best Made cookware line that Sears marketed. This pan is identical in size and shape to the No 2700 Wheat Stick Pan that Griswold sold. The number of the patent (73,326) that Griswold obtained on the wheat stick pan design also appears on this pan.

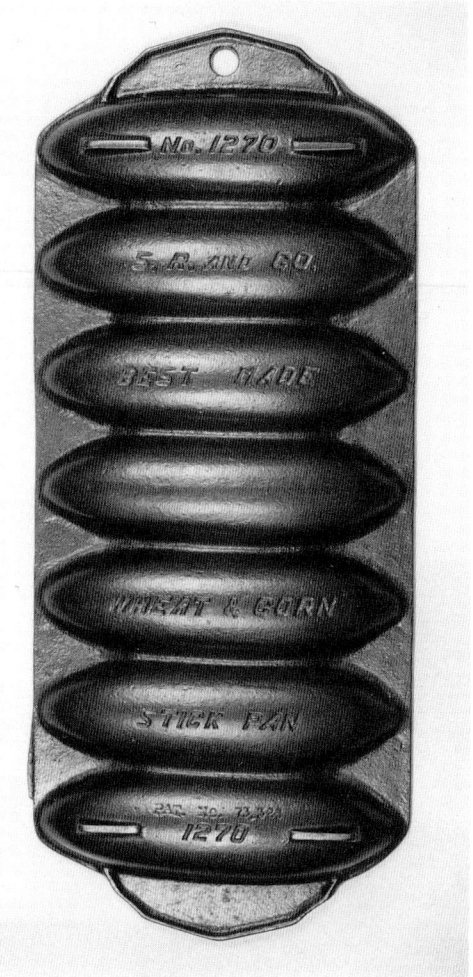

Underside of No 1270 Wheat Stick Pan (Best Made)

NO 1270 WHEAT STICK PAN (BEST MADE) P/N 1270

Top view of No 1270 Wheat Stick Pan (Best Made)

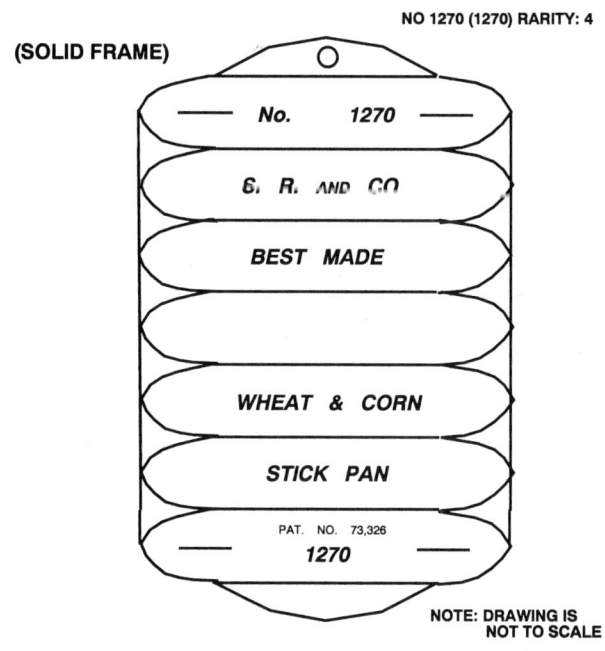

NO 1270 (1270) RARITY: 4

(SOLID FRAME)

No. 1270

S. R. AND CO

BEST MADE

WHEAT & CORN

STICK PAN

PAT. NO. 73,326

1270

NOTE: DRAWING IS NOT TO SCALE

VIEW OF UNDERSIDE

No 1270 Wheat Stick Pan, Merit for Sears

P/N 1513
No. of cups: 7
Dimensions: 13 1/16" x 5 1/2"
Production Date: 1930s
Rarity: 5
Value: $120 to $140

The Merit Wheat Stick Pan was made by Griswold for Sears. This was part of the Merit line of cookware that Sears sold in the late 1930s, primarily through their catalogs.

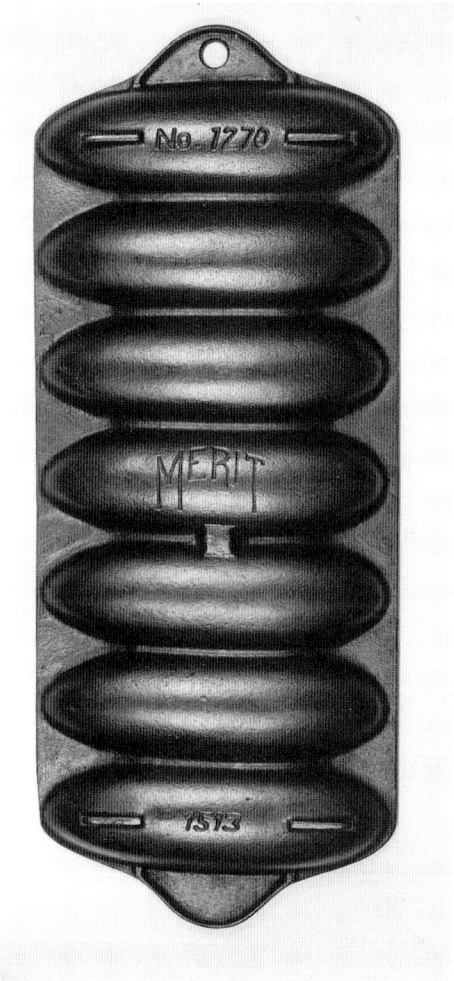

Underside of No 1270 Wheat Stick Pan (Merit)

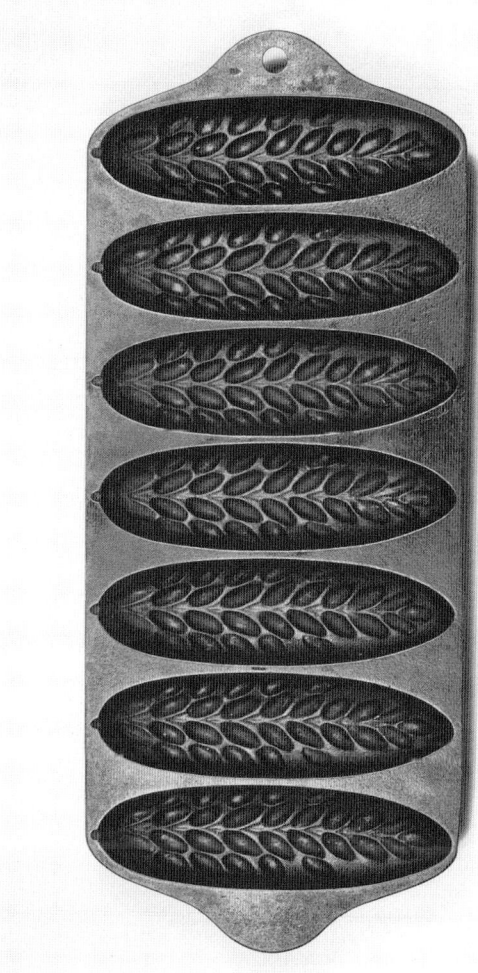

Top view of No 1270 Wheat Stick Pan (Merit)

NO 1270 WHEAT STICK PAN (MERIT)
P/N 1513

NO 1270 (1513 - MERIT) RARITY: 5

(SOLID FRAME)

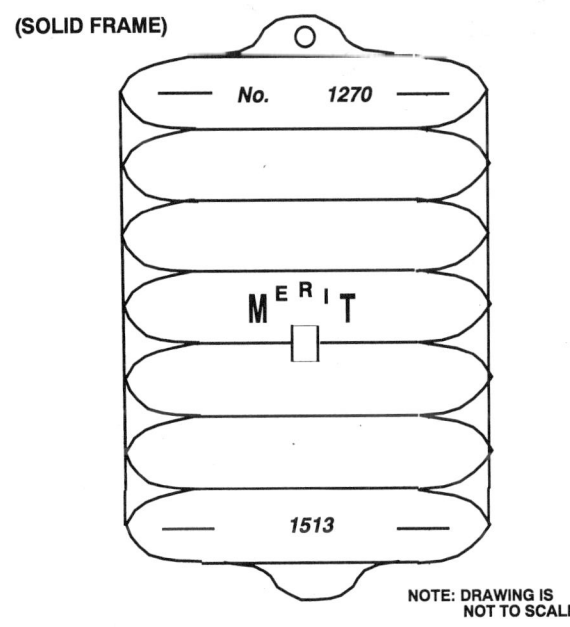

NOTE: DRAWING IS
NOT TO SCALE

VIEW OF UNDERSIDE

No 1270 Wheat Stick Pan, Puritan for Sears

P/N 1513
No. of cups: 7
Dimensions: 13 1/16" x 5 1/2"
Production Date: 1930s
Rarity: 4
Value: $90 to $110

The Puritan Wheat Stick Pan was made by Griswold for Sears. Sears had a line of Puritan cookware and this pan was part of that product line. These appeared in the Sears catalogs in the early 1930s.

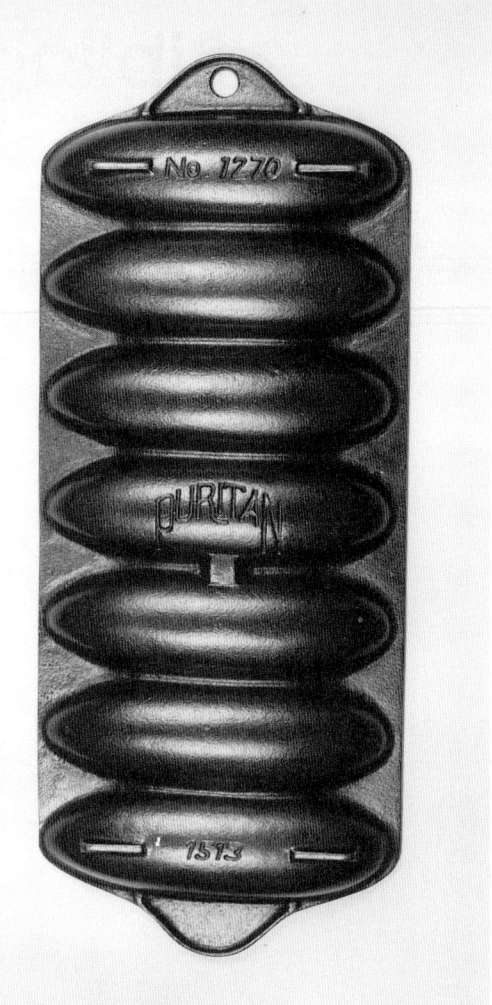

Underside of No 1270 Wheat Stick Pan (Puritan)

NO 1270 WHEAT STICK PAN (PURITAN)
P/N 1513

NO 1270 (1513 - PURITAN) RARITY: 5

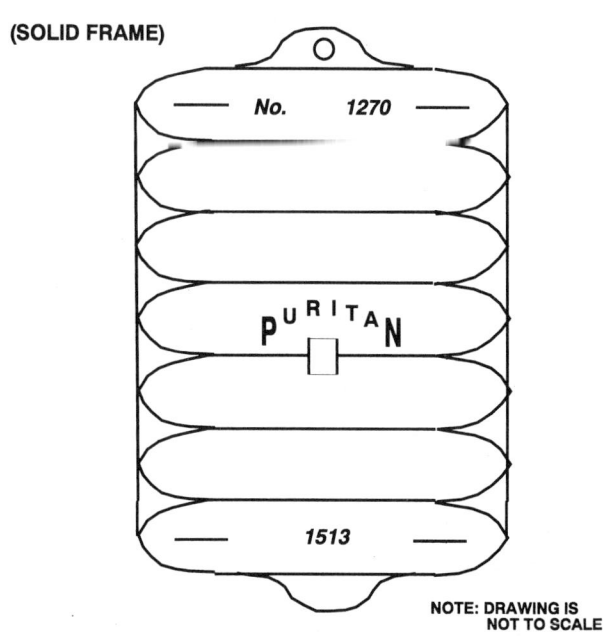

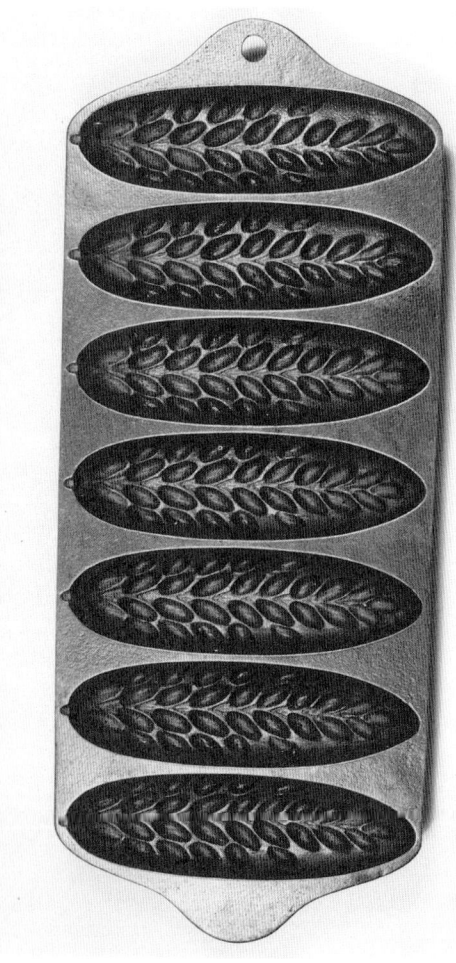

Top view of No 1270 Wheat Stick Pan (Puritan)

Bibliography

Cast Iron Cookware News, Vol. 1 No.1 to Vol. 3 No.3, January 1988 to March 1994.

Cast Iron Marketplace, Volume 1 Issue 1 to Volume 2 Issue 3, July 1995 to September 1996.

Griswold Cast Iron, Gas City, Indiana: L-W Book Sales, 1993.

Griswold Manufacturing Co., Catalog, 1890 - 1891.

Griswold Manufacturing Co., Catalog 40.

Griswold Manufacturing Co., Catalog 45.

Griswold Manufacturing Co., Catalog 47.

Griswold Manufacturing Co., Catalog 49.

Griswold Manufacturing Co., Catalog 55.

Griswold Manufacturing Co., Extra Finish Cast Iron Cooking Utensils.

Kettles 'n Cookware, Vol. 1 No. 1 to Vol. 5 No. 3, 1992 - 1996.

Smith, David G. & Charles Wafford. *The Book of Griswold & Wagner*. Atglen, Pennsylvania: Schiffer Publishing Ltd., 1995.

Appendix

Pattern Numbers of Griswold Cast Iron Muffin Pans

623	Unnumbered Corn or Wheat Stick Pan
625	No 262 Corn Stick Pan
629	No 272 Corn or Wheat Stick Pan
630	No 282 Corn or Wheat Stick Pan
631	No 240 Turk Head Pan
632	No 2700 Wheat Stick Pan
633	No 2800 Wheat Stick Pan
634	No 130 Turk Head Pan
635	No 140 Turk Head Pan
636	No 270 Corn or Wheat Stick Pan
637	No 280 Corn or Wheat Stick Pan
638	No 27 Wheat Sick Pan
639	No 28 Wheat Stick Pan
640	No 13 Turk Head Pan
641	No 14 Turk Head Pan
930	No 273 Corn Stick Pan
931	No 283 Corn Stick Pan
940	No 1 Gem Pan
941	No 2 Gem Pan
942	No 3 Gem Pan
943	No 5 Gem Pan
944	No 6 Gem Pan
945	No 7 Gem Pan
946	No 8 Gem Pan
947	No 9 Golfball Pan (10 Cup)
947	No 9 Golfball Pan
948	No 10 Popover Pan
949*	No 11 French Roll Pan (H Pattern)
949	No 10 Popover Pan
950	No 11 French Roll Pan
951	No 12 Gem Pan
952	No 14 Gem Pan
953	No 20 Turk Head Pan
954	No 22 Bread Stick Pan
955*	No 1 Vienna Roll Pan
955	No 23 Bread Stick Pan
956	No 2 Vienna Roll Pan
957	No 4 Vienna Roll Pan
957	No 24 Bread Stick Pan

958	No 6 Vienna Roll Pan
958	No 26 Vienna Roll Pan
959	No 24 Bread Pan
959	No 50 Hearts/Star Pan
960	No 26 Bread Pan
960	No 100 Hearts/Star Pan
961*	No 28 Bread Pan
961	No 21 Bread Stick Pan
962	No 32 Danish Cake Pan
963	No 31 Danish Cake Pan
966	No 19 Golfball Pan
969	No 34 Plett Pan (Milled Bottom)
2070	No 10 Popover Pan (Hammered)
2073	No 273 Corn Stick Pan (Hammered)
2980	No 34 Plett Pan
2992	No 33 Munk Pan
6138	No 15 French Roll Pan
6139	No 16 French Roll Pan
6140	No 17 French Roll Pan
6141	No 18 Popover Pan

*These pattern numbers are not known to be found on these pans. If a variation of any of these pans was made with a pattern number, it is believed that these would be the pattern numbers used.

Pattern Numbers of Griswold Cast Iron Muffin Pans made for Others

962	No 32 Danish Cake Pan for Favoritt Piqua Ware
1253	No 10 Popover Pan, Best Made for Sears
1270	No 1270 Wheat Stick Pan, Best Made for Sears
1512	No 10 Popover Pan, Puritan for Sears
1513	No 1270 Wheat Stick Pan, Merit for Sears
1513	No 1270 Wheat Stick Pan, Puritan for Sears
2980	No 34 Plett Pan for Alfred Andresen Co.
2980	No 34 Plett Pan for Sandvik Saw & Tool Corp.
2980	No 34 Plett Pan for Scandinavian Importing Co.
2980	No 34 Plett Pan for Western Importing Co.
2992	No 33 Munk Pan for Alfred Andresen Co.
2992	No 33 Munk Pan for Western Importing Co.